Wellsprings
of the Great Perfection

RANGJUNG YESHE BOOKS • WWW.RANGJUNG.COM

Wellsprings
of the
Great Perfection

Lives and Insights of the
Early Masters in the Dzogchen Lineage

compiler & translator
Erik Pema Kunsang

editors
Michael Tweed
& Marcia Binder Schmidt

artwork
Ngawang Zangpo

Rangjung Yeshe
PUBLICATIONS
Boudhanath, Hong Kong & Esby
2006

Rangjung Yeshe Publications
Flat 5a, Greenview Garden,
125 Robinson Road, Hong Kong

Address letters to:
Rangjung Yeshe Publications
p.o. box 1200
Kathmandu, Nepal
www.rangjung.com
wellsprings@rangjung.com

Distributed to the book trade by:
north atlantic books

1 3 5 7 9 8 6 4 2

First edition 2006
Printed in Canada on recycled acid-free paper

Publication Data:
translated from the Tibetan by Erik Pema Kunsang,
(Erik Hein Schmidt).
Edited by Michael Tweed and Marcia Binder Schmidt.
Artwork by Ngawang Zangpo.
isbn-10: 962-7341-57-6
isbn-13: 978-962-7341-57-4
1. Eastern philosophy—Buddhism.
3. Vajrayana—Dzogchen (Nyingma).
I. Title.

Cover art detail: icon of Shri Singha from the archives of
Tulku Urgyen Rinpoche
Design: Michael Tweed

When I have passed beyond this world of sorrow,
Three hundred sixty years from now,
In Uddiyana, land of braided people,
To the daughter of the monarch Uparaja,
Will appear a yogi-child, without a father,
Who is blessed by buddha Vajrasattva
And bears the name Delightful Vajra.
He will spread the doctrine of the Ati teachings.

*Buddha Shakyamuni foretold the coming of Prahevajra in
the Nirvana Sutra.*

Contents

ILLUSTRATIONS

Without explaining the meaning of the history,
The blemish of mistrust may then arise
Towards the teachings of the *Certain Greatest Secret*.

—*The Tantra of the Union of the Sun and Moon*

NAMO GHURU DHEVA DAKKINI HUNG

Our teacher, the truly and completely awakened one, teaches an inconceivable number of entranceways to the Dharma, but it is the Mahayana itself that lets you awaken to buddhahood.

For those of the highest capacity he teaches the sacred Great Perfection, Ati Yoga, the quintessence of which is contained in the Seventeen Tantras. The life-blood of these seventeen tantras is contained in two paths: Trekchö and Tögal.

Trekchö liberates through the sudden path beyond cultivation, upon having left mental assumptions behind; and through practicing the path of Tögal the material aggregates vanish within this same body and life so that one attains enlightenment freed from the illusory form of the four elements.

—*Padmasambhava*
from the revelations of Sangye Lingpa

Foreword

The Dzogchen teachings of the Greatest Secret, also known as the Great Perfection, are the words of the compassionate buddha, and among the causal and resultant vehicles, they are of the type that employ the fruition as the path.

This book describes the origin, and gives both short and detailed historical accounts and teachings. They were revealed by the five tertöns kings, the eight masters with the name Lingpa and others.

These revelations and other authentic narrations are translated into the English language by my late father Tulku Urgyen Rinpoche's and my personal disciple of unique dedication, Erik Pema Kunsang, who is rich in trust and respect towards the Buddha and his teachings, and whose flowers of experience and realization are blooming. On this endeavor I repeatedly throw flowers of praise and honor.

I see a profound importance in studying, reflecting upon and practicing the authentic statements and explanations of the Dzogchen lineage masters—especially for people who aspire to realize the Great Perfection—the Thorough Cut of primordial purity, the view of Trekchö. I therefore request readers to keep these scriptures in the center of their hearts.

—*Written by Tulku Chokyi Nyima on the 20th of May, 2006.*

Preface

Throughout history great individuals have appeared to inspire others. They formulate their insights to help others transform their lives, and find meaning and happiness, even liberation and enlightenment. The philosophy and stories of these great ones, passed down by the first recipients, often have such a force and strength that thousands of years later, their lives and values continue to be sources of inspiration. The present recipient—always at the end of a long line, like at the water tap from a pipe originating at a mountain spring—must hear of the origin of the teaching and its teacher, to know and have trust in its authenticity, before turning on the water and drinking. This book contains the origins and early history of the Dzogchen lineage in the hopes that it will inspire trust and confidence in those who are fortunate enough to meet the present holders of this remarkable lineage.

Wellsprings of the Great Perfection is the culmination of aspirations formed over many years. In the 1970s, the emissaries of Padmasambhava—Dudjom Rinpoche, Dilgo Khyentse Rinpoche and the Karmapa—blessed the West with their visits. At that time, my Dharma friends and I repeatedly received Prahevajra's Three Words from these kind lineage masters. Some years later, Tulku Urgyen Rinpoche explained the three lineages of Dzogchen and how these extraordinary teachings were taught in three divine realms before reaching this world. These auspicious coincidences gave rise within me to a recurring deep and heartfelt wish to document the original sources that explain how the Dzogchen teachings came into this world: who of the early masters in India and in the country of Uddiyana received them; and through whom they passed.

One of the first translations of Dzogchen scriptures to reach the English language was Padmasambhava's concise meditation advice in the *Tibetan Book of the Great Liberation*, showing how to see awareness directly, and the more famous *Tibetan Book of Liberation Through Hearing in the Bardo*. Both of these appeared via a lama from Sikkim who dictated a translation to W.Y.

Evans-Wentz, an Englishman, and had a tremendous impact. Since that time the Dzogchen teachings have continually spread throughout the West. In fact now it is not uncommon for people interested in Tibetan Buddhism to attend seminars and lectures on the Great Perfection.

Over the last couple of years I succeeded in locating a vast number of original documents, all written in classical Tibetan—some were old hand-written documents, some wood carvings and some recently published books from India and China. Several years went by while comparing and selecting the manuscripts that are now included below.

Wellsprings not only documents the lives of the early masters in the Dzogchen lineage; it also contains selections of songs of realization by a good number of them. Many of these incredibly beautiful songs are still used today during tantric feast gatherings and during empowerment ceremonies.

With this collection I have attempted to help fill a gap that other translated works in English have missed. Many short segments have been published already and these were additional catalysts that triggered undertaking this project. However, we have not yet seen a comprehensive selection that documents not only the early Dzogchen masters' lives and what they taught, but also the transmission of the Dzogchen teachings that took place *before* it entered the human realm. In many of these early documents, I was able to find narrations of events that took place on the summit of Mount Sumeru, inside the palace of Indra the king of gods, and some even earlier than that in the various Buddha realms. Sometimes it felt as if I were a witness to intimate conversations between celestial beings, buddhas and bodhisattvas.

In the process of collecting these pieces, I consulted almost every major Nyingma master including my own personal teachers, to make sure that I had cast out a wide net of opinions. Such eminent lamas included Chatral Rinpoche, Trulshik Rinpoche, Thinley Norbu Rinpoche, Tulku Thondup, Tulku Pema Wangyal, Orgyen Tobgyal Rinpoche and Chökyi Nyima Rinpoche. Many stated that their personal choice of preference would be the histories contained in the *Four Branches of Heart Essence (Nyingtig Yabzhi)*, the sources that trace back to Padmasambhava and Vimalamitra—containing the famous *Heart Essence of the Dakinis* that came to Tibet through Padmasambhava, as well as the *Heart Essence of Vimalamitra.*

In order to expand the breadth of this work I decided to include line drawings. It is often said that one picture is worth a thousand words. Line drawings fill the need for intimacy, since they did not have snapshots two thousand years ago. Line drawings are both important and inspirational in order to get the feeling that we are talking about real people who lived and taught. Many of these images I found in original scriptures, which I then had reproduced by Ngawang Zangpo, an excellent contemporary artist. Other drawings were redrawn based on empowerment icons. In addition, wherever possible I have also included some of the mystic script of the dakinis that has a profound and symbolic significance. Only a select few enlightened masters can read this mystical script.

In short, this book is a sacred document. For an outsider, a book like this would be a valuable collection of historical fragments from early manuscripts interspersed with spiritual poetry. Nevertheless, for someone who has received instruction or who simply possesses a deep-felt yearning to do so, this book will likely be respected as a "holy scripture." Whatever the case, it is my hope that many will find the texts contained here profoundly inspiring.

Searching through the many volumes of ancient scriptures has often had the atmosphere of an enchanted adventure—of exploring uncharted territory—full of mysterious delights and profound wonders. My poor translation abilities were steadily ignored by a resolute and blind will to see "what was behind the next range of snow mountains." Call it love of the subject or an obsession; I would happily have continued researching these topics for many more years as it felt like being in the company of the buddhas and the great vidyadharas themselves. This book contains a mere fraction of what could have been—and should be—translated. Therefore, if it had not been for my partner Marcia's ability to bring projects to completion, this book might never have been published.

Being able to offer this book to you, the reader, is the outcome of not only my aspirations and effort, but also the result of the dedication of my close friend Michael Tweed. Words of praise and gratitude cannot equal the sweat and toil he put into this project and without him it would not have happened. Special thanks also go to Tulku Thondup whose kind words of encouragement and guidance reminds me of the pleasure it is to work with such sacred texts; to James Valby who kindly lend an early draft of his translation of the history of *Vima Nyingtik;* to my Dharma friends Mads Julius Nielsen, Tom Nygaard, Danny and Tara Goleman, David Cowey, Zachary Beer, Cortland Dahl and others who patiently listened to the many readings and offered useful help; and the proofreaders Michael Yockey, Lynn Schroeder, Claude Herail, Rinchen Lhamo, and Zachary Beer who stepped in at the last minute and improved the manuscript. Cheers to the typesetter Joan Olson who withstood the distant sporadic communication and was a pleasure to work with. Finally, this book would not have seen the light of day without the generous support of Richard Gere and the Gere Foundation.

By the virtue of this book's stories, insights and connection with real, authentic masters, directly and in many other ways, it is my deep-felt wish, prayer, and belief that people in the thousands, and through them beings beyond number, may feel inspired to discover in themselves the true Samantabhadra—the awakened state.

—*Erik Pema Kunsang*
Nagi Gompa Hermitage

Translator's Introduction

The source of the Dzogchen teachings can be traced back not to some ancient country lost to modern historians, but to the truly and completely awakened mind of the primordial buddha Samantabhadra. All the Dzogchen history books and tantras agree on this point. Who other than Samantabhadra could actually know this far back in such infinite detail? In terms of time, it was before our galaxy or even our universe unfolded from the Big Bang. Actually, it was before ten trillion Big Bangs or the immense dramas and subsequent implosions, occurring in parallel, in staggered sequence or within each other. The Dzogchen perspective is awesome and its scope inconceivably vast. As Tulku Urgyen Rinpoche said:

> In Dzogchen all phenomena of samsara and nirvana are completed or perfected in the expanse of the single sphere of dharmakaya awareness.[1]

Longchenpa, the 12th century Dzogchen master begins his history of Buddhism, *Illuminating Sunlight*, with a radical statement that contextualizes this primordial reality as being the basis for everything:

> Every type of experiential content belonging to samsara and nirvana has, as its very basis, a natural state that is a spontaneously present *buddha*—a dimension of purity and perfection,[2] that is perfect by nature. This natural state is not created by a profound buddha nor by a clever sentient being. Independent of causality, causes did not produce it and conditions can not make it perish. This state is one of self-existing wakefulness, defying all that words can describe, in a way that also transcends the reach of the intellect and thoughts. It is within the nonarising vastness of such a basic natural state that all phenomena belonging to samsara and nirvana are, essentially and without any exception, a state of *buddha*—purity and perfection.

This original and timeless nature of reality—which is Longchenpa's baseline for all history—a nature in which samsara and nirvana are not two, contains every virtue to be realized and thus is the source and origin of every buddha as well. This state of self-existing wakefulness (*rangjung yeshe*) is the very heart of all the Dzogchen tantras, the awakened state realized by all the masters of this lineage, and the natural state to be uncovered within the experience of every practitioner on this path—it is the cord that ties every chapter in this book together.

The reader will notice that *dharmakaya* is the starting point of almost every chapter. The primordial buddha Samantabhadra's awakened mind is known as dharmakaya and from this dharmakaya countless buddhas and manifestations appeared and still appear—first as sambhogakaya, and then as nirmanakaya.

These three kayas—dharmakaya, sambhogakaya and nirmanakaya—will gradually be explained by some of the greatest masters of the millennium. The 16th century master Tashi Tobgyal summarizes the Dzogchen tantras' view of how Samantabhadra awakened to enlightenment:

> Let me briefly describe this perspective according to the Luminous Vajra Essence, the tradition of the sublime vehicle. Long before there had ever been or was to be any division between samsara and nirvana, as ground-displays began to manifest from the primordial ground—the basic space of self-existing wakefulness which is the sugata-essence—in that instant Samantabhadra, the teacher of perfect mastery, ascended from the ground and recognized the ground-displays to be self-displays. Through those three self-existing principles,[3] he captured the stronghold of great primordial purity within the precious sphere of spontaneous presence, the timeless resolution that is the realms of the Youthful Vase Body. Thus, having perfected the virtues of abandonment and realization, he had awakened within the nature of dharmakaya and so remained as the state of inner brilliance.

In Tulku Urgyen Rinpoche's words, here is how the realms subsequently unfolded for the benefit of beings:

Dharmakaya is like space. You cannot say there is any limit to space in any direction. No matter how far you go, you never reach a point where space stops and that is the end of space. Space is infinite in all directions; so is dharmakaya. Dharmakaya is all-pervasive and totally infinite, beyond any confines or limitations. This is so for the dharmakaya of all buddhas. There is no individual dharmakaya for each buddha, as there is no individual space for each country. You cannot say there is more than one space, can you? It is all-pervasive and wide open. It's the same with the dharmakaya level of all buddhas. That is the dharmakaya sphere within which sambhogakaya manifests. No world anywhere in the universe takes form outside of the three kayas—it is simply not possible. The three kayas are the basic dimension within which all mundane worlds manifest and disappear.[4]

One of the first times I heard Tulku Urgyen Rinpoche explain the greater sambhogakaya my mind was stunned. Who can grasp such vast dimensions?

The greater sambhogakaya is a fivefold mandala of the buddha Vairochana known as Immense Ocean. He is seated in vajra-posture in the center of the mandala, holding a begging bowl within which is a great lake called Immense Ocean. In the center of this lake are twenty-five lotus flowers in full bloom, one above the other. Each lotus flower has a thousand petals, in the center of which there are a thousand pistils. On each tip of these thousand pistils there are one trillion nirmanakaya realms. Likewise, there are trillions of nirmanakaya realms on each of the other pistils, as well as in each of the trillion pores of this buddha's body. The world we presently reside in is located on the thirteenth lotus flower, which is exactly level with Vairochana's heart.

Among the thousands of trillions of nirmanakaya realms, ours is but one of those within which one-thousand buddhas will appear in this present aeon. Sometimes, a scripture mentions that there are one billion and sometimes a trillion worlds or "one hundred times one hundred times one billion" simultaneous world-systems. All of them added together, comprise the activity-sphere of a single one of the

Vairochana Immense Ocean

countless supreme nirmanakaya buddhas. Yet Vairochana Immense Ocean in the center is not the only such buddha—in the eastern, in the southern, in the western and in the northern directions, there is also a buddha Immense Ocean for each of the other four families.[5]

To explain nirmanakaya, I will rely on a poetic saying,

> Within the all-pervasive space of dharmakaya,
> Sambhogakaya manifests distinctly, like the light of the sun,
> While nirmanakaya, like a rainbow, acts for the welfare of beings.

Within the perspective of the *Brilliant Expanse* we find the Lotus-Born master of Uddiyana described as indivisible from the buddha Samantabhadra, already from the very first, and so it is this primordial buddha who appears in the form of Padmasambhava. The drama being played out in our world is—to paraphrase Jamgön Kongtrül—only one of many trillion among the oceanlike cloud banks of buddhafields, bodily forms and Dharma-doors which the conquerors of the three kayas display in ways that utterly defy the mind's comprehension.

As witnessed in the records that we, with our mundane intellects, can perceive, Padmasambhava met Shri Singha, a great master who had accomplished the rainbow body of the great transformation, and in his company he enacted the drama of perfecting the great strength of realization in the Luminous Vajra Essence, which is a synonym for the innermost part of the Great Perfection. It is from Shri Singha that the Lotus Master received not only the seventeen great tantras that are the quintessence of the six million four hundred thousand stanzas of the Great Perfection, but in particular the Mother Tantras known as the *Sun of the Brilliant Expanse* and the *Blazing Lamp*. Having integrated these tantras and pith instructions within his own experience, the Lotus-Born (the literal translation of the name Padmasambhava) composed three cycles of the most profound heart essence, including the *Heart Essence of Dakinis*.

When he later arrived in Tibet, he perceived that the time was ready for Vimalamitra to teach the Great Perfection, and therefore bestowed his lineage of *Heart Essence* upon only a few worthy disciples. The wisdom dakini Yeshe Tsogyal then concealed his teachings in the form of terma treasures for future generations. Padmasambhava's profound hidden treasures containing his instructions on the Great Perfection are therefore primarily found among the revelations of the major tertön masters who have appeared over the centuries since the fifty-five years and six months Padmasambhava spent among the snowy ranges of Tibet.

In trying to organize this book in a way that was true to the subject matter and easy for the reader, I rearranged it seemingly countless times. Finally, I came up with a simple solution: to assemble the material the same way it was transmitted. So, in the end what we have is the historical unfolding of the Dzogchen teachings and when they each appeared in our human realm.

I feel very fortunate to be able to present this collection in five parts with a prelude at the beginning and an aspiration at the end.

To mentally set the tone, at the start of each part, I chose a pithy piece that embodies the intent of the section. Before the individual selections, wherever possible, I have included a brief description. This serves the purpose of explaining where the text fits in the general scheme of Dzogchen, the lineage and who discovered it and when. If it is an excerpt, I refer to the complete text. Finally, I tried to note important facets unique to this selection.

In a more detailed way, let me clarify section by section.

To give an overview, there is an essay by Tsele Natsok Rangdröl, which is a condensed teaching of the meaning of the Great Perfection. To instill a positive connection to this book as a practice, there is the prelude, which I will go into more detail about later.

THE GRAND VISTA

The first of the five parts consists mainly of translations from the early period, approximately when the Dharma was brought to Tibet at the invitation of the great Dharma-king Trisong Deutsen. This was the period when the Samye temple was built and consecrated by the Padmasambhava. The great scholar Vimalamitra arrived from India, and the Tibetan translator Vairotsana had been sent to India and returned. These three masters—Padmasambhava, Vimalamitra and Vairotsana—are pivotal figures throughout this book and you will see their names repeatedly. Due to their kindness, we have the Dzogchen teachings presented not only here, but also in all the Buddhist lineages that have developed in Tibet.

The Grand Vista's five chapters contain a tantra from the Mind Section, songs of realization, an excerpt from the opening chapter of the primary tantra of the Space Section, and an excerpt from the Oral Lineage of history of the Vajra Bridge, the *Journey to the Golden Sanctuary*. This is followed by Realization Songs of Awakened Mind from Longchenpa's *Illuminating Sunlight,* which he, frankly speaking, copied from the autobiography of the Tibetan translator Vairotsana. It contains the songs of all the masters of the combined lineage of the Mind Section and the Space Section from the primordial Buddha down to Vairotsana's own teacher, Shri Singha.

REVELATIONS FROM THE EARLY TREASURE MASTERS
The next part begins with two excerpts from the *Heart Essence of Vimalamitra.* The first describes the mind transmission of the conquerors and the twelve Dzogchen buddhas, next *The Great History of the Heart Essence* contains the history Vimalamitra brought to Tibet that was concealed to be revealed at a later, more opportune time.

The Songs of the Buddhas and Bodhisattvas contains a record of a visionary journey taken by the great treasure revealer known as the King of Nyang.

After this comes *Shri Singha Confers the Eighteen Dzogchen Tantras, The Heart Essence of the Dakinis* and *The Essence Tantra of Liberation through Wearing.* These three are teachings that Padmasambhava gave to the King of Tibet, Yeshe Tsogyal and the king's daughter who unfortunately died young. The story goes that in a past life, during the building of the great stupa in Boudhanath, each participant of the building made a profound wish upon completion. The three brothers who contributed the majority of the work joined their palms and made the wish to establish the Dharma in Tibet. A bee stung one of the brothers and he slapped the bee and killed it. This brother later became the king of Tibet and the bee his daughter. Due to their karmic link, this daughter's had a short life. Nevertheless, she was blessed by Padmasambhava to reveal *The Heart Essence of the Dakinis* in a future life as a tertön. That tertön was reborn as the illustrious master Longchenpa.

7

The Tibetan treasure revealer Rinchen Lingpa traveled to India where he revealed *The Great Single Cut of Complete Liberation.* He was a reincarnation of the Indian master Prajnakara.

The last two chapters are by Longchenpa. *The Jewel Garland Records* shows how the manifestations of enlightenment appear for the benefit of beings, while *Illuminating Sunlight* deals more specifically with the origin of the Dzogchen teachings in our world.

FROM THE REVELATIONS OF SAMANTABHADRA'S MIND

Part Three has six chapters from the well-known terma *Gongpa Zangtal,* revealed by Rigdzin Gödem who was one of the famous five tertön kings. The collection of treasures *Gongpa Zangtal* is an abbreviation that literally means "the teachings that directly reveal the realization of the primordial Buddha Samantabhadra." It consists of four volumes. Here, I have selected six excerpts that mainly contain historical records of transmission. The special feature is that these teachings were taught while the three masters—Padmasambhava, Vimalamitra and Vairotsana—were together in the caverns above Samye. These teachings were then given to the King of Tibet, Yeshe Tsogyal and very few others and later concealed as a terma treasure for the benefit of beings in the future.

FROM THE LATER TREASURE MASTERS

The first chapter in the fourth section is from the *Golden Garland Chronicles* and is comprised of excerpts from the extensive version of Padmasambhava's life story. Here, we are presented fabulous examples of how Padmasambhava received transmissions directly from buddhas and bodhisattvas in divine dreams and became a holder of these lineages without going through any other masters. These are some of the teachings he brought to Tibet.

In the following chapter, *The Single Golden Letter of the Black Quintessence*—the famous *Yangti Nagpo*—we see a similar example of how Padmasambhava received teachings from the buddhas of dharmakaya and sambhogakaya.

Transmitting the Brilliant Expanse is a terma revealed by Ratna Lingpa. The Lotus-Born master received this collection of teachings directly from his teacher, Shri Singha. The special feature is that they originated from the female Buddha Samantabhadri, the consort of Samantabhadra. Even though predominantly, Dzogchen teachings seem to originate from a male buddha, the dharmakaya is neither male nor female. However, when appearing in an anthropomorphic form for our benefit, names, places, attributes and so forth are attached. *Brilliant Expanse* is known as a mother tantra of Dzogchen. It has appeared in several versions—one by Dorje Lingpa, one by Ratna Lingpa, and another by Pema Lingpa. The most famous version is of course the *Heart Essence of the Dakinis.*

Next, the *Brilliant Expanse* includes an intriguing record of how Padmasambhava received the symbolic transmission from Shri Singha.

Shri Singha's *Heart Mirror* follows it, which is a concise summary of all the Dzogchen teachings.

After that comes *The Heart Essence of Vajrasattva* and *The Quintessence of All Vehicles*—two excerpts from a terma that Padmasambhava gave to the Tibetan translator Vairotsana. They focus on the Buddha Vajrasattva, containing a treasury of various Dzogchen teachings.

The Written Narration: Tibet is a shorter version of *The Heart Essence of Vimalamitra*, which explains how Vimalamitra gave teachings while he was in Tibet.

It is followed by a testament of the knowledge-holders, containing Prahevajra's *Three Words Striking the Vital Point* and *The Seven Spikes of Shri Singha*, both in their original form.

The Twenty-One Songs of Self-Existing Oneness is from a seventeenth century treasury revealer named Longsal Nyingpo. He received these in a vision of Vimalamitra. They contain the songs of realization of the early lineage masters in Uddiyana and India. These versions are different from those in other records, which is why I decided to include them.

Lastly, we have the chapter entitled *The Golden Sun that Dispels Darkness* which is the extensive version of the history of the twelve Dzogchen buddhas. These accounts of the Mahasandhi sugatas of prehistory are found in various sources—including the writings of both Vimalamitra and Padmasambhava. This version is from Padmasambhava, which is quite different from the long version in the *Heart Essence of Vimalamitra.*

The importance of these twelve buddhas is manifold. Not only are they emanations of Samantabhadra, the first of them appeared at the beginning of this eon when the lifespan of beings lasted for a duration known as "incalculable"—which is actually ten followed by fifty zeros. Slowly the lifespan decreased, according to Mipham Rinpoche, with one year for each hundred years, until the time of Buddha Shakyamuni when the average lifespan of a human being was one hundred years.

Vajradhara was the first of these twelve buddhas. He taught the one thousand and two buddhas who will appear in this world during this cycle. He gave us the first Dzogchen tantra known as the *Dra Talgyur*. From these accounts it is quite obvious that the Dzogchen teachings have an ancient history, indeed.

From Chokgyur Lingpa's Revelations

The fifth and last section contains more recent revelations from Chokgyur Lingpa (1829-1870), the great revealer of seven types of heart essence. The songs of realization in the four excerpts are from the terma known as the *Three Sections of the Great Perfection (Dzogchen Desum)*.

Aspiration

The book ends with an aspiration from the famous *Heart Essence of the Vast Expanse,* the *Longchen Nyingtig,* revealed by the great knowledge-holder Jigmey Lingpa two centuries ago. It expresses the wish that everyone might realize the ground, path and fruition of the great perfection.

Lastly, there is the index of people, places and texts. On our website you can find a bibliography, an extensive index, as well as other resources and material are for easy digital searches:

WWW.RANGJUNG.COM/WELLSPRINGS/

This book needn't be read from front to back but can be dipped into wherever one would like, depending on what inspires, interests or moves the reader at any particular time; if something is too dense move on to a song. I encourage the reader to ask the lineage-holders for teachings and explanations, and to use these selections as a basis of further learning and clarification.

I would like to conclude by answering a question I have often been asked as to whether there is any prophecy about the Dzogchen teachings coming to the West. And here's an indication, from the prophetic dream of Khenpo Ngakchung, (also known as Ngawang Palzang), who is well-known for his excellent *Notes to The Words of My Perfect Teacher.*[6] I take the liberty of quoting from *A Marvelous Garland of Rare Gems* by Nyoshul Khenpo:

> On the evening that Lungtok finished giving him the teachings concerning the main body of practice, he instructed Ngawang Palzang, "Pay attention to your dreams." That night, Ngawang Palzang dreamed that Yeshe Tsogyal gave him a volume of scripture, telling him that it was the treasury of the enlightened minds of the masters of awareness, the gurus of the three lineages. Later that night he dreamed about an ancient monument, a stupa built by the Indian Buddhist king Ashoka, which crumbled from the spire downward and fell into the western ocean (is still carried) by a great flood, the ocean turning a murky red. From the sky, a voice said, "Millions of beings living in the ocean have seen the truth." This second dream seemed to have been an omen foretelling the destruction of the teachings in Tibet and their dissemination in the foreign lands of the Western Hemisphere.

Most of the writings by the seventeenth century master Tsele Natsok Rangdröl came about in response to questions. This reply to the problem of understanding Vajradhara, the dharmakaya buddha, is most appropriate to include here as he brings into the discussion not only Buddha Samantabhadra and the teachers of the three kayas, but also covers the relationship between them, as well as the origin of the tantras in both the Old and New schools.

He begins in his usually self-effacing style:

"You raise the question about the definition of the name Vajradhara, the Sixth, as well as the explanation of the word 'the sixth.' You also ask about how it could be that he has a form with color, arms, attributes and ornaments when his identity is supposed to be dharmakaya, the natural state of the sugata-essence that transcends constructs and attributes.

"In order to give a sequence of thorough answers to this issue, it is indeed a topic that must be covered with detailed explanations, using the great authoritative expositions of the sutras and tantras as the framework, a feat beyond the limited abilities of an ignorant person such as me who lacks eloquence and confidence, hence, all I can offer you is this brief summary as a temporary reply."

And then he continues with a most profound and articulate answer, in the lucid style for which he became known and loved by all—both great masters and simple practitioners— up to this very day.

COLLECTED REPLIES

Samantabhadra's Infinite Realms

An introductory essay
by Tsele Natsok Rangdröl

Long ago, before the split between samsara and nirvana occurred, within the basic spaciousness that is the natural state of everything, exactly as it was since the beginning, glorious Samantabhadra, the self-existing buddha of natural awareness, awakened to true enlightenment in the nature of equality—the very state within which both samsara and nirvana first arise and then again subside. This is why he is known as the primordial buddha, original protector, and as the universal forefather of all of samsara and nirvana.

Samantabhadra is not a buddha who—from a temporal perspective—journeyed through a gradual sequence of levels and paths, gathering accumulations and purifying obscurations. He is the dharmakaya itself and since the very beginning has never been subject to confusion. Therefore, he is compared to the source of all conquerors, their creator or the basis for their emanations. All the realms and teachers, their retinues, activities and spheres of influence—in short every possible phenomena within samsara and nirvana—are included within this buddha, without a single exception.

Dharmadhatu is also known as the realm of the Luminous Vajra Essence in that it is indivisible from the kayas and realms throughout the unfathomable and infinite universe, and present without change or alteration throughout the four times. Indeed it is utterly impossible for anything belonging to the whole of samsara and nirvana, all that appears and exists, to be excluded

Samantabhadra

from it. This is why we have the statements: "The sugata-essence is present throughout all beings," and "The triple levels of existence are all awakened realms; and since the very first the body, speech and mind of the victorious ones." Other passages include: "While dharmadhatu in itself is neither good nor bad, we are mistaken to believe in the duality of good and evil things" and "Samantabhadra is the all-pervasive dharmakaya." In short, it is from this principle we should understand the reasons for the phrase "all-encompassing purity of appearance and existence."

It is also from within this state that sentient beings fail to recognize their own nature when the ground displays manifest from the ground and instead apprehend their own natural display as being "something other," causing confusion to perpetuate incessantly. And so, all the beings of the three realms experience samsara—just like the sceneries of a dream, a magical show that is "perceived while non-existent."

Inspired by nonconceptual great compassion for all these beings, Samantabhadra, the dharmakaya itself, magically emanated the realms and bodily forms of sambhogakaya in ways that transcend numbers and dimensions, and extend as far as space can reach. These realms include the Thunder of the Drum of Purity, which is a densely arrayed self-display of spontaneous presence. And the bodily forms include the five families of Immense Ocean and of Vajradhara, the Great Sixth. Within the area of a single pore on each of their bodily forms, there are inconceivable numbers of realms with beings to be guided and teachers to guide them. Each of these teachers carry out activities to benefit beings by means of "never-ending adornment-wheels" of body, speech, mind, qualities and activities, the extent of which cannot possibly be fathomed by the minds of ordinary beings like us since it completely transcends the reach of thought and description.

Manifestations of sublime nirmanakaya realms to guide beings appear as the natural expressions of these sambhogakayas, including the Array of Great Purity. Here the teachers manifest in ways that correspond to all the possible degrees of karmic fortune of those to be guided, both the general and the extraordinary types.

In particular, in our universe, Flower-Adorned Base and Center, there is a buddha known as Vairochana Immense Ocean who holds a begging-bowl containing a fragrant ocean from which grows a lotus tree with twenty-five flowers, tiered one above the other. The thirteenth contains our present Saha world-system, known as Endurance.[7] Within just this single realm, this buddha unceasingly carries out activities to benefit beings in the infinite ocean of eons throughout the past, present and future.[8]

In our present Good Eon, in general he magically appears as the one thousand buddhas, and specifically as the widely renowned twelve teachers. Moreover, he displays the myriad forms of nirmanakaya manifestations that are the chief figures of the various mandalas of the Dharma—adorned and unadorned, peaceful, wrathful and semi-wrathful. For beings that lack the fortune to behold these displays he appears in other ways corresponding to each of their individual karmic fortunes. These activities to guide beings by means of boundless manifestations—from the crafted, incarnated and mahabodhi nirmanakayas, to the displays consisting of the five elements, worlds and inhabitants—are all without exception the compassionate play of glorious Samantabhadra.

In order to guide individuals of the gradual type through the paths and levels there may exist teachings on how the teacher Vajradhara and the buddhas of the five families were once ordinary beings who formed the resolve set upon enlightenment and then gradually awakened to true enlightenment. On the level of the definite meaning, however, all these manifestations are never different from the dharmakaya Samantabhadra himself.[9]

The great Vajradhara, the lord who encompasses all families, is, among his various names and forms, known in the context of dharmakaya as Samantabhadra; while when manifesting as a form-body with the major and minor marks he is called Vajradhara or the buddhas of the five families. At the time of appearing as the nirmanakayas to guide beings he is the King of the Shakyas and the other buddhas of the ten directions. When magically emanating the mandalas of the tantras of Secret Mantra, he is the one who appears as Chakrasamvara, Hevajra, Guhya Samaja, Kalachakra, and countless other forms and manifestations. When for a specific purpose he needed to appear as a requester or compiler, he is the one who manifests in the forms of Vajrasattva, Vajra Garbha, Dharmevajra, Vajrapani and so forth.

Furthermore, since this buddha also displays himself in the countless forms, names and skillful manifestations that are required to guide sentient beings with all their individual dispositions, capacities and inclinations— one of us, who is densely obscured by the veil of habitual tendencies, may surely wonder, "Who are Samantabhadra, Vajradhara and Shakyamuni?" The answer is this: we must understand that they are no other than the teacher who shows us the path to awakening. And while he indeed is a symbolic or temporary teacher who shows us the path, the ultimate teacher is the real substance or identity that is supposed to be shown. This ultimate teacher—the true Samantabhadra—is present, fresh wakefulness, untainted by good or evil. This is undoubtedly so, but failing to recognize this nature is the basis for delusion, and so we have experienced false phenomena, which "while nonexistent are mistakenly believed to be what they seem." In spite of this, since the very beginning we have never been apart from dharmakaya, not even for a single moment.

Considering this state of affairs, Gyalwa Yangönpa wrote in his specific treatise on Secret Mantra, the *Seven Vajra Words:*

The word *vajra* is used since it connotes the unchanging identity of all phenomena, which is indivisible from the vajra body, speech and mind. The word *holder* or *bearer*—and therefore the state of vajra holder—is used since it connotes having understood and realized this vajra nature exactly as it is, and, consequently, having eliminated the flaws and veils of the ground and path so that there is no longer any parting or separation from the true nature of the great original wakefulness.[10]

The scriptures belonging to the expedient meaning teach in great detail that Vajradhara's realm with its sceneries and qualities is the Densely Arrayed realm of Akanishtha, located countless leagues[11] above and beyond the Akanishtha that belongs to the Brahma abodes. But according to the definitive meaning, Samantabhadra or Vajradhara is the identity within which self-knowing wakefulness is recognized and the dharmadhatu palace of Akanishtha is the whole of wisdom experience that is his self-display. Taking this vital point into account, every type of practice found on a practitioner's present path is simply a training to grow familiar with this essential nature.

To explain further, when training in development stage, we imagine the environment to be the celestial palace and the inhabitants to be deities. When cultivating a buddhafield, we train in everything being a pure realm—beginning with one's house and home, land and country. When training in the dream state, we imagine the wheel of channels and syllables in the throat to be a pure land; and when training in luminosity, we visualize the heart center in the same way. When training in the bardo state, we imagine that everything we see—all illusory sense objects—to be nothing other than the pure display of a buddhafield. In short, all these methods are exclusively means to transmute distorted and mistaken karmic experience into pure wisdom experience. All these methods are, furthermore, not a case of distorted understanding—an exercise in believing something to be what it is not—but rather ways to purify our habitual tendencies that distort and delude us into failing to see things as they actually are.

Generally speaking, our world-system Endurance is a part of the Great Purity nirmanakaya realms and all the Great Purity nirmanakaya realms are a part of the sambhogakaya realms known as Thunder of the Drum of Purity. All these sambhogakaya realms are a part of the dharmakaya realm Luminous Vajra Essence, and so, there is nothing within the worlds and sentient beings, samsara and nirvana, that is excluded from this dharmakaya realm. All universes and all living beings, without even one atom of exception, are consequently Samantabhadra's display. Hence we hear the statements, "Every being is a buddha, but obscured by passing veils," "I am the teacher and the teaching," "I am the world and its transcendence." These and other quotations all converge in the same meaning.[12]

Even though this is so, the dominance of the positive or negative tendencies of individual sentient beings cause some beings, temporarily and in some world-systems, to enjoy comfort and well-being with increasing lifespans, to witness the appearance of a universal monarch and a buddha, and to experience the higher realms and the states of liberation. In some realms the Conqueror has passed into nirvana, the doctrine has declined, neither the secular rulers nor practitioners follow spiritual principles, the eon is in decline and beings are oppressed by suffering and woes during periods of

Shakyamuni

plague, famine and warfare. All these various experiences are the personal perceptions of sentient beings, which is why one and the same realm can be seen in a variety of ways.

This is illustrated by the story from a sutra in which the bodhisattva Braided Brahma asked Shariputra the following question:

"Elder, how do you behold this, the world of the exalted Shakyamuni, and with which attributes?"

Shariputra replied, "I see this world of Shakyamuni as utterly horrid, so full of cliffs and canyons, precipices and spiked thickets."

The bodhisattva responded, "You perceive the world in an ignoble way. Elder One, you see it thus because your mind is full of the cliffs of conceptual clinging, the canyons of ignorance, the precipices of self-oriented views, and the spiked thickets of negative emotions. I see this world as adorned with boundless sublime decorations—made of precious gemstones and as level as the smooth palm of my hand."

To summarize, the basic nature of things, Samantabhadra's wisdom mind of great equality, pervades the whole of samsaric existence and nirvana's peace. It encompasses everything, yet sentient beings still fail to acknowledge this, their own nature, obscuring this fact from themselves. Hence they go through the illusory endless circle of samsara's three realms. Though they suffer in this way, their basic wakefulness, dharmakaya, never undergoes any change or transformation, increase or decrease. Even while beings experience the infernal suffering of the deepest hell, their buddha-nature's basic wakefulness remains unimpaired and vividly present. Their momentary experiences are merely the reflected images of suffering—the expressions of dependent origination that are the consequence of having engaged in unvirtuous actions—while in reality they have not separated from dharmakaya by as much as a hair's tip.

It is for this reason that under the dense veil of ignorance we only experience samsara's distorted, karmic displays. As the veil grows gradually thinner through familiarity with the pith instructions, the experience of basic wakefulness becomes increasingly clearer. Finally, when the obscuring factors are permanently eliminated, the kayas and wisdoms, buddhafields and enlightened qualities that are all perfectly present within us become evident. The phrase 'awakening to enlightenment' is just a label for this and a buddhafield is not some faraway place that you must undergo an arduous journey to reach.

In this context, some writers in the Sarma traditions feel it unreasonable to describe Vajradhara as being sambhogakaya when he is the dharmakaya buddha. In such cases please understand that, essentially, the three kayas do not have separate identities. Specifically, this is the context in which Samantabhadra, the identity that is present throughout all of samsaric existence and nirvana's peace, turns the unexcelled Dharma-wheels of sublime secrets. Consequently it is Samantabhadra's unobstructed and natural radiance that appears as the sambhogakaya's forms with their major and minor marks, and which spontaneously manifests as the self-displays of retinue, buddhafield and the rest of the mandala's five perfections. Essentially, these manifestations have never parted from dharmakaya, which is why there is no conflict between the Sarma and Nyingma perspectives.

This is also the reason why the source of the Nyingma tantras is the glorious Samantabhadra who, having awakened within the ground in the primordial eon, taught through the blessings of his ineffable realization the six million four hundred thousand tantras of the effortless Ati vehicle to his retinue of self-radiant awareness, the ocean-like assembly of original wakefulness. Afterwards, the glorious Vajrasattva taught these tantras to the assembly of vidyadharas, including the nirmanakaya Prahevajra, so that they might gradually flourish in the human world.

The source of the Sarma tantras is also Samantabhadra manifest in the form of Vajradhara who throughout the three times incessantly turns the Dharma wheels of infinite tantras to his retinues of bodhisattvas on the ten levels, the wisdom dakinis of dharmadhatu and oceans of other pure assemblies. These tantras were then transmitted by the wisdom dakinis to their respective vidyadhara masters in the human realm.

You should therefore understand that the names "Sarma" and "Nyingma" stem from the origins of these tantras. The specific and diverse ways in which teachers and retinues are magically manifested, as you see in the opening chapters of the respective tantras, are innumerable and all part of the compassionate play to guide whoever needs in whichever way is necessary.

You may wonder how there could be any need for such a long-winded explanation since you inquired about just the meaning of Vajradhara's name. Nevertheless I wrote this down, feeling it might be somewhat beneficial for people in future generations who are unable to receive teachings or reflect upon the major tantric treatises.

And, by the way, since this explanation reveals my feeble scope of learning and is primarily about the Nyingma perspective, if anyone from a different Dharma lineage is offended, then I ask their forgiveness.

Longchenpa the Omniscient

It has always been the tradition that the students and practitioners of the teachings of the Great Perfection begin by forming the resolve set upon supreme enlightenment. Therefore before embarking on reading this book I would like to request you, the reader, to join your palms before your heart and say the following words from Longchenpa's opening verses of poetic invocation from the Heart Essence of the Dakinis and the brief practice with good wishes from his Collected Works, which in themselves will set the authentic tone for proceeding.

Or if you prefer a shorter more condensed supplication, simply repeat:

All sentient beings, as infinite in number as the sky is vast, have been my own parents. It is my wish to liberate every one of them from the ocean of samsara and establish them firmly in the state of the primordial enlightenment of Buddha Samantabhadra, the Ever-Excellent. In order to be able to do so, I will read this book in a respectful and open frame of mind so that the blessings of the lineage masters may inspire me to pursue, receive, understand and practice the teachings of the Great Perfection. As soon as possible may my experience deepen and may authentic realization blossom in me to benefit all other beings.

Prelude

That I and all the countless sentient beings
Are since primeval time awakened ones,
In knowing this to be just what it is,
I am resolved towards supreme enlightenment.

—*The bodhichitta resolve from the*
Guhyagarbha Tantra

Continuous
Stream of Nectar

an invocation by Longchen Rabjam

OM AH HUNG
Your blessings fill the sky, like clouds of nectar
Pouring down an ocean of accomplishments.
All noble masters, hear this supplication,
Bless me and fulfill my every wish.

Within the timeless palace of the natural state,
The kayas undivided from the wisdoms,
Ever-Excellent and consort, hear this supplication,
And bless me to be freed within the ground.

In the Akanishtha palace of the Greatest Bliss,
Vajradhara, sugatas of the fivefold families,
And Vajrasattva, hear this supplication,
Bless me to behold the natural presence.

Within the palace of the Blazing Fire Mountain,
Passionate cloud banks of skillful means,
Prahevajra, hear this supplication,
Bless me to attain the vidyadhara stage.

Within the palace of the Rugged Grove,
Lord of beings with five sets of fivefold wisdoms,

Yeshe Tsogyal the Dakini

Splendid Lion, hear this supplication,
And bless me to realize the natural state.

Within the palace of the Sosa Sanctuary,
You attained supreme and common siddhis,
Padma Tötreng, hear this supplication,
And bless me to attain the triple kayas.

Within the palace in the land of Uddiyana,
You are the queen of infinite dakinis,
Yeshe Tsogyal, hear this supplication,
And bless me to unchain my stream of being.

Within the palace of the self-existing wisdom,
With blessings to make real the basic state,
Flawless Light Ray, hear this supplication,[13]
And bless me to achieve the rainbow body.

ᛦ

Atop my head, upon a throne of sun and moon,
Master of the highest siddhi, ripening and freedom,
O root guru, hear this supplication,
And bless me to perfect the fivefold kayas naturally.

৯

Within the palace on the Multicolored Cliff
Supreme *upaya* to awaken in a single lifetime,
Heart Essence of Dakinis, hear this supplication,
And bless me to attain the siddhi that transcends remainder.
Within the palace where the destined gather,
With unobstructed miracles and strength,
Protectors of the terma treasures, hear this supplication,
And bless me so that hindrances subside.

Within the Dharma palace, everywhere you dwell,
You hoist the triumph banner of the triple trainings,
All true practitioners, please hear this supplication,
And bless me to uphold the Dharma teachings.

Within the divine palace of my body,
Seen yet empty, timeless, natural presence,
All-embracing peaceful-wrathful devas, hear this supplication,
And bless me to gain mastery in wakefulness.

Within the palace of resounding empty speech,
Inside channels, wheels of letters dwell.
Self-existing, timeless presence, hear this supplication,
And bless me to attain a purity of voice.

Within the palace of the mind's most basic nature,
The nonarising, equal nature of all things,
Empty rigpa, dharmakaya, hear this supplication,
And bless me to behold the self-arising natural freedom.

Within the palace of the world and beings, all that may exist
and may appear,
Everything is timelessly a realm of buddhas.
Totality of threefold levels, hear this supplication,
And bless me to make real the nature of equality.

Within the palace of the unbound vastness,
The nature of nondual, open space,
Supreme view, hear this supplication,
And bless me to be free of prejudice.

Within the palace of the basic, lucid wisdom,
The timeless nature of nondual, empty knowing,
Supreme training, hear this supplication,
And bless me to transcend increase and decrease.

Within the palace beyond taking and rejecting,
Continuum where all is wisdom magic,
Supreme conduct, hear this supplication,
And bless me with duality's collapse.

Within the palace that transcends all hope and fear,
Where luminous self-knowing is unchanging,
Supreme fruition, hear this supplication,
Bless me to arrive at the exhaustion of all things.

Sugatas of the past, present and future
And everyone worthy of veneration,
With constant honesty, please hear this supplication,
And bless me with fulfillment of activities.

֍

Grant your blessings that I train in kindness and compassion,
Feel disenchantment and renunciation,
Engage each day and night in Dharma practice,
And cut back my mundane pursuits and aims.

Grant your blessings to regard appearance and existence as my
  teacher,
And so receive unceasing inspiration,
To experience with pure perception, free of bias,
And to feel devotion with sincerity.

Grant your blessings to remain in quiet places,
Undistracted and without diversions,
To destroy deluded clinging to the solid and the real,
And to firmly place my feet upon the path.

Grant your blessings that I use this life for Dharma practice
To ensure my masters will always be pleased,
That I reach perfection in my training
To ensure the benefit of everyone.

Grant your blessings to exhaust my kleshas and my karmas,
And to persevere upon the bodhi path,
To journey to the end of all the paths and levels,
And achieve the state of buddhahood.

Grant your blessings in this life to gain the rainbow body,
To recognize the bardo's natural state,
To take rebirth in nirmanakaya's natural realms,
And to accomplish both the twofold goals.

By virtue of this prayer, a *Continuous Stream of Nectar*,
May the beings in all worlds, in all existence,
Fully traverse the ocean of samsara
And, all together, realize the state of buddhahood.

This supplication entitled the Continuous Stream of Nectar was composed by Drimey Özer (Flawless Light Ray), a yogi of the Heart Essence of the Dakinis, on the slope of Gangri Tökar, during the third month of autumn when flowers and fruit were fully ripened. May it be virtuous!

ॐ

The Yoga of the Early Dawn

Sit cross-legged on a comfortable seat
and form this attitude from the very core of your heart:

> While all phenomena are states of pure perfection
> since the very first,
> I pity any sentient beings who fail to realize this fact
> and wander through samsara!
> Now I must bring every one of them to the state
> of perfect buddhahood!

Then continue with this chant:

> In all the hosts of gurus, yidams and dakinis,
> And in the Buddha, Dharma and the noble Sangha,
> Filling all of space throughout the sky,
> The six beings and I respectfully take refuge.
>
> That I and all the countless sentient beings
> Are since primeval time awakened ones,
> In knowing this to be just what it is,
> I am resolved towards supreme enlightenment.

OM SVABHAVA SHUDDHO SARVA DHARMA SVABHAVA
SHUDDHOH HAM

> All phenomena, internal and external,
> Are great equality and indestructible as basic space—

Their nature nonarising in the state of great perfection,
From here appears the whitest lotus flower and a full moon disc.

Upon this I appear as Vajrasattva, white in form, one face, two
hands,
My right hand holds a vajra at my heart, my left supports a bell
upon my thigh.
I am adorned with silken garments and ornaments of precious
gems.
With my legs in vajra posture I am seated.

In the curl of hair between my eyebrows,
Inside a sphere of five-hued lights, is a white OM.
And in my throat, inside a sphere of five-hued lights, is a red
AH.
At the center of my heart, inside a sphere of five-hued lights, is
a blue HUNG.

Above my head, upon a lotus and a jeweled throne,
With layers of a sun and moon, is my personal root guru,
Together with the Flawless Kinsman Vimala, Lotus-Born of
Uddiyana,
And all the lineage masters, up to Samantabhadra, and the
yidam deities and dakinis.
Present as the roots of every siddhi, they are no other than the
Triple Gems.

Rays of light shine forth from the syllables in my triple places;
They invoke from Akanishtha, from all buddhafields throughout
the ten directions,
Endless hosts of gurus, yidams and dakinis, and the Triple
Gems.
Each accompanied by a retinue, in spheres of effulgence and
rainbows, they arrive.

Now every one of them remains, having melted indivisibly,
Into the guru who is present right above my head.

Prahevajra

Mentally, I pay respect, make offerings, apologize, beseech.
Then from my guru's body, speech and mind, shine forth
Streams of light rays with ambrosia, in colors white, red and
 blue.
They shower through me, purifying body, speech and mind,
Of all diseases, evil influences, veils and harmful actions.
The ambrosia fills me, from head to toe, completely.
Blessing me so I become the nature of the vajra body, speech,
 mind and wisdom,
And, receiving all the four empowerments,
I realize the nature of the Great Perfection's basic state.

From within this state, perfect in view and in samadhi, chant:

OM AH HUNG
Saviors from the terrors of the lower realms,
Triple Gem, in you I place my refuge.
Having resolved to know the actual nature,
I will practice guru yoga for the sake of beings.

From the palace of the basic space of dharmas
Gurus, nonarising, please approach.
From the palace of sambhogakaya
Gurus, lucid purity, come close.

From the palace of nirmanakaya
All of you, who have compassion, please approach.
From the fivefold mountain peak in China,
Flawless Kinsman Vimala, come close.

From the mansion known as Lotus Light,
Uddiyana master and your consort, please approach.
From the mansion glowing in a mass of brilliance,
Flawless Light Ray, please come close.

From the throne of sun and moon above my head,
Fundamental guru please approach.
Swirling in your effulgence and rainbows,

Swarmed with groups of rainbow lights and spheres,
On the throne of sun and moon above my head,
Please remain with me, steadfast and nondual.

I pay homage with respectful body, speech and mind,
Present you offerings--both outer, inner and the secret,
I apologize for the breaches against body, speech and mind,
Please empower me, instruct me, make me ripened, set me free.
OM AH HUNG

OM
Dazzling radiance, transcending birth and death,
Vajra body, heed my supplication.
Bless me so my body fills with ease.

AH
Voice of Dharma that transcends cessation,
Ali Kali, heed my supplication.
Bless me so my voice has energy.

HUNG
Timeless purity, Samantabhadra's vastness,
Transcending every type of thought, please heed my
    supplication.
Bless me that I reach dharmata, the exhausted stage.

O my guru, vajra-bearer,
Single kinsman of samsara's threefold realms,
Savior of all defenseless beings,
Supreme destiny on liberation's path.

You, the lamp that clears away unknowing,
Are the refuge in my darkness' gloom.
When I am sinking down and I am helpless,
Please rescue me from samsara's muddy swamps.

When I am scorched by searing flames of passion,
Please cool me with the rain of your compassion.

Since eons that transcend a first beginning
I have been chained in bodies made of solid substance.
Please purify this stream of karmic skandhas
So I obtain a flawless form of shining light.

My voice that has been bound by verbalizing—
Please clear this stream of clinging speech,
So I achieve the speech of dharmata, ineffable.

My mind that by deluded thinking has been bound—
Please let attachment to the thought activity be cleared,
So I attain the nonconceptual heart of wisdom.

O my guru, precious buddha,
I have no one else to trust than you,
From this moment and until supreme enlightenment,
Witness all my joys and sorrows, hopes and aims.

Please embrace with your compassion my defenseless self.
Clear away my illness, evil influences, and hindrances.
Grant the blessings of your body, speech and mind.
And bestow the common and supreme accomplishments.
OM AH HUNG MAHAGURU SARVA SIDDHI PHALA HUNG

Chant this as many times as you can. Then continue:

Namo,
Sublime root guru, every master of the lineage,
Hosts of yidam deities of every mandala,
Together with your retinues of dakas and dakinis,
You are the owners of the wisdom knowledge,
Compassionate affection, activity of the enlightened deeds,
The power and the strength that grant protection,
The siddhis to be given, and the noble words of truth,
As well as other virtues that defy all count.
Since I and others who have now begun
To realize the sacred Dharma that brings liberation,
Please ensure that all the demons have no way to hinder us.

For the qualities that we promote in practice,
Such as view and meditation, conduct and the rest,
Please ensure that they continue to increase
So the unexcelled enlightenment is rapidly attained.

Within this life, make sure as well that we do not encounter
The harms and dangers, both the outer and the inner,
Unfortunate events when practicing the sacred Dharma,
Such as illness, evil influences, the hindrances and obstacles.

May we never be in want of anything we need
Such as food and drink, possessions, clothing, and a dwelling
    place.
Instead ensure that we make use of every type of resource,
Just like the jewel that fulfills all wishes,
To provide spontaneous accomplishment of offerings,
For our teachers and all the yogi lords.

As we realize the meaning of the natural Great Perfection,
Please ensure that, effortless and free from struggle,
All our actions, every thought, and our words and deeds,
Every utterance, intention and perception,
May arise as mandalas of dharmata,
So that ongoing samadhi and a perfect recall,
Intelligence with no obstruction, liberated wakefulness,
Eloquence like flowing rivers, life-span like the king of stones,
Spontaneously accomplished actions, strength to challenge every
    thought,
Boundless miracles, and never-ending treasuries of Dharma,
    most sublime—
Please ensure that we will master all of these.

Once we gain the realization unexcelled,
The secrets of the mind of all tathagatas,
Please ensure that we may reach perfection in the fourfold
    visions,

In the basic space of kayas and of wisdoms, beyond meeting,
    beyond parting,
Within the luminous mandala that is the nature of all things,
So we gain the mastery of birth and of re-entering
And thus attain the body of the greatest transformation.

For as long as this is yet to be attained,
Please ensure that, not even for a moment,
We get swept away into improper modes of thinking,
The distractions of this life and the eight worldly concerns,
But instead maintain the threefold trainings, ocean-treasuries of
    learning,
So that we may please the gurus, most sublime,
Realize the nature of the vast, extensive teachings,
And, apply ourselves whole-heartedly towards essential practice.
May we spend both day and night devoted to the Dharma,
With neither weariness nor partiality, when it is time to work
For sentient beings' benefit through magnetizing with the
    fourfold means.

When on the verge of death, please help make certain
That we neither suffer at the interruption of this life
Nor reconnect to any type of evil fortune.
But may we realize the meaning of the most profound,
So that, full of joy and filled with inspiration,
We are welcomed by the hosts of gurus, yidams and dakinis,
Leading us to timeless, basic space,
From where, with wondrous omens, every being we may guide.

Having realized the nature of dharmata in the bardo,
Please ensure that we don't meet the abyss of the bardo of
    becoming,
But instead find perfect steadiness within spontaneous presence's
    precious sphere.

But if the field of our experience becomes changed,

Please ensure the doors into the wombs are closed,
Leading to the six deluded states of sentient beings,
So instead we journey to the natural realms of the nirmanakayas
Where spontaneously we may accomplish, indivisibly,
The primordial abode, Samantabhadra.

Even if we find ourselves in other states within samsara,
Failing to be confident in view and deed, unending like the
    ocean,
Please ensure that we obtain a special incarnation
That is endowed with all the virtues of the higher realms,
So we may meet the Dharma just as soon as we take birth,
And be free to practice in the most authentic way.

May we thereby please our gurus most sublime,
Be retainers of the threefold training—ethics, insight and
    samadhi,
Mastering the treasury of Dharma, in its full entirety,
By earnestly applying ourselves to practice,
May we find the nectar of the unexcelled,
That is the siddhi of reality, the sacred Secret Mantra,
And within this very life attain the state
Of supreme enlightenment, Samantabhadra.

These were the supplications to be made.

૭

Part I begins with excerpts from tantras and songs of realization. There is also a selection from the Nyingma Kahma that belongs to the oral transmission and was passed down from teacher to student over many generations. Hence, the style and language is quite different from the other terma selections in the book.

PART I
The Grand Vista

ཀ྅ྃ྅ྃ྅ྃ྅ཿ ཀ྅ཿ྄ྃ྅ྃ྅ཿ

All things have no identity, are insubstantial,
So, cultivate the notion of intangibility.

All things have nothing tangible to grasp at,
So, cultivate the notion of their nonduality.

All things have no observable identity,
So, cultivate the notion of their pure and lucid emptiness.

All things have no identity to cultivate,
So, cultivate the notion that transcends all reference points.

All things have no identity with fixed positions,
So, cultivate the notion that transcends all notions.

All things have no identity within the known,
So, cultivate the notion that transcends all effort.

Lovingly Playful Wisdom, one of the twelve Dzogchen buddhas, who in a past aeon also taught the Kulayaraja Tantra, spoke this testament of the Six Vajra Words on the verge of passing. It is part of a collection brought to Tibet by Padmasambhava and later revealed by Dorje Lingpa in the Father Tantra View of Vastness.

࿄

Yudra Nyingpo of Gyalmo

The next source text is the opening chapter from the Kulayaraja Tantra, famed as the primary tantra of the Mind Section (Semde). Its colophon mentions that it was explained by the Indian pandita Shri Singha Prabha and translated into Tibetan by Vairotsana of Pagor.[14]

Dilgo Khyentse Rinpoche, one of the most extraordinary masters in recent times, describes the Mind Section in the following words:

"The Vajra Vehicle of the Early Translations contains three main transmissions— the oral lineage of Kahma, the treasure lineage of Terma and the visionary lineage of Dagnang—all of which are permeated by the [three inner tantras] known as development, completion and Great Perfection. Like a victorious mountain peak among the nine vehicles, Ati is also called luminous Great Perfection from "Mahasandhi" which means Great State of Perfect Mental Stability[15]—the single, unexcelled wakefulness for which all phenomena of samsara and nirvana are self-displayed within the sole expanse of the natural state, beyond the conceptual positions of the eight vehicles. Ati of the luminous Great Perfection has three major divisions: the Outer Cycle, the Inner Cycle and the Secret Cycle. The Mind Section, belonging to the Outer Cycle, is compared to the body.

The Mind Section consists of tantras, scriptures and instructions that state the intent of the Eighteen Marvels of Mind—the Five Early Translations and the Eight Later Translations—all branching out from the Kulayaraja Tantra, the King of Marvels, and the Ten Scriptures, twenty-one in all. In summary: the Mind Section teaches liberation from the limit of discards[16] through realizing all phenomena to be the magical play of the single mind—beyond cause and effect, effort and achievement.

"The Mind Section, along with its seven subcategories, were transmitted by the great translator Vairotsana to the king of Tibet, to Yudra Nyingpo of Gyalmo, and others, five people in all. There is also Jnana Kumara of Nyak's lineage, which he received through both Vairotsana and Yudra Nyingpo. Both of these belong to the Kahma, the oral lineage. Besides this, there are various terma cycles containing Mahamudra teachings."

Kulayaraja Tantra, the opening chapter

In the language of India: SARVA DHARMA MAHASANDI BODHICHITTA KULAYARAJA.

In the language of Tibet: *chos thams cad rdzogs pa chen po byang chub kyi sems kun byed gyal po.*

In the English language: *The All-Creating King of Awakened Mind, the Great Perfection of all Things.*

Homage to the perfect conqueror, the All-Creating King, Awakened Mind.

Once upon a time, these were words that I expounded.

In Akanishtha's realm, the sky of dharmata, the vast expanse of basic space, domain of mind itself, within a palace beyond measure, of wisdom unobscured,

They were my nature, my identity and my capacity, my wakefulness appearing as a retinue:

The retinue known as dharmakaya, the retinue that is my nature,

The retinue known as sambhogakaya earth, a retinue of my identity,

The retinue known as sambhogakaya water, a retinue of my identity,

The retinue known as sambhogakaya fire, a retinue of my identity,

The retinue known as sambhogakaya wind, a retinue of my identity,

The retinue known as sambhogakaya space, a retinue of my identity.

And furthermore, there were the emanated retinues, capacity of wakefulness all manifest:
The retinue known as the beings of the Kama Loka,
The retinue known as the beings of the Rupa Loka,
The retinue known as the beings of Arupa Loka.

And also, as my nature, these were the fourfold retinues of views:
The retinue known as Ati Yoga,
The retinue known as Anu Yoga,
The retinue known as Mahayoga,
The retinue known as Sattvayoga,
And they were all together, as my nature, my identity and my capacity, having no division within me.

And furthermore, there was the retinue that realizes this—my very nature:
The retinue remaining as the buddhas of the past, the retinue fulfilling aims of buddhas dwelling in the present, the retinue arising from the buddhas yet to come,
And they remained together, since in my nature there is no division.

Then, in order to infuse the retinues with blessings of his nature, the All-Creating King, Awakened Mind, dissolved all retinues within the state of his awakened mind, and thus illuminated self-existing wakefulness.

And so that everyone may be endowed with dharmata, he gathered everyone within him and remained as the single vastness of the sphere.

It was then that Vajra Being, remaining as this single vastness of the sphere, arose,
And in the presence of the All-Creating King, Awakened Mind,
With joyful spirit, his face all jubilant, took seat.

The All-Creating King, Awakened Mind,
Addressed the Vajra Being in these words:

Vajra Being, emaho, how wonderful!
With joy your mind is filled, how wonderful!

Your face all jubilant, how wonderful!
And yet you sprung from me, how wonderful!

The Vajra Being then put forth these words:

Hear me, teacher of all teachers, All-Creating King,
Is my teacher not this sphere, beyond all constructs?
Is the retinue as well no other than this unconstructed sphere?
Is the doctrine also not this unconstructed sphere?
Is the time and place no other than this unconstructed sphere?

When everything is of the nature of this sphere,
Then why, oh teacher of all teachers, do you take the role of
    teacher?
And why are you encircled by this retinue?
How come you teach the doctrine to this retinue?
And how, as well, are time and place all one?

To Vajra Being, in these very words,
The All-Creating King, Awakened Mind, then spoke:

Great Being, listen, keep these sounds in mind,
Through sounds I shall here clarify the meaning, listen
    Mahasattva.

As I, the All-Creating King, awakened mind itself,
The essence of all dharmas, everything,
Am a timeless sphere, an essence beyond constructs,
Thus, this unconstructed nature, this primordial dimension,
This timeless sphere, this self-existing state,
Is the teacher and the teaching, and the retinue, the time and
    place,
And so I teach this sphere to be my nature.

Thus he spoke.

From the *All-Creating King, Awakened Mind,* this was the first, the chapter on the Setting.

According to the early Mind Section sources, "King Dhahena Telo (Dhanadala) was the son of Moonlight, a king in the eastern direction. He attained accomplishment through the Magical Net of Vajrasattva and had a vision of the forty-two peaceful buddhas. He became the teacher of Rajahasti in the Sandalwood Forest of Gorshikha."

Rajahasti the senior prince was the son of King Shakyapuri. He was learned in the Eighteen Tantras and attained accomplishment through glorious Guhya Samaja and was able to display the mandala of the thirteen deities. Rajahasti taught his daughter Sarani in the Garden of Udumvara Flowers.

Sarani, the daughter of Rajahasti, realized the unconditioned nature of equality while practicing close to her father. She attained accomplishment through Guhya Samaja and had a vision of Amrita Kundali. No one was able to cross the boundary line of her mandala. She could employ spirits and dakinis as her servants and travel through the charnel grounds in the company of Ekajati. This yogini also composed the scripture on the Great Perfection known as Jewel Studded Bliss of Awakened Mind. She became the teacher of Takshaka on the shore of the Sindhu ocean.

Takshaka, the son of the naga king Maladhara, was a disciple of the Buddha. He guided beings through his bodhisattva activities and became a teacher for the all the nagas. He displayed miracles in order to teach, maintain and protect the Mahayana teachings. Then in turn he became the teacher of Bodhi the Yakshini, in Serenity, a town in the valley of Magata.

Literally known as the Realizations of the Eighteen Scriptures of the Mind Section Expressed in Song by the Vidyadharas, these songs of the early masters of the Great Perfection express the realization of the famous Eighteen Scriptures of the Mind Section, one after the other. These scriptures are contained in the Nyingma Kahma, the canonical scriptures of the Nyingma School, a precious collection which in recent years was expanded, codified and published by Kyabje Dudjom Rinpoche. The lineage passes from Samantabhadra to the buddhas of the five families. From them the lineage went to Vajrapani the Lord of Secrets, who is the nirmanakaya, and from him to Prahevajra. From Prahevajra the teachings went through the twenty-one learned masters of the Mind Section to the Tibetan translator Vairotsana who passed them to his gifted disciple, Yudra Nyingpo.

Jamgön Kongtrül, who received this lineage from Jamyang Khyentse Wangpo, included these songs in his Treasury of Instructions as did Kyungtrul Rinpoche in his Treasury of Songs, a compilation of the most essential vajra songs of the Nyingma lineage. These songs are moreover an indelible part of the transmission of the Dzogchen Desum, a treasure of Chokgyur Lingpa. There is a tradition for receiving the insights these songs reveal in an elaborate empowerment ceremony where each song is introduced with a lucid pointing-out instruction and accompanied by a guidance in its meditation practice.

The Eighteen
Songs of Realization

I.

The intent of the *Great Garuda*, the spontaneous meditation song about dharmata, was sung in these words by Dhahena Talo, the king, in the Sandalwood Forest at midnight.

> HUNG
> This dharmata, unchanging,
> The all-ground uncontrived, is the awakened mind,
> Beyond the reach of dualistic thought.
>
> Awakened mind, transcending forms to see,
> Cannot be discerned nor can it be caught by thought.
>
> This mind itself, ineffable like space,
> I leave without distraction—unpolluted, uncontrived.
>
> In dharmadhatu's vastness, unformed by meditation,
> Unthinkable awareness, undistracted now remains.
> To train forth—surely there is not the slightest beyond this.
>
> In my successive rebirths I as a king was born,
> But singing out this *doha*, my conceit has now collapsed.
>
> Formerly I resolved to gain supreme enlightenment,
> And have relinked with mingling the Dharma with my mind.

Bhashi the Rishi

For when this body, an illusion, crumbles into dust,
The light rays of Samantabhadra's mind will dawn within me.
GHITAMA KOLASA A HOH

Moreover, these are the words spoken by Bhashi the Rishi:

Do not conceptualize attention, in any way at all;
Let be just as it is, natural, uncontrived.

This was the first; the realization of the *Great Garuda*. ITHI.

2.

The realization of the *Cuckoo of Awareness*, the spontaneous meditation song about rigpa, was sung in these words by Rajahasti the senior prince in the Sandalwood Forest of Gorshikha during the first watch of the night.

HUNG
Uncontrived and timeless all-ground, suchness' basic space,
Self-existing wakefulness, a great equality, like space,

Beyond the sounds of words and names—such is the Ever-
Excellent.

And once your mind and dharmata are equal and nondual,
No matter what conceptual trait of body, speech and mind may
interfere,
The dharmata of mind awakened is unchanging.

This all-ground of awakened mind, beyond the flaws of thought,
Without contrivance, settled in itself.
Surely meditation training is nothing else but this.

And when these aggregates, illusions, crumble,
The light rays of Samantabhadra's mind will dawn within me.
GHITAMA KOLASA A HOH

Moreover, Shri Singha stated:

Within the self-aware diversity of wakefulness,
Remain unwavering, just as it is.

This was the second; the realization of the *Cuckoo of Awareness.*
ITHI. 𑁍

𑁋

3.

The realization of the *Great Space,* the spontaneous meditation song about
original wakefulness, was sung in these words by Princess Sarani in the
Garden of Udumvara Flowers during the last watch of the night.

The all-ground uncontrived, the timeless dharmadhatu,
Is not produced from causes or conditions
And so is not apart nor does it perish.

This self-existing conqueror, spontaneously perfected,
Vajrasattva's self-existing mind, beyond all things,
Is surely nothing other than my state, now realized.

And when these aggregates, illusions, crumble,
Samantabhadra's mind, a treasure unexcelled, will dawn within.
GHITAMA KOLA HOH

Moreover, Aryadeva has stated:

Awareness in itself is not some other thing,
So let it be as thoughtfree, lucid knowing.

This was the third; the essential realization of the *Great Space.*
ITHI. 🕉

🕉

4.

The realization of the *Sixfold Sphere,* the spontaneous meditation song about space, was sung in these words by Nagaraja at Ocean Depth during the first phase of dawn.

Without center, without edge, just like the sky,
Dharmakaya lies beyond the reach of thoughts and words.

To purify all beings within the threefold realms,
Within the all-ground of awakened mind, be uncontrived and
    wholly pure,
Remain composed and without seeking; that's the meditation
    most supreme.

Not contriving rigpa, not departing from the sphere of
    everything,
For paths of liberation there is none more eminent.

This is the insight of sugatas in the triad of time;
Beyond both weight and measure, I have found that there is
    simply this.

And when these aggregates, material, are crumbling,
I reach the state of never parting from the Ever-Excellent.
GHITAMA KOLASA A HOH

Kukkuraja the Dog King

Moreover, the *Spontaneous Prophecy* states:

> Since all phenomena are timeless, perfect purity,
> Be free from hope and seeking something other.

This was the fourth; the essential realization of the *Sixfold Sphere.*
ITHI. 𑁍

𑁍

5.

The realization of the *Great Strength,* the spontaneous meditation song
about awakened mind, was sung in these words by Kukkuraja the Dog King
on the Ocean Isle during the second phase of dawn.

> HUNG
> Samantabhadra, timeless and spontaneously perfected,
> Lucid, thoughtfree, unconstructed, is awakened mind.

> While awareness stays unmoved—composed and uncorrupted—
> From dharmadhatu, free of reference and unchanging,
> No thought is formed, no concept held at all.

This wondrous mind itself, a mystery supreme,
Lies not within the reach of hearing nor of other senses.

Within the changeless all-ground's great space
Let awareness stay unchanged and undistracted.
Apart from this I found no other meditation.

The triple realms dissolved unto themselves,
So striving and achieving are no longer needed.
Transcending hope and fear, truly have I awakened.

GHITIMA KOLA HOH

Moreover Aryadeva declared:

Free from accepting good, rejecting evil—an unimpeded
wakefulness,
Like on the Golden Isle, this wakefulness in itself delights.

This was the fifth; the essential realization of the *Great Strength.*
ITHI. 卐

卐

6.

The realization of the *Training in Awakened Mind,* the spontaneous meditation song about basic space, was sung in these words by Nagarjuna in the
garlanded forest of Glorious Mountain during the third phase of dawn.

Upon the pyre of the perceived, the timeless vastness of the basic
space,
I lay unchanging rigpa for its final rest.
Now basic space remains unchanged and rigpa uncorrupted.

Unwavering and unaffected, the purity of space,
This wakefulness is lucid, undistracted, uncontrived.
Naught but this I label "meditation."

This body, of brute stuff composed,
Has now arrived at the nondual stage.

Bodhi the Yakshini

GHITAMA KOLASA HOH

Moreover, the instruction entitled *White Crystal Garland* states:

Appearance and existence, dharmata from the first,
Are therefore dharmata experiencing itself.

This was the sixth; the essential realization of the *Training in Awakened Mind.* ITHI.

7.

The realization of the *Marvels,* the spontaneous meditation song about the wisdoms of the five elements, was sung in these words by Kukkuraja the Younger at the shore of the ocean as the first hint of redness appeared in the sky.

The nature of awakened mind has these five elements:
Lucid naturally and uncontrived, like space.
Consuming beings' dualistic clinging, it resembles fire.
Its timeless, undirected purity is like the wind.
Like water, it is free from dualistic dirt.

Its firm and utter flawlessness is like the earth.
The mind's awakened nature has these five traits from the first.

Pure and timeless, like the sky,
Without distraction, free of reference point—
I have found the meditation to be simply this.

My body, forged from solid matter,
Has now arrived at the nondual stage.
GHITAMA KOLASA A HOH

The *Vajra Mound* moreover states:

Within the timeless, wakeful state conceptual thinking clears;
Therefore reject not thoughts, but let them naturally subside.

This was the seventh; the essential realization of the *King of Marvels.*
ITHI. 卐

🌀

8.

The realization of the *Wishfulfilling Jewel,* the spontaneous meditation song
about accomplishment, was sung in these words by Bodhi the Yakshini as
the second glimpse of redness appeared in the sky.

The nature of awakened mind, neither clung to nor beheld,
Yet it appears to all as something to be seen.
Undisturbed by anything, it cannot be dissected.
Such natural mind, on nothing does it dwell.
This knowing is the nature of awakened mind.

However modified, this space is unaffected,
And rigpa need not seek this basic space.

Mind-essence's pure reality, like space,
Is uncontrived, devoid of true existence.
The training, I have realized, is simply this.

Buddhamati the Courtesan

When this body made of matter falls apart,
Samantabhadra's heart will shine within me.
GHITAMA KOLASA A HOH

Moreover, Maha Rahula has said:

Samsara clears without being rejected,
And in its place the sun of wisdom dawns.

This was the eighth; the essential realization of the *Wishfulfilling Jewel*.
ITHI.

9.

The realization of *Spontaneous Summit*, the spontaneous meditation song about effortlessness, was sung in these words by Buddhamati the Courtesan, among trees where birds alight as the third glimpse of redness appeared in the sky.

O wonder, the dharmata of awakened mind
Can neither be dissected nor examined,
Nor found or changed by any remedy.

Apart from mind there is no other buddha.
Not found by seeking, he is naught but mind.
This buddha is mind's nature uncontrived.

And this awakened essence, timeless and unsought,
Unstained by concentration, present by itself,
I realize the buddha-mind is simply nothing else.

When my material body crumbles into dust,
Samantabhadra's heart will shine within me.
GHITAMA KOLASA A HOH

Moreover, Mahaguru exclaimed:

All is an adornment for clarifying wisdom,
And is purified by simply realizing this.

Manjushrimitra

This was the ninth; the essential realization of *Spontaneous Summit*.
ITHI.

ᠪ

10.

The realization of *Comprehension*, the spontaneous meditation song about mystery, was sung in these words by Manjushrimitra the Younger at the base of a *nyagrodha* tree during the time of dusk.

> HUNG
> On all-ground's vast and lonely plains
> The sun has risen upon its pure expanse,
> It rises once and never sets.
> And having risen, its light is uncontrived and bright.
>
> The buddha, dharmata and sequence, three,
> Cannot be found however hard you try.
>
> In the nature of the all-ground's vastness,
> The sun of wakeful rigpa shines,
> And, uncontrived, it never sets.
> The meditation, I have seen, is none apart from this.
>
> If you wish to taste, taste this: the mind's own nectar.
> If you wish to see, look into this: the wakeful knowing.
> PADMA KOLASHA A HOH

Moreover, the *Subsequent Scripture* states:

> This—the greatest bliss that can be tasted—
> Is the ultimate for clarifying all.

This was the tenth; the essential realization of the *Perfect Comprehension*.
ITHI.

ᠪ

11.

The realization of *Framework*, the spontaneous meditation song about space, was sung in these words by Aryapalo in the shade under the wishful-filling tree at the break of dawn.

HUNG
Awakened mind, a space-like vastness,
Is wakeful, lucid and thoughtfree,
Neither outside nor within, though all-pervasive.

Within this basic purity, a vast and open sky,
A wakeful knowing blazes, incinerating thoughts.
'Arising,' 'ceasing,' 'narrow,' 'vast' are but empty words.
Apart from this no buddha mind I see.

For food, eat this ambrosia of mind's own nature.
For dress, wear this, the raiment of dharmata.
EMA KOLASHA A HOH

Moreover, the *Kingly Scripture* states:

The dharmata of mind is present, uncontrived.
Since this is so, there is no thought formation.

This was the eleventh; the essential realization of the *Framework*.
ITHI.

12.

The realization of *Jewel Studded Bliss,* the spontaneous meditation song about activity, was sung in these words by Dhahe the scholar of Uddiyana on Jewel Isle just after midnight.

HUNG
Since mind itself is the awakened state
The buddha is nowhere apart from mind.

The nature of the mind—the timeless buddha,

Aryapalo

Awareness, insubstantial, and free from change;
Forget not dharmadhatu's depth, the ultimate lies clear.

Just like an ocean's vastness, the spacious depth of things,
Awareness—unchanged, tolerant—shines forth within.

Majestic sun, the ground-of-all perfected from its base,
Is pure like space, suffusing everything.

This dharmata, a timeless purity, need not be purified.
Awareness is unchanging and present from the first.

Untainted by distortions and present vividly,
The Sugata's realization is simply this, I see.

On garuda wings this yogi freely soars
Through the vastness of dharmata's open skies.

KARMA KOLASHA A HOH

Moreover, the *Scripture of Great Vastness* states:

Nonconceptual, like the sky, mind itself remains.
This fact is obvious when free of thought and uncontrived.

This was the twelfth; the essential realization of *Jewel Studded Bliss.*
ITHI.

᠖

13.

The realization of *Wheel of Life-Force,* the spontaneous meditation song
about self-existence, was sung in these words by Bhashita the Rishi at Nyagrodha Hermitage just after dusk.

HUNG
As stars and planets course across the natural sky,
Ineffable this space of timeless purity remains.

Within awakened mind, sky-like and pristine,
Thought-illusions may attempt to taint

But the space of this pure mind remains unchanged.[17]

Upon the mandala, immensity of basic space,
I lay this wakeful knowing for its final rest.
Clear and present, this mandala's mystic light.

While undistracted from the nature of this presence,
I have found the very insight of all buddhas.

The forceful gusts of wakeful knowing
Disperse the shadows of conceptual thought.
AKASHA KOLA MANGHA A HOH

Moreover, the instruction entitled *Swirling Vastness* states:

In mind all is complete, perfected in itself,
Nothing to approve and nothing to refute,
Not modified, not tampered with, just a wakeful presence.

This was the thirteenth; the essential realization of *Wheel of Life-Force.*
ITHI.

14.

The realization of the *Collection of Precious Gemstones,* the spontaneous
meditation song about nonarising, was sung in these words by Princess
Gomadevi at the Hermitage of Conquerors during the latter half of night.

HUNG
The mind of all the buddhas is the letter A.
The nature of this A is timeless, insubstantial.

This A, the source of all sugatas and the twofold truths
Also takes the form of what appears and what exists.

The substance of this A is timeless, the awakened mind.
By seeing its unchanging presence, beyond parting, I awakened.

In this awakened space transcending words and thoughts,
Awakened mind is nonarising like this A.

Stay composed and undistracted, uncontrived—
Realization I have found is simply this.

The stallion of wakeful knowing
Now gallops on the plains of dharmata.
KAPALA KAMAPASHA A HOH

Moreover, the *Amrita Kundali* states:

Awakened mind, as we all realize,
Resides as nonexistence within everything.

This was the fourteenth; the essential realization of the *Collection of Precious Gemstones*. ITHI.

15.
The realization of *Nonarising Natural Mind,* the spontaneous meditation song about dharmakaya, was sung in these words by Brilliance the king of Kashmir, at the base of a sandalwood tree during the early afternoon session.

HUNG
Awakened mind, from the beginning dharmakaya,
An all-pervasive presence, like the sky.

This presence, in itself an emptiness,
Which magically appears in every way.

Let not the slightest thought imagine this,
Instead remain, without description or distraction.

This dharmata, the mind's ambrosia,
Cures all ills of those within the triple realms.
KALAPA KOSHA A HOH

Devaraja the King

Moreover, the *Rampant Elephant* states:

As great bliss shines, simple and nondual,
Remain authentic, suchness uncontrived.

This was the fifteenth; the essential realization of *Nonarising Natural Mind.* ITHI.

16.

The realization of *All-Encompassing Bliss,* the spontaneous meditation song about the three kayas, was sung in these words by King Devaraja in the city of Gunashri at the time of dusk.

HUNG
I bring within the perfect natural state
The urge to focus on apparent and existent things.

Worlds and beings, Samantabhadra from the first,
Nothing else than this, so undistracted I repose.

The training, I have realized, is simply this.

This body, made of matter, just a label for illusion,
My mind has reached the greatest wakefulness.
CHANDRA DEVA KOSALA A HO

Moreover, the *Instructions of Vimalamitra* states:

The poisons five are present as five wisdoms,
Seeing this is knowledge most sublime.

This was the sixteenth; the essential realization of the *All-Encompassing Bliss*. ITHI.

17.

The realization of *Sky King*, the spontaneous meditation song about liberation, was sung in these words by Dharmaraja in a flower garden during the first period of the night.

HUNG
The nature of this mind, a timeless treasury,
However one may know, however one perceives,
Always Ever-Excellent, even when thoughtfree.

This awareness, having no duality,
Is the mind awakened of the Ever-Excellent.

As the basic space of knowing stays untainted
Both training and abiding are transcended.

Alas, I pity those who fail to see.
Hey ho, for now I naturally am free.
DHOHA KOPASHA A HOH

Moreover, the *Instructions of Rishi the Seer* states:

One-pointed, undistracted and thoughtfree,
By being so, the wakeful state is unimpeded.

This was the seventeenth; the essential realization of *Sky King*.
ITHI. 𑁍

𑁍

18.

The realization of *Sublime King*, the spontaneous meditation song about discriminating insight, was sung in these words by Buddhagupta in the Great Hermitage during the first period of the night.

> HUNG
> Samantabhadra, everything left uncontrived,
> The lucid mind awakened, free of change.

> Repose while uninvolved in thoughts of solid concepts
> Always rising and subsiding in this state itself.
> The training, I have seen, is simply this.

> Unless you gaze into the mind's own mirror
> By thoughts you will surely remain obscured.
> PRAJNA KOSALA A HOH

Moreover, the *Great Scripture on Meditation Training* states:

> In uncontrived primordial purity
> Gone by itself all clinging to duality.

This was the eighteenth; the essential realization of *Sublime King*.
ITHI. 𑁍

𑁍

19.

The general realization of the Mind Section, the spontaneous meditation song about the precious jewel, was sung in these words by Shri Singha in his meditation hut during a feast offering.

Buddhagupta

HUNG
However thought of, it defies imagination;
However spoken of, it cannot be discerned;
But from the basic space of wakeful vastness
Shines forth a light that never need be sought.

In dharmata which thoughts can never fathom
Remain unwavering and evenly composed.
There is, I see, no other training.

The spear tip of my wakeful knowing
Rents asunder my enemy, my thoughts.
RATNA KOSALA A HOH

This was the nineteenth; the essential realization of the general Mind Section. ITHI.

This completes the essential realizations of the *Eighteen Scriptures of the Mind Section* expressed in vajra song by the vidyadharas. SHUBAM.

To introduce the history of the Space Section (Longde), I will begin with Dudjom Rinpoche's summary describing the context for this tantra that points out the infinite or all-inclusive vastness that is our basic nature:

"*Among the famous nine gradual vehicles of the Nyingma School's early translations, the most eminent are the inner vehicles that master the profound methods—the triple yogas of Maha, Anu and Ati—based on practices that emphasize skillful means, insight or their unity. And it is Ati Yoga, the pinnacle among them all, which consists of three sections: the outer Mind Section, the inner Space Section and the secret Instruction Section.*

"*Here, the inner Space Section (Longde) is described as the heart—the intent stated in such tantras and scriptures as* Samantabhadra's Royal Tantra of All-Inclusive Vastness *and others. It is the teachings within the Space Section that declare the fact that all phenomena never depart from the unconditioned nature of Samantabhadri's vast expanse.*

"*The Space Section has innumerable tantras, scriptures and instructions. For the most part, Shri Singha who attained the indestructible form of the rainbow body and has remained as the crown ornament of all vidyadhara masters transmitted these to the great translator Vairotsana, himself an incarnation of Buddha Vairochana. Vairotsana received these teachings after undergoing numerous difficulties and translated the* Samantabhadra's Royal Tantra of All-Inclusive Vastness *into Tibetan. This lotsawa was at a level of accomplishment known as the rainbow body. He imparted the pith instructions upon Mipham Gönpo, as a one-to-one lineage. For five generations every master who obtained these instructions departed in a body of rainbow light. It is this long lineage of the oral transmission—known as the* Vajra Bridge of the Symbolic Transmission—*which has continued unimpaired, through an unbroken line of siddhas who all recaptured their primordial kingdom.*"

The Samantabhadra's Royal Tantra of All-Inclusive Vastness *is renowned as the "king" of tantras belonging to the Space Section (Longde). Even though the tantra lacks the traditional colophon that mentions who explained and translated it, we can safely assume that it made its transition into Tibetan in a similar fashion to many of the other Longde tantras: in the capable hands of the "Indian pandita Shri Singha and the Tibetan lotsawa Vairotsana inside the gandola at Dhahena."*

The Royal Tantra
of
All-Inclusive Vastness

In the language of India: MAHA AVARNTA PRASARANI RAJA TANTRA NAMA.

In the language of Tibet: *klong chen rab 'byams rgyal po'i rgyud ces bya ba bzhugs so.*

In the English language: *The Royal Tantra of All-Inclusive Vastness.*

Homage to the perfect conqueror, glorious Samantabhadra.

Upon a time when these were words that I heard from myself,

Remaining as the sovereign, unmoving from the single sphere, the state continuous,

And not divided from the body, speech and mind, nor from the qualities or the activities of all the bliss-gone ones throughout the ten directions and in the triple times,

Where all is one within an equal vastness.

And yet, in order to bring forth a certainty about this nature,

It was within the realm, the place of Akanishtha, not separated from the basis of the three realms,

That a retinue appeared, self-manifest and undivided—not separated from the awakened ones throughout the three times nor from the sentient beings of the three triple realms,

Together with the retinues, both those mundane and those beyond all worlds,

All of whom are indivisible from me and from my nature,

Who ceaselessly fulfill the aims of beings, through emanations of themselves and of their nature.

For all of them I then proclaimed the lion's roar of truth, in a voice melodious,

Fully explaining the reality of natural mind which is the meaning of the King of All-Inclusive Vastness.

Every type of thing and every kind of name
Are one within the timeless vastness, beyond basis for a label.
Within this single vastness, both samsara and nirvana,
Every momentary thing, all that rises from their circumstance,
Like clouds in heaven, like rainbows in the sky,
Appears within awareness, and thus is but the state of basic space.

This boundless natural knowing, unobscured and flawless,
Subject not to thought, precious, timeless wakefulness,
Insubstantial in itself, yet from it everything arises,
For all is but the vastness of awakened mind.

The mandalas of conquerors, the bliss-gone ones,
And all things samsaric, sprouting from mistaken thinking
When deluded ignorance holds sway,
Since these phenomena, whatever may appear,
Are all identical in being the awakened state,
To form the concept, the duality, of being and not being,
And the dualistic view of good and evil, is mistaken.

Believing in one-sidedness within the nature of equality,
Forms the incidence for self and other to appear divided.
Holding concepts of the absent being present,
Reinforced, this clinging caused the body to appear.

The painful trust in a personal identity
Is why the basic nature still remains unknown.
The failure to find comfort in the nature that is true
Lets emptiness lie latent and concreteness hence begins.

Samantabhadra the Primordial Buddha

All things when probed no concreteness can be found.
And yet this absence takes the form of everything.
In the vastness of self-knowing neither empty nor concrete exist,
To know this absence liberates all of samsara's ways.
This, the state of realization, is the most sublime.

§

After this excerpt from the opening chapter, this tantra continues with forty-eight chapters detailing the viewpoint of the Space Section.

§

The following text is from the Nyingma Kahma, the canonical scriptures of the Nyingma School, which contains the oral records of teachings given by Vairotsana to his Tibetan disciples Yudra Nyingpo, Mipham Gönpo the mendicant of Pang and others.

From the long history I have selected two excerpts from the Oral Lineage for the Vajra Bridge. It describes Prahevajra's birth and Manjushrimitra's perilous journey to Uddiyana in order to receive the Dzogchen teachings from him. The special feature here is the transmission of insight by means of the four syllables A HA HO I, *the symbols and most explicit description of these two masters' enlightenment.*

The accounts were recorded by Lobpön Kunsang, a disciple of the lineage master Dzeng. Between Vairotsana and Dzeng, seven lineage masters departed in a rainbow body at the end of their life.

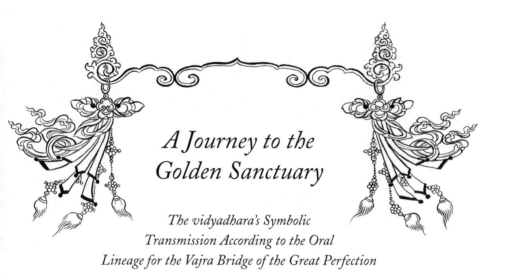

A Journey to the
Golden Sanctuary

*The vidyadhara's Symbolic
Transmission According to the Oral
Lineage for the Vajra Bridge of the Great Perfection*

To understand the transmission of the vidyadharas that liberates through symbols, *vidyadhara* means upholder of the family line of the resultant vajra vehicle of Secret Mantra. *Liberated through symbols* means to be freed simply through the master showing a symbol without him needing to explain with many words. *Transmission* means that this has been passed on from one to another, from Vajrasattva down to Vairotsana, like the links in an unbroken chain.

Here are the accounts that were later given as to the ways and methods this transmission took place.

To begin the story, these teachings trace their source back to the Indian continent, a land that has nine major countries. To the east lies the country of Bhangala, to the south Bhetala, to the west Uddiyana, to the north Kashmir, to the southeast Khangbu,[18] to the southwest Zangling, to the northwest Zahor, to the northeast Kamarupa, and in the middle is the Vajra Throne. Among these, this Dharma originated in the western country of Uddiyana.

These Indian countries typically have two kinds of rulers. One is the Dharmaraja, the royal caste who governs religious affairs. The other is the Uparaja, also of the royal caste, but who governs secular affairs. The kings who uphold religion become Dharmarajas in succession, the sons the succeeding their fathers. They involve themselves in only virtuous pursuits, and no misdeeds even cross their minds, much less are actually done. They would have no right to rule over secular affairs even if they wished to, and if they were to try, they would fail. The kings who govern the secular affairs also become Uparajas in succession, the sons after their fathers. They supposedly involve themselves in nothing other than waging wars and other unvirtuous activities. No virtuous actions even cross their minds, much less are actually done. They have no right to rule over the spiritual affairs of the kingdom even if they wish to, and if they were to do so, they would be unable. That which in the Indian language is called *Dharma* is *Chö* in Tibetan, while the Indian word for king—*raja*—is *gyalpo* in Tibetan.

Now it happened that the Dharma-upholding king of the Shakya clan was Flawless Crest, Excellent among the Shakyas. His queen Sublime gave birth to a daughter who was so stunningly beautiful and radiant that she captivated everyone's sight. One could never get enough of gazing upon her. Her name was Sarani, which in Indian means Lovely.

"I cannot bear to show my daughter to other people," her father exclaimed, and so he made her live in the top story of a nine-storied palace together with her nursemaid. Since at this time the Dharma-king had no son to succeed him, his bloodline was in danger of being broken.

Meanwhile, glorious Mahasukha was the dharmakaya of dharmakaya, glorious Samantabhadra was the sambhogakaya of dharmakaya, and glorious Vajrasattva was the nirmanakaya of dharmakaya. Their compassionate capacity for the benefit of beings was about to manifest an emanation to teach the meaning of the resultant Secret Mantra from the utterly pure continuity of Vajrasattva's body, speech and mind, since Vajrasattva's mind is dharmakaya, his speech sambhogakaya, and his body nirmanakaya. This emanation was to be known as Noble Spirit Devaputra.

While remaining in the god realm of Akanishtha, Shakra, the king of the gods, perceived this emanation and exhorted him, "Devaputra, you are meant to be emanated by Vajrasattva to teach the Dharma of the resultant Secret Mantra in the world of men." On hearing this reminder, Noble Spirit Devaputra recognized his identity as being Vajrasattva's emanation, and for

Shakra the King of the Gods

the sake of continuing the bloodline of the Dharma-king Flawless Crest, Excellent among the Shakyas, on the southern Jambu continent, he then entered the womb of Princess Sarani the Lovely. This is mentioned in the *Empowerment Instruction of the Great Bridge:*

> Prahevajra's later emanation[19]
> Revives the dynasty on Jambu Isle.

This happened in the following way. It was in the Year of the Ox, in the third month of spring, under the Victorious constellation and the parasol of the full moon as the sun was about to rise, that Noble Spirit magically transformed himself into a turquoise-colored cuckoo bird, which, in front of Princess Sarani the Lovely, sang "cu-coo" three times and then vanished. This was to indicate, "I will come tonight."

That same evening a radiant youth came to her. He was adorned with the major and minor marks, and so amazing was his beauty that her eyes were held captive, she could never get enough of watching him. His full set of teeth was like the whitest conch, his brows like lines of turquoise, and locks flowed freely from his head. They joined in union and at the break of dawn the next morning he flew into the sky and vanished.

The following year the princess gave birth to a son who was also adorned with the major and minor marks. Ashamed to face her father, she kept the child a secret for seven years.

Then one day she introduced the child to the king, admitting, "Father, I have a son." The very moment he beheld the child's perfect features, he fell into a faint. The princess helped the king to regain his senses and asked, "Father King, are you displeased?" The king replied:

"How could I possibly be displeased? He must be an emanation of the celestial beings who rekindle bloodlines and so he is here to revive the lineage of this Mahayana family. So beautiful is he, and conceived without a father, that he must be an emanation of a god. A Dharma is meant to appear in our bloodline through the grace of such a being—a teaching for realizing the greater vehicle in a single instant and awakening to enlightenment in a single lifetime. Tears flow from the eyes of this old man. These tears of joy flow because I am delighted with that boy. Daughter, you are totally blameless since this child is an emanation of Vajrasattva. This being so, he should be named Prahevajra, Delightful Vajra."

๑

Eventually Prahevajra reached the age of eight. One day he declared:

"Please stay well, mother. I am going north to the Dhanakosha region of this country Uddiyana, to the shore of the great ocean, where in the Enchanting Forest of Exquisite Taste, the udumvara flowers grow. In that forest lies the great charnel ground Golden Sanctuary of Expanding Delight with its sacred practice place known as Hooked Cave of Golden Rock. There is my place of practice. Unless I reach accomplishment in the sacred Dharma right now, this worldly kingdom may be mighty, but it is nothing more than one night's dream, and completely worthless when the time of death arrives."

Having paid his respects to his mother, Prahevajra set out to practice in Hooked Cave of Golden Rock.

Now, it was in the Year of the Ox, in the third month of spring, under the Victorious constellation and the parasol of the full moon, at the first rays of the sun, that the utterly pure emanation of the exalted Vajrasattva's body, speech and mind known as Noble Spirit Devaputra, appeared to Prahevajra. His form was visible but intangible—a body of light adorned with the major and minor marks, naked, with hair in free-flowing locks, wearing just a blue skirt, while holding a golden vajra in his right hand and supporting a crystal bell on his thigh. He placed the vajra in his right hand at the crown of Prahevajra's head, blessing him, and with a smiling face exclaimed, "A HA HO I."

A—nonarising
HA—unceasing
HO—nondual
I—indivisible

At the moment of realizing the indivisible nature, Prahevajra stayed for seven days in a single stretch of samadhi—within the natural sound of dharmata's unbroken continuity, in which neither the limited concepts of being separate or not separate, nor limited words, however profound and subtle they might be, remained.

When he at last arose, in his ensuing insight he continued to experience and realize the intrinsic nature of things, as unfabricated and vivid self-knowing, just like when a torch is lit in a room that once lay in darkness.

As a reminder, to stabilize this meaning so that it would not be forgotten or dissipate, Noble Spirit Devaputra exclaimed "AWANDHARA" and showed a symbol. In Tibetan, it meant, "Look at this radiant rainbow in the clear sky!" As he pointed, a bright rainbow appeared in the middle of the clear sky.

While Prahevajra looked, he realized that the clear sky that has no observable reference points symbolized dharmadhatu's space. The rainbow appearing unobstructedly with five colors within this unobservable nature was a symbol for wakefulness that is aware and cognizant. These two are not separate but indivisible and are the symbol for the nonduality of dharmadhatu's space and wakefulness.

Noble Spirit Devaputra and the rainbow appearing unobstructedly in a visible form symbolized the means for indicating. His form that was intangible and without observable reference points symbolized knowledge. That these two were not separate but a single identity, symbolized the nonduality of means and knowledge, and the nonduality of space and wakefulness. In this way, Prahevajra realized the nature of mind that is the basic state of all things—as a single identity possessing four principles—like the radiant rainbow in the clear sky.

This was when three dakinis—Blazing Face, the chief of the realm-born dakinis; Sky-Farer, the chief of the action-born dakinis; and Sky-Soarer, the chief of the mantra-born dakinis—suddenly appeared in front of Prahevajra and declared, "We will serve as your Dharma protectors and guard these profound teachings. We will bestow the siddhis on practitioners who observe the samayas, and we will punish those who flout their practice or desert their samayas."

Having spoken these words, the dakinis gave Prahevajra their blessings and offered him the essence of their life-force. Thus they are known as "the dakinis who pledged themselves without being exhorted by others" and as "the three guardian dakinis of the teachings who took the oath by themselves." The dakinis also announced, "The teachings possess extremely great blessings. They have immense potential and are very powerful, so it is of utmost importance to keep the samayas completely pure."

Merely by being shown the symbol by Noble Spirit Devaputra, the master Prahevajra understood. Simply by having understood, he realized the meaning. At that very moment, he cleared away the obscurations that are difficult to purify—the emotional and cognitive obscurations. Simultaneously he attained the accomplishments that are difficult to attain—the supreme and common siddhis. This was like the metaphor of a successful rice harvest where the stalks for roofing and mats are naturally obtained, or that of honoring a wishfulfilling jewel one has previously obtained which spontaneously fulfills needs and wants all at once.

After this, inspired by the master Prahevajra's blessings for the welfare of beings, faith spontaneously arose in the master Manjushrimitra's heart. This was like the metaphor of the sun that can reflect itself in a clean vessel no matter whether the vessel is near or far. It happened like this:

One morning, at the break of day, Manjushrimitra thought to himself:

"I wonder, even though one may have gathered the accumulations for eons on end and purified the obscurations for eon after eon, does one ever become liberated from samsara's misery, even after one or two incalculable eons?[20] Since one cannot be liberated any sooner, there should be a teaching for realizing the unconditioned nature in a single instant and awakening to enlightenment in a single lifetime.

"There is no one else to ask about this, so I must go to the glorious Nalanda temple at the gateway to the city of Kapilavastu where five hundred panditas of the causal teachings of philosophy and five hundred panditas of the resultant Secret Mantra reside. If such a teaching does exist, surely I will be able to verify it there."

At Nalanda he looked at the five hundred panditas of the causal teach-ings of philosophy with his right eye and the five hundred panditas of the resultant Secret Mantra with his left eye, and inquired:

"O panditas, I wonder, even though one may have gathered the accu-mulations for eons on end and purified the obscurations for eon after eon, does one ever become liberated from samsara's misery, even after one or two incalculable eons? Since one cannot be liberated any sooner, shouldn't there be a teaching for realizing the unconditioned nature in a single instant and awakening to enlightenment in a single lifetime?[21]

The panditas of the causal teachings of philosophy remained silent, but the scholars of the resultant Secret Mantra looked to one side to exhort the last pandita, who then spoke:

"No one among us knows such a teaching. However, make a journey to the west of here. Go to the glorious country of Uddiyana. There, in the region of Dhanakosha, on the shore of the great ocean in the Enchanting Forest of Exquisite Taste, the udumvara flowers grow. In that forest lies the great charnel ground Golden Sanctuary of Expanding Delight with its sacred practice place known as Hooked Cave of Golden Rock.

There resides the great master Prahevajra, the magical incarnation of a celestial being who rekindles bloodlines. He has been blessed by an emanation of Vajrasattva known as Noble Spirit Devaputra. He possesses a teaching for realizing the unconditioned nature in a single instant and awakening to enlightenment in a single lifetime. If you go there, you can receive it. Since no one else claims to know it, such a teaching cannot be found anywhere else, so you must surely make this journey!"

"To the west," where the sun appears to set, means to the west of the Vajra Throne. However, it could also mean the direction where disturbing emotions have set and no longer arise. "The glorious country of Uddiyana" refers to the place where there is the glory of realization for oneself and the glory of compassion for others. It is where those born as males are dakas and those as females are dakinis, and it is adorned with udumvara flowers.

In "the region of Dhanakosha," *dhana* means to ease the mind, while *kosha* means to protect the mind. "Ocean" means the water is salty and not suitable to drink. The shore lies a little higher up than the bank of the ocean itself. "The Enchanting Forest of Exquisite Taste" is a jungle and forest with fruit trees, the eminent taste of which, when eaten, has the power to generate bliss in one's stream-of-being. A little higher up on the outskirts of this forest is a site where only blue udumvara flowers grow.

"Charnel ground" is called *charnel* because conditioned thoughts dissolve into the unconditioned nature, and *ground* because it is where wakeful knowing transcends arising and ceasing. Like the Golden Isle that has no other earth or stones, in this "Golden Sanctuary" charnel ground no ordinary thoughts arise in one's stream-of-being. It is known as "Expanding Delight" because immense delight in the nondual nature of dharmata expands beyond direction and partiality.

This sacred practice place is the location where without exception one attains every supreme and common siddhi. It is called "Golden Rock" because of the unchanging nature of dharmata, "Cave" because of the deep meaning, and "Hooked" because of the lineage of masters who attain accomplishment in the profound nature of dharmata, the unchanging *Vajra Bridge,* are like uninterrupted hooks, one after the other.

Manjushrimitra then asked, "Well tell me then, how great is the difficulty and how long is the journey to such a perfect place?" The panditas are said to have given this reply:

"The difficulty is enormous. There are unpopulated areas with savage beasts, poisonous snakes, nonhuman spirits, demonic beings and other horrors. If you encounter the savage beasts, they will devour you on the spot. If you meet the poisonous snakes, they will bite you and suck your bones dry, leaving them in a pale heap. If you cross paths with the nonhuman spirits, they will swallow you whole. If you come face-to-face with the demonic beings, their shrieks will strike you dead while blood oozes from your eyes. As for distance, you must travel for thirteen whole months through such desolate areas free of human habitation. If it were not for such difficulty and distance, we would also make the journey."

The master Manjushrimitra then thought to himself:

"In the past, this body of mine has died for nothing more than samsaric emotions, now I will sacrifice it in pursuit of the Dharma. Even if my body dies once in this type of circumstance, without a doubt my mind must aim at Prahevajra's abode. The master will know this and bless my mind. If I can definitively interrupt this mind's perpetual roaming through samsara, then what does it matter if my body dies this once?"

With this thought in mind, Manjushrimitra resolutely began the journey. After thirteen full months, he reached a cliff where he met a tattered monk holding five arrows and a bow in his hands, while wearing his skirt tied around his head. Manjushrimitra thought, "I wonder—no one else comes here, so this must be the master Prahevajra."

When he was about to present the master with a mandala of gold, he did not find any water with which to sprinkle it. The master said, "You do have a body."

"But of course!" Manjushrimitra thought. "I have a body, the body has veins, and in the veins there is blood." He cut the vein commonly used for blood-letting with a *kamali* razor, arranged the mandala and sprinkled it with his own blood. Having arranged the heaps of gold, he bowed down innumerable times, circumambulated the master thrice and supplicated, "Great master, please let your realization dawn within me." Prahevajra simply left the great charnel ground without uttering a word.

Manjushrimitra followed him, circumambulating the master three times every day and three times every night, and prostrating to him three times a day and three times a night. Once a month he presented his request but still Prahevajra remained silent. Then Manjushrimitra thought, "He will not give me the instruction. If I return home, I may die on the road and risk roaming forever in samsara. Better if I kill myself right here. Even if my body dies, the master will bless my mind so that I will not continue wandering through samsara."

With this thought, he took out the *kamali* razor from his *kapali* pouch, and raised it with the intention of cutting his own throat. The master Prahevajra perceived this and exclaimed, "Manjushrimitra!"

"Yes," he replied.

"What do you want?" the master asked.

Manjushrimitra responded, "I want a teaching for realizing the unconditioned nature in a single instant and awakening to enlightenment in a single lifetime."

Prahevajra said, "Haven't you understood yet?"

"No, I don't see it. I don't understand it," Manjushrimitra replied. Then Prahevajra placed his right hand at the crown of Manjushrimitra's head and blessed him while uttering, "A HA HO I."

A means nonarising, HA means unceasing, HO means nondual and I means that the nondual nature is indivisible. At the moment of realizing the indivisible nature, Manjushrimitra stayed for seven days in a single stretch of samadhi—within the natural sound of dharmata's unbroken continuity, in which neither the limited concepts of being separate or not separate, nor limited words, however profound and subtle they may be, remain.

When he at last arose, in his ensuing insight he continued to experience and realize a vast self-existing wakefulness as unfabricated self-knowing—the intrinsic nature of mind that is the natural state of all things—just like when a torch has been brought into a room that once lay in darkness.

As a reminder, in order to stabilize this meaning, so that it would not be forgotten or dissipate, Prahevajra exclaimed "SURYADHARA" and made a gesture. Manjushrimitra understood this to mean, "Look up at the sun itself!" He looked up and saw that the sun itself transcends presence and absence throughout the three times, does not become clearer or dimmer, come or go, and is beyond arising and ceasing. He realized it to be one identity possessing these four principles.

Just like in that example, Manjushrimitra realized that his mind too is one identity endowed with these four principles; that like the sun, it is lucid yet free of thought. He understood this by simply being shown a gesture. By simply understanding, he realized the meaning. At that very moment, he cleared the obscurations that are difficult to purify—the emotional and cognitive obscurations. And simultaneously he attained the accomplishment that is difficult to attain—the supreme siddhi. The common accomplishments were attained incidentally like the metaphor of a successful rice harvest where the stalks for roofing and mats are naturally obtained.

Manjushrimitra understood Prahevajra holding the five arrows in his hand to indicate the five wisdoms. Putting them together with the bow indicated that means and knowledge are to be a unity without separation. He understood the skirt tied around Prahevajra's head to mean that the lower vehicles should not be rejected but be absorbed into the sphere of the higher. The three dakinis guarding the teaching then pledged to serve him and gave him their blessings.

Eventually the master Manjushrimitra, like the flight of a bird or like a breeze, left the charnel ground Golden Sanctuary and, arrived directly at the city Glorious Source of Qualities, which was situated thirteen whole months' journey away.

Now, through the spontaneous blessings of master Manjushrimitra, an inspiration formed in master Shri Singha's mind. Just like the sun or moon that can reflect itself in a clean vessel with pure water whether it be near or far, in the same manner however near or far, a true inspiration spontaneously dawned in Shri Singha's mind.

☙

The story continues with how Shri Singha is inspired to seek out the teaching that grants enlightenment in one lifetime. The panditas at Nalanda tell that Prahevajra is no longer among human beings, but before then a certain Manjushrimitra went to Uddiyana and received it. He supposedly flew to Glorious Source of Qualities, a city that lies to the south of the Vajra Throne, in the warriors' land of Bhetala, within a jungle of nine types of trees. It is a place that, in addition to the same list of hazards Manjushrimitra faced, can only be reached after crossing through a vast area infested by bloodthirsty yakshas who enjoy

Dharmaraja the King

feasting on live roasted travelers. Shri Singha escapes dreadful vipers by smearing his body with a special magic tonic. Then, using an oil lamp fueled by human grease to find his way through a maze of caverns he finally met Manjushrimitra. After several trials, he receives the transmission of the four syllables and is shown the symbol of the sky itself. Foremost among five hundred arhats, Shri Singha later became renowned as the defender of the northern gate of the Vajra Throne in debates with non-Buddhist teachers.

Vairotsana is the next master in this lineage whose records are better known from his biography. He also receives the transmission of the four syllables from Shri Singha but with the symbol being the crystal.

The early Mind Section source texts give more details about the masters in this lineage of transmission. We hear, for instance, that Kukkuraja the second Dog King was the son of Beta, the king of Mekhyo. Having learned all available tantras of Secret Mantra he became a renowned holder of the pith instructions. He composed sadhanas and commentaries on one hundred tantras, as well as the scripture on the Great Perfection known as Comprehension of Awakened Mind. This Kukkuraja in turn taught Maharaja in the town Source of Splendor.

Maharaja, son of the king Dong of Uddiyana, was a master endowed with the six types of higher perception by which he could see not only his own deaths and rebirths but that of others as well. He attained a vision of Manjushri and composed the scripture on the Great Perfection known as Spontaneous Summit of Awakened Mind. *Maharaja became the teacher of Aloke the Atsantra.*

Aloke the Atsantra, the son of the householder Mangala, was a master learned in grammar, logic and various philosophical positions. He was capable of rebutting attacks from non-Buddhist teachers and became a most excellent scholar. He had visions of the bodhisattvas Samantabhadra and Avalokiteshvara, held conversations on the Dharma with them and resolved profound topics. This master composed the scripture on the Great Perfection known as Wishfulfilling Jewel of Awakened Mind *and became the teacher of Dharmaraja at Radiant Vajra in the land of Zahor.*

Dharmaraja was the son of Lucid Brightness, the king of Golden Sanctuary. He was also a king, a guardian of the teachings, who inspired others to embrace Dharma of the ten virtuous actions and the six paramitas. By simply beseeching his yidam deity, he was able to fulfill his every need. Having attained a vision of the buddha Dharmevajra, he received teachings and empowerment. This master composed the scripture on the Great Perfection known as All-Encompassing Bliss of Awakened Mind *and in turn became the teacher of Devaraja on the sandy shore of the river Ganges.*

Devaraja, the son of King Courage from the western region, was learned in both Mahayana and Secret Mantra. Through the practice of Nectar Medicine he had a vision of the heruka and received a prophecy. He composed the scripture on the Great Perfection known as the Golden Razor of Awakened Mind *and in Dhanakosha of Uddiyana he taught the seven later panditas: Kukkuraja the Younger, Manjushrimitra the Younger, Bhashita the Rishi, Buddhagupta, Shri Singha the Younger, virtuous Kungamo the Younger, and Purasati the Courtesan.*

Among them, Shri Singha the Younger, who attained accomplishment through the nine deities of Vishuddha, composed the scripture on the Great Perfection known as Sun Mountain of Awakened Mind *as well as commentaries on Five Early Translations.*

Buddhagupta had a vision of vajradhatu mandala's thirty-seven deities through the Tatvasamgraha Tantra and attained accomplishment.

Bhashita the Rishi had a vision of glorious While Garland's mandala. Kukkuraja the Younger had a vision of the dakini.

Manjushrimitra the Younger is regarded as a miraculous reincarnation of the first Manjushrimitra and was born one hundred and twenty-five years after the passing of the first. He received the lineage from Kukkuraja the Younger, attained accomplishment through Awesome Wisdom Lightning and was able to employ the five rahulas and the five yamas as his servants. According to Jigmey Lingpa, this was the Manjushrimitra who secretly transmitted the Heart Essence to Aryadeva through which the great pandita attained rainbow body, and who taught Padmasambhava the Mahayoga tantras.

Kungamo the Younger attained accomplishment through White Ushnika and Vasundra. Purasati the Courtesan attained accomplishment through Vajra Tikshana.

In the following excerpt from Longchenpa's Illuminating Sunlight, which he had copied from Vairotsana's Autobiography,[22] we find songs of pithy instruction in which the early masters of the Dzogchen lineage in India and Uddiyana imparted vital insights and also spontaneous verse expressing their disciples' realization

Realization Songs of Awakened Mind

King Dhahena Talo—who was himself the son of King Helu Bhade and the brahmini Constant—was a direct disciple of Prahevajra, the nirmanakaya, from whom he received the essential realization. Nonetheless he received it in full from Manjushrimitra.

It was around that time that Manjushrimitra condensed the meaning of the realized state for Dhahena Talo in song:

> Awakened mind, endowed with major elements, these five:
> Unmanifest and all-pervasive, it is space.
> Wisdom earth supports the buddha of the mind.
> Wisdom water washes off the tendency for thought.
> Wisdom fire burns away all dualistic concepts,
> And to the goal, unshakable, the wisdom wind conveys.
> Mind's nature may appear as five such elements.
> Once you realize this lucid state—thinking and its source
>   nondual,
> Rest then uncontrived, while training in its self-occurring, self-
>   subsiding.

On hearing this song, Dhahena Talo, among others understood the intent of the realized state and he then expressed his understanding in these words:

Dhahena Talo the King

For I, by name Dhahena Talo,
Whose mind is like the sky's expanse,
This spacious vastness has no end or center,
No end nor center has awakened mind.
Within this centerless and endless nature,
My training now is nondistraction.

Having realized the essential meaning, he attained mastery over longevity.

Rajahasti the senior prince was the son of the king Dhahena Talo and his queen Victorious Perseverance. He had understood the essential realization from Prahevajra the nirmanakaya but received it in full from his father, King Dhahena Talo, who in song condensed the meaning of the realized state for Rajahasti, his older son:

The buddhas of the threefold time are the awakened mind.
From it arose all buddhas of past ages.
The buddhas of the present within this state abide.
And buddhas to appear, they will awaken there.
Your mind is thus the state awakened
Of all buddhas in the triple times.

On hearing this, Rajahasti the senior prince understood the meaning of the realized state and then expressed his understanding:

For I, by name Prince Rajahasti,
See awakened mind, self-knowing, nonarising,
And hold the line of Vajrasattva and the Ever-Excellent.
Without a journey, all at once, I reached the threefold
    buddhahood.
In this awakened state the buddhas of the triple time are
    equaled.

Princess Parani had understood the essential realization from the nirmanakaya Prahevajra but she received it in full from her older brother Rajahasti, the senior prince, who condensed the meaning of the realized state for her in song:

Since mind is free of matter's mass, neither grows nor crumbles,
Mind neither takes rebirth nor dies, and no one can injure or
    slay it.
Everything this mind contains; its nature is the dharmakaya.
To see this is the true awakened state--the Buddha.

On hearing this song, Princess Parani understood the meaning of the realized state and then expressed her understanding:

I am the princess Parani
For whom awakened mind does not arise and does not cease.
Once I realized this mind beyond arising, beyond ceasing,
The victors of the triple time are seen within this mind
And I am never separate from their realized expanse.

About then, Nanda the naga king, a bodhisattva emanation whose task it was to benefit the nagas, perceived that in the human world there was a wondrous essence of the doctrine, the nature of the Great Perfection. He then took birth as the son of Apardharmu Jnana and his wife Sagara, both of lowly caste, and they named him Naga King and also Nagaraja Sitrita. He met Prahevajra the nirmanakaya and heard his words, but the ripening empowerments he received from Rajahasti the senior prince. The meaning of the realized state he requested from Princess Parani who condensed its meaning for him in song:

> Do not block your senses six; delight in them with joy and ease.
> All that you take pleasure in will strengthen the awakened state.
> With such a confidence, empowered to the regal state of natural mind,
> The training now is simply this: let your six senses be at ease and free.

On hearing this song, Nagaraja understood the basic intent of the realized state and then expressed his understanding:

> I am Nanda, king of nagas,
> For whom emotions, unrejected, are the noble fivefold wisdoms.
> The three poisons, unrejected, are perfected as the body, speech and mind,
> And samsara, unrejected, the awakened path of greatest bliss.
> The awakened state within me shines—all the buddhas of the triple times.

It was then that Bodhi the Yakshini, the talented daughter of King Atharva, who was extremely devoted and intelligent, requested the meaning of the realized state from Nagaraja Nanda who then bestowed it in full and condensed the meaning for her in this song:

> Awakened mind, the never-lowered flag of victory,
> A changeless cross, unshakable throughout the triple time,[23]
> A triumph banner hoisted high in the battle with samsara,
> Once realized, keep it as the sovereign of insights.

On hearing this song, Bodhi the Yakshini glimpsed the basic intent of realization and then expressed her understanding:

> My name is Bodhi the Yakshini,
> One whose mind is timelessly awakened.
> Self-existing vastness is itself the Conqueror,

The purity, primordial, of all samsara;
Realizing natural mind, the awakened state I now have found.

About then, the commoner Rahuta and his wife Joyful Dhari had a daughter, known as Barani the Courtesan,[24] whose mind was bright and sharp and who definitely had the Mahayana potential. She requested the meaning of the realized state from Bodhi the Yakshini who then bestowed it in full and condensed the meaning for her in song:

Buddhas and all beings are no different from the first;
Realize this fact, the state sublime.
Once you realize nondual mind to be the dharmakaya,
Apart from this there is no higher training.

The courtesan understood the basic intent and then expressed her realization:

I am Barani the Courtesan
Who fully sees awakened mind, the sovereign of every view.
Mind is neither male nor female, so union I fear not.
Mind knows neither birth nor death, it does not die by slaying.
Worlds and beings are all nectar, timelessly transcending clean
and unclean.

It was then that Bhibhi Rahula, the king of Kashmir, and his wife Shila Kumara had a son who was known as Brilliance, the Kashmiri scholar. He became a pandita of the most erudite learning, and requested the meaning of the realized state from Barani the Courtesan which she bestowed in full and then condensed the meaning for him in song:

Awakened mind is the fruition resulting from no cause.
Awakened mind is the instruction that does not come from
words.
Awakened mind is the buddha who does not stem from
thought.
Like space, awakened mind is not a thing that can be seen.
Devoid of color, it is not a thing to be singled out as *this*.

On hearing this, Brilliance understood the basic intent and then expressed his realization:

> For I whose name is Brilliance the scholar,
> Within my state of fearless courage[25] whatever may occur,
> All apparent and existent things, in any way perceived,
> This mind lies far beyond both increase and decrease,
> As I have realized the self-existing, simple calm of dharmakaya's
>   vastness.

It was after this in the land of Uddiyana that Shri Raja and his wife Renowned had a son who had become known as Maharaja the Uddiyana scholar. He was a great pandita, fully learned in the five topics of knowledge in Uddiyana, the land where people wear their hair tied up in top-knots. Yearning to know the essential nature, he requested the meaning of the realized state from Brilliance the Kashmiri scholar who then bestowed it in full and condensed the meaning for him in song:

> The mind's nature is timelessly the buddha;
> When training cultivate just that.
> This training object is not found through reason.
> The training is: be undistracted from this nature.

On hearing this, Maharaja the Uddiyana scholar understood the basic intent and then expressed his realization:

> For I whose name is Maharaja,
> The training in awakened mind has gone beyond an object.
> By looking into mind, I found no thing to see.
> But seeing there's no thing to see is the very sight.
> The training now is nondistraction from this state of nothing
>   seen.

About then, the talented Princess Gomadevi yearned deeply to know the essential nature. She requested the meaning of the realized state from Maharaja the Uddiyana scholar who then bestowed it in full and condensed the meaning for her in song:

A single sphere, continuous, and not apart throughout the triple
    time,
A single sphere of natural freedom, beyond a path to travel,
Not bound by words, beyond a nature to be grasped,
Free from meditation object, I see the state beyond confines.

On hearing this, Princess Gomadevi understood the basic intent and
then expressed her realization:

I am the one whose name is Gomadevi.
The elements, all five, are consorts of the fivefold families.
The aggregates are the five buddha lords.
The elements and sense-bases are male and female bodhisattvas.
Samantabhadri is the ground-of-all.
Samantabhadra is the knowing mind.
Attainment is these lords and ladies in nondual union.

It was then that the rishi Paraja and his wife Youthful Bliss-Giver had
a son by the name Aloke the Atsantra, who was highly educated in the
causal and resultant teachings. Feeling deep yearning to know the essential nature, he requested the meaning of the realized state from Princess
Gomadevi who then bestowed it in full and condensed the meaning for
him in song:

To yearn for freedom and the levels delays enlightenment.
To yearn for gaining happiness is deeply painful.
To yearn for reaching nonthought is itself a thought.
Gain this insight and remain devoid of seeking.

Upon hearing this, Aloke the Atsantra understood the basic intent and
then expressed his realization:

I am Aloke, the learned.
Skilled in liberation, I cut arising's stream,
Skilled in union, the confine of ceasing is removed.
Skilled in the activities, effortlessly I achieve.
Skilled in siddhi, I depend on nothing else.
And skilled in meditation, uncontrived I now remain.

It was about then that Kukkuraja the Elder, the son of Kukkuraja Gatu and his wife Crescent Moon, who was a monk learned in the five topics of knowledge and especially learned in the *Eighteen Tantras of Mahayoga* of Secret Mantra, felt deep yearning to know the essential nature. He requested the meaning of the realized state from Aloke the Atsantra who then bestowed it in full and condensed the meaning for him in song:

> To see with mind and object split in two is just conceptual
> thought.
> To see them as nondual is the wakefulness pristine.
> To see while uninvolved in thought is meditation training.
> To see devoid of clinging is the natural liberation.

On hearing this, Kukkuraja resolved that his mind and all appearances were a state of natural freedom. He understood the basic intent and then expressed his realization:

> I am the one whose name is Kukkuraja.
> Mind transcends both birth and death, it is the vajra being.
> The form of vajra being is all-pervasiveness;
> Even the metaphor of space does not suffice.
> See this nature, stay unswayed—that is the meditation.

It was then that Bhashita the Rishi, the son of the rishi Kumara and his wife Dhari, who possessed the seven branches of the Vedas and who, in order to perfect the strength of original wakefulness, yearned deeply to know the essential nature. He requested the meaning of the realized state from Kukkuraja the Dog King, who then bestowed it in full and condensed the meaning for him in song:

> Awakened mind beyond arising, beyond ceasing,
> Perceives and yet transcends substantial nature.
> Awakened mind is not a thing that need be cultivated;
> Take rest within a state of ease, that is the meditation.

On hearing this, Bhashita the Rishi realized his mind to be beyond seeking. He understood the basic intent and then expressed his realization:

I am Bhashita the Rishi.
Just as the sky's expanse contains five elements,
The essence of all yanas is contained in Ati Yoga,
And the essence of all buddhas in the triple times within
    awakened mind.
To realize awakened mind is bodhi, great perfection.

Free of seeking, free of trying, mind itself is the Awakened One.
Beyond center, beyond edge, mind is such a vast immensity.
This mind, beyond arising, beyond ceasing, is the great
    accomplishment.
Apart from this there is no nature to be cultivated.

About then, Purasati the Courtesan, in order to realize that all phenomena exist within the profound continuum of the *bhaga* of the Mother, had a strong yearning to know the essential nature. She requested the meaning of the realized state from Bhashita the Rishi who then bestowed it in full and condensed the meaning for her in song:

You can realize the greatest knowledge
Within the state of total non-premeditation.
And when there is no thing to which you cling,
Then in the training you have reached perfection.

On hearing this, the virtuous Purasati understood the basic intent and then expressed her realization:

For I the courtesan Purasati,
The elements, all five, are the vastness of the consorts of the five
    families,
And this vastness is the basic space, Samantabhadri.
The all-ground of the Ever-Excellent,
I see as indivisible from basic space.
Awakened mind now shines just like the sun within the sky.
The meditator is the one who realizes mind itself.

It was about then that Nagarjuna, a monk learned in the five topics of knowledge, who had understood the meaning of the *Tripitaka,* and who

Nagarjuna the Learned

knew numerous resultant teachings on Secret Mantra, went in search of the nature of the effortless Great Perfection. After meeting the virtuous Purasati, he requested the meaning of the realized state from her. She bestowed it in full and condensed the meaning for him in song:

> While knowing, you may know that things are empty, yet be in
>   delusion.
> While holding, you may hold the view, but it is still a bind.
> While thinking, you may ponder dharmakaya, it is still a
>   thought.
> While meditating, you may nurture nonthought, but it's still
>   conceptual.

On hearing this, Nagarjuna understood the basic intent and then expressed his realization:

> For I whose name is Nagarjuna,
> My ease transcends a body, since dharmakaya is beyond the
>   aggregates,
> My ease transcends a voice, since speech unceasing is beyond
>   conceptual attributes,
> My ease transcends a mind, since wisdom mind surpasses birth
>   and death.
> Awakened mind I realize is the greatest ease.

About then, Kukkuraja the Younger, the son of Gyuhe Nagatama and his wife Mahena Charama, a man with deep devotion and broad knowledge, had become a pandita and understood without exception all the causal and resultant teachings. He yearned deeply to know the essential nature and requested the nature of the realized state from Nagarjuna who then bestowed it in full and condensed the meaning for him in song:

> The empty state means empty of perceiver and the thing
>   perceived.
> To understand it means a freedom from both names and
>   designations.

But emptiness means to be free of clinging even to this state.
And training in this emptiness means to remain like that.

On hearing this, Kukkuraja the Younger understood the basic intent and then expressed his realization:

My name is Dhahuna, the learned,
Who sees the skandhas and the dhatus, five, and all the rest,
As lords and consorts, male and female devas of the families,
Their nonduality, the all-ground of awakened mind.
The purity of worlds and beings is the mandala of conquerors.

It was about then that Manjushrimitra the Younger, the son of the rishi Lahina and his wife Highest Grace, had become a pandita in the causal and resultant vehicles. Yearning deeply to know the essential nature, he requested the meaning of the realized state from Kukkuraja the Younger who then bestowed it in full and condensed the meaning for him in song:

Mind is named with labels, yet transcends confines of names.
Mind is shown by an analogy, yet lies beyond examples.
Nondual, beyond objects to observe or to conceive—
While seeing this, the training is to be unswayed from
    nonobserving.

On hearing this, Manjushrimitra the Younger understood the basic intent and then expressed his realization:

For I, by name Manjushri Bhadra,
While training in the tantras of the twofold knowledge,
My aims achieved, the root of mind is cut.
And in this very moment, completely free of thought,
The fruit of the awakened state is none apart from that.

About then, the rishi Bhahi and his wife Bhagula Ocean Queen had an extremely gifted and intelligent son whom they named Devaraja. After seeking the essential nature, he requested the meaning of the realized state from Manjushri Bhadra who then bestowed it in full and condensed the essential meaning for him in song:

The reach of space transcends both ends and center,
But even that is not a match for the awakened mind.
Seeing that awakened mind transcends a thing to show,
The training is to stay composed while free of effort.

Upon hearing this, Devaraja understood the basic intent and then expressed his realization:

For I whose name is Devaraja,
Instruction in the greatest bliss, resulting from the statements,
Dwells in the deepest depths of mind and not in spoken words.
The Ati Yoga nature of Samantabhadra's mind,
This basic meaning, I have seen is changeless dharmakaya.

It was about then that there was a monk by the name Buddhagupta who was learned in the five topics of knowledge, but especially learned in the meaning of Mahayoga of Secret Mantra. After seeking the essential nature, he met Devaraja and requested the meaning of the realized state from him who then bestowed it in full and condensed the essential meaning for him in song:

This mind from which you never part, it is the great eternity.
And rigpa manifesting within mind is the awareness king.
Since mind transcends samsara, it is ambrosia most sublime.
The greatest mandala is mind, transcending edge and center.

Upon hearing this, Buddhagupta understood the basic intent and then expressed his realization:

For I whose name is Buddhagupta,
From time primordial, this mind is greatest bliss.
Since unknowing has concealed it from us all, it is the greatest
    secret.
But when this effortless awakened state is seen, it is the greatest
    training,
Yet buddhahood transcends both training and nontraining.

It was about then that King Accomplisher and his wife Nantaka had a son named Splendid Lion Prapata (Shri Singha) who refined his insight with five hundred panditas and became a great monk learned in the five topics of knowledge. He requested the meaning of the realized state from Buddhagupta who then bestowed it in full and condensed the essential meaning for him in song:

> This natural mind, invisible,
> Forever present in all things, the visible,
> But once you have resolved unchanging mind,
> The buddha is not gained elsewhere.

On hearing this, Shri Singha understood the basic intent and then expressed his realization:

> For I whose name is Splendid Lion
> Awakened mind transcends conceptual limits,
> Nondwelling actuality pervading all, samsara and nirvana.
> This wakefulness, self-knowing, beyond all limitation,
> Cannot be shown as tangible even by Vajrasattva.

About then Chamkha and his wife, the courtesan Patu, had a daughter, a nun by the name Kungamo. She was learned in the five topics of knowledge and, yearning deeply to know the essential nature, she decided to seek it out. She met Shri Singha and requested the meaning of the realized state from him which he then bestowed in full and condensed the meaning for her in song:

> Remain composed within the frame of mind
> Of someone who has done his task.
> And this, endowed with strength of presence,
> For certain is the state the Buddha realized.

On hearing this, Kungamo understood the basic intent and then expressed her realization:

> My name is Kungamo the virtuous.
> Just like a mighty river

Includes all smaller streams,
The teachings of the nine progressive yanas
Are all included in the Great Perfection.

It was about then that the son of the king Dhahena Chadu and his wife Singha Shipitika, a monk known as Vimalamitra who was learned in the five topics of knowledge, yearned deeply to know the essential nature. He met Shri Singha and requested the meaning of the realized state, who then bestowed it in full and condensed the essential meaning for him in song:

Five poisons, unrejected, are the five great wisdoms,
While samsara, unrejected, is a timeless, perfect purity.
And once you realize your mind itself is buddha,
There is no state to realize apart from this awakened mind.

On hearing this, Vimalamitra understood the basic intent and then expressed his realization:

A spacious vast is dharmata, ungrasped by thought.
This space of mind itself defies imagination.
Within awakened mind which is no object to conceive,
The basic nature is not gained through cultivation.
Not wrought by meditation, timeless, empty, not apart,
The training is this sameness free of thinking.

With this song the general story of the lineage masters is completed.

§

Among the early treasure masters who revealed the hidden teachings of the Great Perfection, two of the most noteworthy are Nyang Ral Nyima Özer and Guru Chöwang. Several of the tantras on Dzogchen that they revealed were later included in the Nyingma Gyübum, the Collection of Tantras of the Old School which was kept as a canon of scriptures separate from the Translated Words, the Tripitaka of Buddha Shakyamuni's teachings.

The following chapter contains selections from the famous Four Branches of Heart Essence (Nyingtig Yabzhi) compiled by Longchenpa, as well as selections from the revelations of Rinchen Lingpa.

The Four Branches of Heart Essence owes its name to the two mothers and two children. The mothers are the Secret Heart Essence of Vimalamitra, combining the intent of the Eighteen Dzogchen Tantras, and Padmasambhava's Heart Essence of the Dakinis, emphasizing the intent of the Tantra of the Blazing Brilliant Expanse. The two children are Longchenpa's compositions—the Quintessence of the Guru (Lama Yangtig), explaining the Secret Heart Essence of Vimalamitra, and the Quintessence of the Dakinis (Khandro Yangtig), explaining Padmasambhava's Heart Essence of the Dakinis. The Four branches also includes Longchenpa's Profound Quintessence (Zabmo Yangtig) which combines their most vital points.

The tradition of transmitting and teaching these wonderful and profound instructions and practices has continued to this very day.

PART II
Early Treasure Masters

up to the 14th Century

A

The perfected buddhas rise from A.

This A is most sublime of all the letters.

The A can conquer all samsaric and nirvanic states.

The A is like the mother giving birth to everything.

The A is like the father all-creating, magical.

The A is tantras of the Ati Yoga.

The A is tantras of the Chiti Yoga.[26]

The A is also truly known as Yangti.

Arising from within, the A is nonarising.

The A is ultimate of every utterance.

Self-existing, A transcends arising.

Knowing one, the A can liberate in everything.

Everything without exception is perfected in the A.

Nothing in itself, the self-existing A appears in every way.

Samsara, nirvana and the path are all mastered in the A.

—From *Equalizing of Buddhahood (Sangye Nyamjor),*
a terma treasure revealed by Guru Chöwang.

To introduce the perspective of the twelve Dzogchen buddhas, I would like to quote Dilgo Khyentse Rinpoche:

"The Ocean of Magical Display scripture describes how the sugatas of the ten directions, in their infinite manifestations of teachers to guide beings throughout three times, teach the luminous Great Perfection that is the very essence of the teachings of the three kayas:"

The conquerors, the sattvas and the yogis
Transmit through mind, through knowledge and through spoken words.

"According to this statement, our Buddha—the dharmakaya Samantabhadra—who is himself never moved from the state of realization in which the kayas and wisdoms are beyond meeting and parting, appears as the five families of sambhogakaya buddhas, as Vajrasattva and others. And it is the play of their compassionate capacity that appears in all the realms throughout the ten directions performing the deeds that benefit beings.

"Specifically in our Saha world-system they appear in two ways: as the supreme emanations of blessings and as the sublime emanations of wisdom. The latter (the twelve Dzogchen buddhas)—from Youth of Sublime Light in the realm Abundant Delight when a lifespan could last an incalculable number of years down to a hundred years when Shakyamuni lived in Anathapindada's pleasure grove in the land of Kapilavastu—the twelve teachers who appeared in the worlds of gods and humans to turn the Dharma wheel of the natural Great Perfection, as indicated by the Dra Talgyur Root Tantra are here regarded as the mind transmission of the conquerors.

"The lineage of symbolic transmission refers to glorious Vajrasattva's passing the teachings to the vidyadhara Prahevajra and down to Padmasambhava and Vairotsana. The transmission of sublime individuals is from then until now.

"The twelve buddhas are counted within the first of these three great ways of transmissions as their identity is at no time any other than the original wakefulness of the dharmakaya Samantabhadra. Nevertheless, their manifestations, names and physical forms appeared in various ways to guide beings in accordance with their needs."

A more detailed version of the twelve buddhas, phrased in Padmasambhava's words, is included in the chapter below entitled "The Golden Sun that Dispels Darkness."

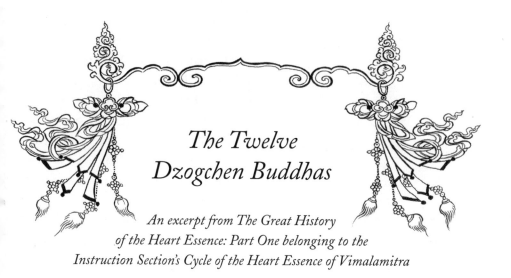

The Twelve
Dzogchen Buddhas

*An excerpt from The Great History
of the Heart Essence: Part One belonging to the
Instruction Section's Cycle of the Heart Essence of Vimalamitra*

Thus, for the sake of an inconceivable number of disciples, Vajradhara, the Great, the truly and completely awakened conqueror, magically conjured forth guides in forms that corresponded to those to be guided. And these emanations were all endowed with five perfections in the following way in order to purify the five aggregates of their retinues.

First, the perfect teacher Great Vajradhara appeared in the realm Abundant Delight, in the perfect palace of a lotus flower. Here, as the teacher Youth of Inconceivable Sublime Light, he taught the *Dra Talgyur*—the tantra that preceded all others, the root of all teachings—to a retinue of one thousand and two buddhas. The tantra's compiler was the celestial youth Mighty Bringer of Joy whose companions included the deva youth Brilliant Sun. This was during the time when a lifespan could last an incalculable number of years.

Youth of Immutable Light

Youth Playful Grace

Powerful Warrior Youth

Second, the place was the realm of the Saha world where the teacher Youth of Immutable Light taught a retinue of two hundred thousand dakinis the teachings of the five tantras of body, speech, mind, qualities and activities in the language of the five-braided Vishnu, the method being the natural sounds of the elements. This was during the time when a lifespan could last one million years.

Third, in Mass of Light a place composed of warmth and moisture, the teacher Gentle Splendor Protector Against Fear taught a retinue of six hundred thousand bodhisattvas the teachings known as *Overturning the Depth of Samsara, Peacocks with Entwined Necks,* and the *Glorious Tantra of the Resolution of the Four Elements,* while descending into midair and, using the wind's gentle *marshashu* whisper, he translated them into the language of the three-tufted garudas. This was during the time when a lifespan could last one hundred thousand years.

Fourth, in the place of the material womb, the source of passions, the teacher Youth Playful Grace taught a retinue of five thousand yakshas and cliff-living rakshas the teachings of eleven tantras—the five tantras of Mind Section and the six branch tantras—during the time when a lifespan could last eighty thousand years.

Fifth, in the place Healing Herb Garden of Youth, the teacher Vajradhara the Sixth taught a retinue of the seven successive buddhas the boundless teachings of the six paramitas and so forth, during the time when a lifespan could last seventy thousand years.[27]

Sixth, in the place of the Blazing Fire Mountain in the charnel ground Delighting in the Great Secret, the teacher Great Powerful Warrior Youth taught a retinue of seven, headed by the bodhisattva Vigorous Cloud,[28] numerous tantras including the father tantras and mother tantras, during the time when a lifespan could last sixty thousand years.

Wrathful Sage King

Seventh, in the place Raksha Sound of Rulu, the teacher Wrathful Sage King taught a retinue of ten million rakshas the teachings of the *Ten Tantras for Taming the Rough-Minded* and many others. This was during the time when a lifespan could last ten thousand years.

Eighth, in the place of the Vulture Peak Mountain in Rajgir, the teacher Sublime Golden Light taught a retinue of innumerable noble shravakas endowed with miraculous powers the

Kashyapa the Elder

teachings on the sublime Vinaya in ten thousand and numberless other sections. This was during the time when a lifespan could last five thousand years.

Ninth, in the place of the land of Turquoise-Browed Sogpos, within the palace of Complete Victory at the tree of enlightenment, the teacher Lov-

Hungkara the Indian Siddha

ingly Playful Wisdom taught a retinue of bodhisattvas on the eighth level the teachings of the *Seven Studded Tantras* and others during the time when a lifespan could last one thousand years.

Tenth, again at Vulture Peak, the teacher Kashyapa the Elder taught a retinue of seven venerable arhats the sublime teachings of the sutras and the tantric teachings on Kriya and Anu Yoga in seventy-five thousand parts. This was during the time when a lifespan could last five hundred years.

Eleventh, in the place of the Vajra Throne, the source of enlightenment, the teacher Truly Perfected Father King taught a retinue of lords of the three families[29] the teachings that were exclusively the definitive meaning. This was during the time when a lifespan could last three hundred years.

Again, in the perfect place of Anathapindada's pleasure grove the perfect teacher Shakyamuni taught his retinue of four groups the perfect teachings of the four truths in the manner of the Dharma-wheel turned twelve times. These twelve turnings were on impermanence, suffering, emptiness, ego-lessness, origin, the aspects of causes and conditions, path, reason, cessation, peace and perfection. This was during the time when a lifespan could last one hundred years.

Thus, in each of these twelve places where Vajradhara displayed five perfections, sixty in total, his appearance was for the purpose of purifying the eon's sixty increasing and decreasing segments.[30] ...

The *mind transmission of the buddhas of the three times*[31] is known as a transmission through blessings—the naturally perfect blessings of all the buddhas of the past and future, and of those who reside in the present. Independent of articulated words this transmission is understood and realized through the natural sound of dharmata.

Literally, *times* refers here to changelessness and *three* to the number. The word *cleared* refers to being free of the karmic, emotional and cognitive obscurations. The word *perfected*[32] means that the identity is perfected as kayas so that the three kayas transcend meeting and parting, while knowledge never parts from being the three aspects of original wakefulness; that abode is perfected as samadhi so that there is never any separation from the vajralike samadhi at any time; and that action is perfected as activity so that the thirty-six deeds are completed. The word *mind* here means that at the dharmakaya level mind holds no conceptual focus and therefore remains primordially free; at the sambhogakaya level mind is lucid and thoughtfree and therefore remains as self-liberated experience; and at the nirmanakaya level mind is free of attachment and therefore remains as a succession of arising and ceasing. The word *transmission* means free from omission and duplication so that from eons without beginning until this present yogi the words have neither been added to nor subtracted from and the meaning is unmistaken—just like a mark pressed into a vessel of precious metal or like the royal seal. The word *history* means that even though many *years* have passed, the *account* is like that related by people who were actually present.[33] For this reason the following quote is used:

> Without explaining the meaning of the history,
> The blemish of mistrust may then arise
> Towards the conqueror's teachings of the *Greatest Secret.*

Thus the word *transmission* is used for the statements of past masters being retained without omission or duplication, like a perfect vase filled from another perfect vase. Moreover, every person who understands and comprehends these points will definitely receive the blessings of the buddhas. The instructions of the transmission are therefore of utmost importance. This was about the mind transmission of the conquerors.

ITHI.

ᦡ

The following excerpt also belongs to the collection of sacred scriptures known as Vima Nyingtig, the Heart Essence of Vimalamitra. The Great History of the Heart Essence, also known as the Seven Segments to Establish the Great History, is the most extensive record of how the innermost Dzogchen teachings were transmitted from the primordial buddha Samantabhadra until they reached Tibet. The narration is interspersed with vivid descriptions of charnel grounds. This account was personally dictated by the great master Vimalamitra to two Tibetan translators—Kawa Paltsek and Chokro Lui Gyaltsen—in the hall on the middle floor of Samye.

Vimalamitra is one of the three masters who brought the Dzogchen teachings to Tibet. Padmasambhava describes him in the Sanglingma *biography, which he dictated to Yeshe Tsogyal:*

"The master Vimalamitra was an emanation of the Great Compassionate One. The Indian King Dharma Ashoka had a daughter named Dharmabodhi whose ravishing beauty resembled a divine maiden. Once, while sleeping in a flower garden, she dreamed that an extremely handsome white man came and anointed her with a full vase of nectar. As the liquid passed down through the crown of her head, her whole body was filled with bliss. After twenty-one days, without any physical discomfort, she gave birth to a baby boy. Thinking that it was dreadfully shameful to have given birth to a child without a father, she took the baby and abandoned him in the desert. Later when she looked for the child, she found him sitting with his eyes wide open and wakeful. Out of compassion for the baby, she took him home and nurtured him. Monthly and yearly the boy grew up much faster than other children. When five years had passed he went to the monastery of Nalanda. With the panditas there, he studied the five sciences and the Tripitaka. In particular, he became learned in all the tantras. He took ordination from the master Shri Singha and was given the name Vimalamitra, Immaculate Renown. Following that, he became the most eminent among the learned ones. He acted as the officiating priest for the religious king Dharmachakra and resided in the monastery of Vikramashila in the company of five hundred panditas."

The Heart Essence of Vimalamitra is a collection of many sacred scriptures: for instance, the Self-Existing Single Child of the Doctrine Tantra with its commentary by Prahevajra, the testaments of the past buddhas and the four vidyadharas.

Dilgo Khyentse Rinpoche, summarized Vima Nyingtig in these words:

"The Heart Essence of Vimalamitra consists of four profound cycles and one hundred and nineteen essential instructions on practice. Brought to Tibet by the great master Vimalamitra, crown ornament of five hundred scholars and siddhas, he taught them to Tingdzin Zangpo of Nyang, the Dharma-king Trisong Deutsen and others, after which he concealed these teachings as a terma treasure. Later revealed by Dangma Lhungyal and Chetsün Senge Wangchuk, throughout history these teachings have been regarded as the extraordinary spiritual wealth that was destined for Tibet."

Seven Segments to Establish the Great History

*The Second Part of the Great History
entitled the Seven Segments.*[34]

In the language of India: BHADU PATRI SAKARI NAMAཿ
 In the language of Tibet: *gnas 'byed bdun pa zhes bya ba*ཿ *lo rgyus chen mo gtan la dbab pa'o*ཿ
 In the English language: *Seven Segments to Establish the Great History.*

Great Vajradhara, sovereign of all beings,
Masters, upholders of all buddhas' realization,
Dakinis, adepts of wisdom activities,
And all protectors and venerable ones; homage to you.

This adornment for your eyes was created
To provide knowledge of the authentic historical meaning
And to instill certainty in skeptical people of future generations.

Here is the history of the siddha masters whose aggregates
  vanished,
Of the past knowledge-holders whose taints were naturally
  exhausted
While their bodily forms departed into basic space.

In unmistaken grammar and certainty of words,
With neither omission nor duplication, it is given exactly as
    spoken
In the *Tantra of Secret Sound* and the *Great Array*.[35]

For worthy heart sons who wish to understand it,
And in order to effectuate the key points of direct experience,
Here I shall explain in detail the words of the historical
    meaning.

In this regard, the word *vidya*[36] refers to Great Vajradhara endowed with ninety-six superior qualities. The word *dhara*, upholder, means to do exactly as he did by practicing in accordance with the key points. Who upheld his lineage? The great master Prahevajra and the other nirmanakayas.

After explaining in detail the meaning of various symbols and words, Vimalamitra continued:

To whom has this meaning been transmitted? It was transmitted to the magical emanation Prahevajra. Who transmitted it? It was transmitted by glorious Vajradhara. How or by which method did the transmission take place? The entirety of Secret Mantra is transmitted using innumerable symbols. What analogy can be used to describe how it was transmitted? Like filling a perfect vase from another perfect vase so that transmission takes place with neither remnant nor incompleteness. Why was it transmitted? It was transmitted so that worthy people of future generations can instantly understand the definite meaning. What then is the purpose of this transmission? It is that buddhahood, the fruition, will remain an unmistaken aim and that one's understanding, cleared of all concepts, will be free of distortion.

Three hundred and sixty years after the Buddha had passed beyond this wretched world, this happened in the western direction of the Vajra Throne in India, in the country of Uddiyana where people wear their hair in topknots, in the area known as Dhanakosha. This land was surrounded by sandalwood forests and inhabited by the type of animals known as *koshana*, whose bodies are human with bear-like faces and whose claws are beset with iron spikes. Since all materials are filled with tiny precious gems it is called Dhanakosha. *Dha* refers to all those areas where sandalwood trees grow.

There too was a grand temple, the auspicious Shankara Kuta, surrounded in the cardinal and intermediate directions by six thousand one hundred and eight smaller temples,[37] all exquisite, tasteful and interlaced by garlands of latticework with bells and jingles. The people had beautiful bodies with graceful limbs; their hair tied up in top-knots at the crown of their heads and adorned with gold, silver, sapphire and the like; and they wore garments in various combinations of red and white cotton. The women would tie their hair in two knots, one at the front and one at the back and embellish it with various conch and bone ornaments.

The king of this country had the title Uparaja; and with his wife, Radiant Light, they had a daughter by the name Sudharma. This daughter had become a renunciant and, having recently completed her novicehood, she had become a fully ordained nun. She then lived one league away in the western direction, having built a grass hut on the island known as Covered with Golden Sand, together with her servant Blissful Compassion who was a dakini.

While staying there carrying out her spiritual activities, the princess dreamt that a white man shaped out of precious crystal, tall like a spear, placed a crystal vase at the crown of her head and, uttering the syllables OM AH HUNG SO HA, empowered her with the five buddha families. To signify that she was being sealed with these syllables, he then placed the vase on her head three times and by doing so she saw that the light radiating from the vase simultaneously illuminated the three realms. In the morning the dream filled her with wonder and that noon she related it to her attendant.

"Princess, this is an omen that you will give birth to a nirmanakaya," the servant girl responded. This attendant was the dakini Serene Purna. "How disgraceful!" the princess thought.

Soon the princess became ill at ease and suffered bitterly. At the end of nine months and ten days, she gave birth to an illegitimate child who emerged through an opening in the right side of her ribcage. Appalled with the newborn, the nun exclaimed:

This misbegotten child must be a mundane spirit.
Is it a worldly mara or a brahma?
An evil spirit—gyalpo, tsen or mu?
Which one is he among the triple realms of craving beings?

But if it is a god or demigod,
No one here has ever seen its like.
How can this be possible; there is no example in this land?

Alas, to defeat samsara with uncorrupted ethics was my wish,
But this moral fall will cause disgrace—how dreadful!

She uttered many such sorrowful verses and would not heed even her
servant saying, "This is a child of the buddhas." Instead she replied, "Put it
in the ashes and cover it up." When the newborn was left in the pile of ashes
there were lights, sounds and others auspicious signs.

After three days had passed she looked again, and heard the infant's
clear voice and saw that it was totally safe and sound. So she took him up,
wrapped him in a clean blanket of white silk, and bathed him in scented
water and milk. "I wonder how he survived. He must be an emanation," she
thought. From the sky celestial beings sang these verses of auspiciousness:

Protector and teacher, conqueror,
Naturally manifest lord of the world,
May you safeguard us as well,
And bestow upon us the vajra of space.

While the dakinis amassed cloudbanks of offerings devas, nagas, yakshas
and other beings showered down a rain scented with sandalwood and saffron. In all directions the guardians of the world sounded the great drum of
the Dharma, blew horns, hoisted victory banners and raised standards, and
the great kings of the *rishi* sages filled the air with clouds of manifold herbs
and incense.

Once the infant began feeding he grew up extremely fast; in fact during a
single meal he grew more than others do in an entire day, and in two months
more than others do in a whole year.

When the child had reached the age of seven, he told his mother, "Listen dear mother. I would like to offer my respects to all the learned panditas. I would also like to have a frank discussion with them about the Dharma. So mother, please give me permission."

"How can a child who has not even lost his baby teeth participate in discussions on the Dharma?" the mother responded.

"By all means, give your permission," the boy insisted. The mother then said, "One league from here to the east, in the area known as Brilliant Dhanakosha, lives your grandfather, King Uparaja. You should go there as he has five hundred panditas in his court." Thus she gave her consent.

Overjoyed, the boy went to Brilliant Dhanakosha and met the king. After paying homage he said, "I am your grandson. Great king, since there are five hundred panditas as objects of veneration at your court, I would like to offer my respects to them. I would also like to have a frank discussion with them about the Dharma. So great king, please grant your permission."

The king looked at him and said, "How can a child who has not even lost his baby teeth participate in a discussion on the Dharma? How can he even pay respect?"

The boy then replied, "By all means, Your Majesty, grant your permission." The king then said, "You are merely a young child, but since your body is adorned with many of the signs that mark a buddha, it is possible that you may be an emanation. I shall therefore allow you to meet with the panditas." The king went inside and when the panditas were taking their meal, he related the above story about the boy.

"Nonsense!" one of the panditas exclaimed. "Have you ever heard of anything so frivolous? Don't let him in!" Another said, "How improper!" A third, who was one of the wiser among them, interjected, "Let him come up! Who can be sure that he isn't some kind of emanation? Last night auspicious omens appeared in my dream." "Have him brought up," they agreed, and he was lead in.

The boy paid his respects and then held a discussion with each of the panditas in turn. Not a single one of them could get the better of him and no matter what they asked his answers came freely and unhindered. Now the panditas bowed to him instead, lowering their heads to his feet, offering him their highest praises. Considering his vast wisdom, they named him Prajnabhava, Source of Knowledge. The king was overjoyed, so he named him Prahevajra, Delightful Vajra. Since he had not died even though his mother had buried him in a pile of ashes, she gave him the name Great Master Rolang Taldok, Resurrected Ash-Colored One. And all the people of the country said that since he was the most beautiful and serene among all the children, he should be named Master Rolang Dewa, Serene Resurrected One. His renown under these four names sprung from the powerful merit of having listened to the words of blessed buddhas and attending them while he had been a sentient being belonging to the four types of rebirth.

Prahevajra then went northward to Mount Brilliant Sun, where among its formidable cliffs he built a straw hut above the dwelling of a fierce *preta;* and there he remained composed in samadhi for thirty-two years. This caused the earth to tremble seven times, endless roars to sound from the sky, a multitude of flowers to rain upon the mountain, and the words "heretical doctrines are defeated" to be heard.

A heretical king, a perpetrator of evil, lived in the lower part of the valley and some children herding his cattle came across Prahevajra. They blew a trumpet into his ears but even that did not disturb him. They poked him with a *ubhi* cane, but that did not break his samadhi either. He remained utterly unperturbed and they related this to their king.

"This is someone who will advance the Buddhadharma and cause the doctrines of extremist philosophers to decline," the king exclaimed. "Send two assassins to kill him!"

Two men were given knives and sent on their way. Though the assassins tried their best to murder Prahevajra they could not succeed. When the master departed on a pathway between the clouds, awestruck the king and his entourage bowed in respect and praised him. They then embraced the Buddhadharma.

From the time Prahevajra was thirty-two years old, he taught all the precious *Collections* spoken by former truly and completely awakened ones, and especially the natural Great Perfection in six million four hundred thousand sections that were present in his mind. This took place on Mount Malaya, the peak of heaped jewels where the doctrine flourishes, at the request of Blissful Loka Taste—the vajradhatu dakini with three faces, wearing tiger's skin, her four arms holding a parasol of peacock feathers, and riding tigers and lions when setting out to act—and Yellow Bliss-Giver of Boundless Qualities—a dakini riding a dragon, holding a garland of lightning-bolts and enraptured in wrath.

For three years they recorded and classified what the master and the buddhas had taught. Meticulously and correctly, together with the nirmanakaya, they wrote down the letters of self-occurring naturalness. The wise dakinis then received permission to venerate the teachings and placed them inside the Freedom Cave of Dakinis.

These events demonstrate how the emanation appeared in person to ensure that the teachings would endure and that the short lineage for the teachings would last for a long time.

၆

Now, I shall as well describe the special source,
The place where all awakened ones appear,
In order to bring forth benefit.

After this Prahevajra went five leagues northeast of the Vajra Throne, to the great charnel ground Cool Grove which is one and a half league across, is level like a yard or like the palm of the hand. It has no perimeter or middle part, no highs or lows, but right in its center is the glorious Stupa of the Descent from Heaven made from copper with gilded wheels and a parasol. It resounded with numerous bells and jingles, and on its four sides were stupas each adorned with an image of the Buddha made from different precious substances.

To the northeast of this charnel ground was a wishfulfilling tree Bhisala, the support for mundane celestial beings, where countless winged scavengers would land and dwell. There the mundane celestial being Mighty Bringer of Joy—riding on a black tiger, holding a trident in his hand and wearing a long cape of red silk—was unhindered in collecting the life-force of beings, and lived together with a retinue of ten million.

This was a place where countless dakinis resided. Some were issuing rays of sunlight from their eyes; some were emitting thunderclaps from their mouths while riding on buffalos; some, riding on lions, were raising human corpses in their hands; some were eating entrails while riding on garudas; some were carrying corpses on spears and riding on jackals; some were drinking oceans of blood, having five or ten heads; and some were holding various types of animals in their countless hands. Similarly, others were raising their own decapitated heads in their hands; some had torn their own heart out and were holding it in their hands; some had cut open their bodies and were holding up their entrails to be eaten; some were riding on horses, elephants or oxen.

In the middle of all these and countless others was a delightful lake. Countless creatures lived in the charnel ground, but other beings were unable to go there for even an instant, and if they did their life-force would be seized directly and they would be devoured.

Considering this to be a place for disciples of misguided intelligence, the master Prahevajra went there, flying astride the naked daughter of Vishnu, whose hair flew free. All the terrifying beings living in this charnel ground gathered wonderful fruits that they offered him with deep-felt respect. Then with his back to the central stupa he taught the Dharma to the dakini Rays of Sunlight and countless others.

It was at this very time that to the west of the Vajra Throne, in the city known as Two Stages, the brahmin Benevolent Teacher and his wife Effulgent Lamp had a son, a lord and upholder of the sublime doctrine, by the name Manjushrimitra, a pandita exceedingly learned in the five topics of knowledge. From the sky, he received this prophecy from Manjushri Tikshna in the great charnel ground Excellent Valley, "Pay heed, son of a noble family. If you wish to attain enlightenment within this same body and life, go to the great Cool Grove charnel ground!"

In accordance with this prediction, Manjushrimitra went to the Cool Grove charnel ground where he met the master Prahevajra. Having presented his request, he remained with the nirmanakaya for seventy-five years receiving teachings.

Five hundred and forty-four years since the Buddha had passed beyond the wretched world, Prahevajra displayed the manner of passing into parinirvana by letting his material body disappear at the spring of the river Dantig to the northeast. The earth trembled six times, an immense mass of light rays and thundering sounds occurred, and Manjushrimitra fell to the ground in a faint.

When he had regained his senses, he looked about and saw that his guru was seated amidst a mass of light in the sky. Manjushrimitra then uttered numerous cries of despair:

Alas, alas!
When the teacher, the light of the lamp, has faded,
Who will dispel the darkness in the world?

Having uttered this three times, the guru extended his right arm, up to his elbow, from the effulgent mass of light in the sky. Accompanied by an awesome sound a one-inch casket of precious gold appeared, encircled Manjushrimitra three times, and then landed in the palm of his right hand. When he opened the casket and looked inside, he found that it contained Prahevajra's *Three Words Striking the Vital Point* written with self-engraved letters of refined lapis on paper made of the five precious substances.

By simply beholding these Manjushrimitra became like a perfect vase filled from a perfect vase. Thus, the time of Prahevajra reaching the exhaustion of phenomena coincided with Manjushrimitra's increase of experience.[38]

The emanation's self-display, spontaneous liberation,
Disclosed the topic on the natural emanation
So that the doctrine might remain for an extended time.

ITHI

ᨀ

Homage to the wheel-like nirmanakaya.

Following this, the master Manjushrimitra divided the untold number of millions of teachings into the *Three Sections of the Natural Great Perfection:* the teachings on settling the mind into the Mind Section, those on non-action into the Space Section, and those on the principal key points into the Instruction Section. The teachings among these that were especially condensed, the *Essence of Naturalness,* he divided into two: the *Hearing Lineage* and the *Exposition Tantras.* The *Hearing Lineage* he made into notes, while the *Heart Essence Exposition Tantra,* finding no one to whom he could entrust it, he concealed beneath the Boulder Marked with the Vajra-Cross to the northeast of the Vajra Throne. Together with the seal of the dakinis, he gave it the seal of the lord of the Dharma and made it invisible.

Following this, he proceeded to the great Sosadvipa charnel ground situated one league to the west of the Vajra Throne. Its circumference was one league and in its center was a self-appeared stupa, broad and lofty. It had wheels and a coral parasol and was made from precious silver. Beautifully decorated with bells and networks of jingles, it was ornamented with the sun and moon. On its sides were self-appeared images of the eight keurimas.[39]

To the northeast of this stupa was the lake known as Razor of Darkness in which water monsters and various other types of malignant beasts lived, and it was surrounded by a rocky shore.

There were also peculiar mundane gods and demonic spirits living to its southwest. In the top of a huge black *nyagrodha* tree, the god of trees, was the nest of a winged scavenger. Half way up was the nest of a jet black viper, and at the base a den of black flesh-eating boars. Among the mundane gods were Ananda Kumara whose face was that of a lion; and who was holding a sword, a human head, a wooden spear and a trident with a human head in his four hands. His body was decorated with garlands made from skulls and draped in a cloak of black silk. With a retinue of one hundred thousand slayer mamos, he was riding an ox, while gorging on flesh and blood.

There were also countless gatherings of dakinis. Some of them were riding lions with their hair hanging loose, raising up victory banners of nine stacked skulls. Some were riding on flocks of birds, holding banners of lion skin. Some had one body but eleven heads and were eating from entrails, hearts and various other things. Some were black women brandishing their braided hair while emitting jackals from their mouths. Some had human bodies but with wings and within the immensity of space they were hurling down rainstorms with bolts of lightning, while raising banners of tiger skin in their hands. Some of them were tearing the upper part of their bodies from the lower, and tearing out their lungs and heart. Some were cutting off their own limbs and tossing them in all directions. Thus there were an untold number of dakinis displaying various types of miraculous feats.

There were also winged scavengers, scavenging boars, venomous snakes, jackals in various colors, wolves and *kilikas,* and many other creatures. There were ghastly hornets, and innumerable heaps of fresh and old corpses, bones, pools of blood, huts made of human heads, and piled up houses of dried skulls. Some were scraping, some were eating, some vomiting, some whimpering, some were poking out eyes, some sucking out marrow and gnawing on bone, some were devouring entrails, and so on.

In the middle of all this dwelled the lords of yogis, the many male and female practitioners engaging in the various types of courageous yogic conduct. And here resided the great master Manjushrimitra, seated in the crossed-legged vajra posture upon a lion throne, with various raised banners and open parasols made from gold, silver, peacock feathers etc. He remained within a hut built from stacked skulls and bones, surrounded by a gathering of dakinis, sustaining his samadhi in the state of composure for one hundred and nine years.

§

Meanwhile in the Chinese region known as Soshaling,[40] the householder Virtuous One and his wife Wise Light had a son known as Shri Singha who was most erudite in the qualities of learning. He took birth in the city called Black Sho-Am Jom. From the age of fifteen, he studied the five topics of knowledge including translation, calculations, grammar, logic, treatises, and so forth with the Chinese master Hastibhala under the Tree of Enlightenment in China and became a pandita beyond dispute in just three years.

Shri Singha then resolved to visit the city of Golden Sanctuary situated to the west of the Tree of Enlightenment. He mounted an extremely sturdy black camel and headed west. While he was traveling through the wilderness, he had a vision: The Great Compassionate One, mighty Avalokiteshvara, displayed in actuality his countenance in the sky before Shri Singha and, with the mudra of revealing the truth, gave this direction, "Listen, worthy son of a noble family. If you wish to attain the definitive fruition, in the land of India is the city of Sosadvipa; noble son, go there!"

On receiving this direction Shri Singha was overjoyed and then had this thought, "I am still young, so in order to make it easier to understand this resultant Secret Mantra, I should train in the entirety of the Secret Mantra, both the outer and inner sections, for a duration of seven years."

He then headed back eastward through China to the Five-Peaked Mountain, Wu Tai-Shan, where for seven years under the low-caste master Bhelakirti he studied all the available tantras, statements and instructions of the outer and inner sections of Secret Mantra, as well as all the prevalent sadhanas.

Following this Shri Singha spent years on futile, empty pursuits until at the age of seventy-two, he took ordination at So-Yar Tha in China and observed the precepts for thirty years. Later on, while he was bathing in a quiet pool to the east of the Five-Peaked Mountain in the early morning, Shri Singha was transformed and briefly lost consciousness. When he had regained his senses and stood up, Avalokiteshvara appeared within a mass of light in the sky before him and again gave him a direction. Now Shri Singha thought to himself, "The journey to India from here is fraught with obstacles. I must go after attaining some miraculous powers."

In this frame of mind he procrastinated out of laziness for about another ten years. Then he practiced for three years and attained siddhi. In particular, he attained the vidyadhara level of mastering longevity. Thus it happened that nineteen years after he had attained the bodily support of a vidyadhara and nineteen years after reaching the land of India, he went to Sosadvipa through his miraculous powers—moving with the speed of the wind for nine *day-nights,* one cubit above and not touching the ground, and here met with Manjushrimitra.

Having paid homage, prostrated, presented mandala offerings and done all that is necessary to show respect to a guru, Shri Singha requested, "Please accept me as your disciple," and he was accepted. For twenty-five years he then received all the instructions and practiced them right there. At this point it was eight hundred and thirty years since the Buddha's parinirvana.

It was at the top of the stupa in the center of the charnel ground in Sosa-dvipa that Manjushrimitra displayed the manner of passing away by letting his material body disappear while the sky was filled with lights and sounds, and musical harmonies resounded across the land. Shri Singha fell to the ground in a faint. When he had regained his senses, he looked about and saw that the sublime master was seated amidst a mass of light. Shri Singha uttered these cries of despair:

Alas, alas!
When the teacher, the diamond light, has faded,
Who will dispel the darkness in the world?

When he had uttered this, his guru extended his right arm up to his elbow. A one-inch casket of precious substance with Manjushrimitra's testament entitled the *Sixfold Meditation Experience* then landed in the palm of Shri Singha's right hand. When he opened the casket and looked inside, he found that it contained letters written with one hundred and one gems on paper composed of five types of precious substance. By simply receiving them, Shri Singha attained the confidence of realization, so that, like a perfect vase filled from a perfect vase, he became free from delusion about the meaning while neither missing nor doubling a single word.

Three hundred and twenty-five years after this had happened, this same Manjushrimitra took a miraculous birth in a place in the western part of India known as Adorned with Golden Flowers, where he became renowned as Manjushrimitra the Younger. Following this, he taught Padmasambhava, the master of Uddiyana, the entire *Sadhana Section* of Secret Mantra. Later on, he taught the doctrine of the *Brilliant Essence of Gold* to Aryadeva who persevered in the practice of yoga. On Mount Mass of Cane in the charnel ground known as Fragrant Grass, Aryadeva awakened to true and complete enlightenment while his material body vanished.

This related the topic of the charnel grounds that promote supreme bliss.

ITHI

🌀

Glorious wisdom, endowed with the perfect wheel,
Everywhere throughout the ten directions of the six worlds,
I salute the one who is always difficult to find.

After Manjushrimitra had passed on as related above, Shri Singha took all of the Secret Mantra teachings comprising the secret key points out from beneath the Vajra Throne, and brought them to the Source of Buddhas at the Tree of Enlightenment in China. In the quarters linked to the upper storey of the temple at the Tree of Enlightenment, Shri Singha categorized all these perfect writings—the source of the Buddhadharma—from the Bindu Cycle of the Great Perfection into four: the Outer Cycle, the Inner Cycle, the Secret Cycle and the Secret Unexcelled Cycle.

For the elaborate type of individuals he combined three of the cycles, put them in a copper box and underneath the balcony in the temple, in the intersecting area between four pillars, he concealed them for the sake of future generations. Together with the seal of the dakinis, he gave it the seal of the lord of the Dharma and made it disappear from sight.

After this Shri Singha kept the exceedingly profound key points, the Secret Unexcelled Cycle of the Utterly Great Perfection inseparable from his own body and carried it with him wherever he went.

Once, in a dense dimension of space, Guru Shri Singha was sustaining the secret level of experience and physical types of conduct, when during a night's dream a woman bedecked with ornaments and in the guise of his own mother, told him these words:

Ema! My son, rise up! Esha! Listen!
You must bury the *Essential Heart Essence*, the most secret
    embodiment of all secrets,
And seal it within the Auspicious Ten Thousand Gates Temple.

It will become the seed of the Buddhadharma for future
generations.

The one who gave this prediction was the dakini known as Manifest
Adornment. Three days later, Shri Singha concealed the teachings in the
cavity of a pillar of the Auspicious Ten Thousand Gates Temple. He gave
them the twofold seal of the dakinis and the lord of the Dharma, then made
them invisible. Moreover, entrusting them in the special care of the female
protector Ekajati, he made this aspiration, "May they meet with my worthy
heart son!" Thus he made them vanish from sight.

Furthermore, Shri Singha concealed texts on astrological calculations
in the Trawa Thawa Temple at the Five-Peaked Mountain in China, and
made them also disappear from sight.[41]

Now Shri Singha went to the Cooling charnel ground in China, a place
surrounded with innumerable trees. Inside of which it was encircled by *kara-
vira* trees, and within that there were groves of cane and reed. In the middle
of this were countless corpses, both fresh and old, and here the dakinis were
emitting their many cries, devouring flesh, drinking blood, gnawing on
bones, and flying through the sky in their multifarious forms and variegated
colors, blowing horns and sounding many other kinds of instruments.

Amidst all this was a mansion of piled skulls, blazing at the top with
flames and wafting with strands of varied shapes of smoke, smears of human
fat at the shoulder, and at the base were naga maidens bathing. Here Shri
Singha remained in samadhi; he sat in the cross-legged vajra posture on an
elephant throne and upon a celestial *vishnu* stripped naked. This was when
the devas, asuras and other such beings honored him by holding up parasols,
victory banners, standards, streamers and so forth.

At this very same time, in Elephant Forest in the western part of India, in
an area with nine hundred thousand cities, the householder Blissful Wheel
and his wife Bright Spirit had a son by the name Vimalamitra. And, in the
city by the name Kamalashila in the eastern part of India, the low caste
Shanti Lagpa and his wife Virtuous Mind had a son who became known
as Jnanasutra.[42] During this time five hundred panditas resided at the Vajra
Throne in India among whom these two—Vimalamitra and Jnanasutra—

became the most learned, insightful and educated. They had a karmic connection from a previous rebirth, since they had been born as sons of the brahmin Sattva, and therefore became good friends.

One day, to refresh themselves from the midday heat, they had gone one league to the west of the Vajra Throne, to the most dense Grove of Reed, a place adorned with extremely fragrant flowers. A sound was heard from the sky and they simultaneously looked up and saw the glorious Vajrasattva present in actuality in a rainbow-like form. Vajrasattva then gave them this prophecy:

> Pay heed, you sons of a noble family. Five hundred times you two have lived the lives of panditas and enjoyed the sublime Dharma, but you have not yet attained the fruition of Secret Mantra. So, if you wish to attain the fruition of buddhahood, and within this same life let your material body vanish, you must go to the temple underneath the Tree of Enlightenment in the land of China!

Since Vimalamitra was the more industrious, by simply being given this prediction, he immediately went back, took his begging bowl from his quarters and set out on his way. After arriving in front of the Tree of Enlightenment in the land of China, he met with the learned Shri Singha. The sublime lord was utterly pleased, and for a duration of twenty years, he bestowed the instructions of the Hearing Lineage and the teachings of the Outer, Inner and Innermost Cycles of tantras. He did not however give Vimalamitra the manuscripts. Nonetheless Vimalamitra was satisfied and returned to India.

At the outskirts of the city named Enchanting Grove in India, he met again with the learned Jnanasutra. Jnanasutra remembered the previous prophecy and asked, "Vimala, is the tathagata emanation still alive?" "Yes he is," Vimala replied. Jnanasutra then thought to himself, "What lousy diligence I have!" and he immediately set out to the land of China. Through natural blessings he reached there, covering the distance in a single month which would otherwise take nine months.[43]

Not finding the master when he arrived in front of the Tree of Enlightenment, Jnanasutra became upset. He searched all around but the master was

Jnanasutra

nowhere to be found. As Jnanasutra was thinking to himself, "Earlier I didn't ask Vimala where he stayed," he did not see anyone but a dark and rather graceful woman carrying a water pot on her back. She had a full row of teeth as white as conch and her eyebrows were one unbroken turquoise-colored line. In the middle of her forehead she had wrinkles resembling a vertical vajra. Remarkably radiant, she was holding a turquoise-colored parrot in her hand. She said, "Listen, worthy one! If you wish to receive the sublime and definitive teaching, it will be revealed to you at Auspicious Ten Thousand Gates!" Thus he received a prophecy from the dakini Noble Kindness.

Jnanasutra then went to the center of China where, in the great city known as Auspicious Ten Thousand Gates, you could see two thousand five hundred temples when looking out through the eastern gate. When looking through the gate to the south, west and north, you could also see two thousand five hundred, so that the city was situated in the middle of ten thousand. These temples had stories of shrine rooms with ten thousand different major and minor images. Each of them had a sangha of ten thousand monks, and ten thousand horses and elephants. Since it had a corresponding number of songbirds and musicians, it was known as Ten Thousand Gates.

Jnanasutra did not find the master there either and became deeply discouraged. "What lousy merit I have! No one is more unfortunate than me!" he thought. While he was thinking that he probably would not meet the master, on a balcony to the northeast, he saw a creature with the body of a lion, the neck of a peacock and the head of a scorpion. It had various circles on its body and was holding a staff with three piled skulls. Then it spoke to him:

Ema, you fortunate one!
Until now the master has been in the area of Danti.
Most fortunate one, straight to the north from here,
There is the Cooling charnel ground.
There you will find the gathering place
For affectionate dakinis
And those with the karmic link.
Son, you must go, you must go to that place!
At leisure you will then receive the Secret Mantra.

Having received this prophecy from the dakini Chari, Jnanasutra went and met with Shri Singha. After presenting a mandala offering of precious substances he prostrated, made circumambulations and then begged, "Please accept me!" Shri Singha rose from his seat upon the naked *vishnu* within the mansion of piled skulls, and without saying a word he raised his hand showing three vertical fingers and looked into the sky. At that moment Jnanasutra thought, "I wonder if this means that he will give the teachings in three years." Shri Singha knew what he was thinking and nodded his head three times.

For a period of three years following this, Jnanasutra made mandala offerings, gave massage and applied lotions, attended and served the master in all other necessary ways. When three years had passed, Jnanasutra once more prostrated himself and circumambulated Shri Singha, offered thirty-eight ounces of gold dust and beseeched, "May the master please accept me!" Shri Singha consented and for nine years he bestowed the Hearing Lineage.

At that time Jnanasutra thought, "There must be manuscripts that set down the system of these teachings." He requested them and they were taken out from the Tree of Enlightenment and given to him. The teachings for these *Exposition Tantras* were established over the next eleven years.

As Jnanasutra now was pleased and rejoiced, Shri Singha said, "Are you completely satisfied?" Jnanasutra replied, "Yes, I am completely satisfied." The master said, "That is unfounded!" Jnanasutra then thought, "Now, there must be an extremely profound application of these teachings!" He requested it, and the master said, "For that, one must obtain the empowerment."

Consequently, in the Auspicious Ten Thousand Gates Temple, Shri Singha conferred the complete outer elaborate empowerment and then gave the instructions for the Secret Unexcelled Cycle over a three year period. Then the master said, "There is a manuscript for these teachings that I shall give to you when the time is right." After that he completed giving most of the last pieces of instruction.

Now Jnanasutra thought, "I have completely ascertained all the teachings. I should go to India!" Later he had second thoughts, "It is pointless to go to one's homeland! I have the teaching on awakening to enlightenment. I will practice it right here and attend the master!" Then he said to the master, "I want to practice." The master replied, "In order to practice you must complete the empowerments, since this is the installment-style." Following this Shri Singha conferred the complete unelaborate empowerment within an empty city. For a year after that, on the summit of the great mountain Kosali, he concluded the practices for *separating samsara and nirvana.*[44] Then he was given in completeness the very unelaborate empowerment and attained an extraordinary degree of certainty.

A month later he was conferred the extremely unelaborate empowerment in full and attained mastery over his own mind. For sixteen years after this, he practiced while observing the master's conduct.

During this time, Shri Singha would occasionally engage in the courageous conduct of retaining the breath. Occasionally he would perform the special conduct of riding on a tiger or a buffalo. His body was naked, emitting blood and tallow, with various feathers inserted in the top-knot of his braided hair. As he rode through the charnel grounds, he held a sword in his right hand and in his left, a skull cup filled with blood, which he would drink.

Sometimes, as he toured the charnel grounds, he would ride an elephant while dressed in the skins of a tiger, sounding a damaru in his hand and wearing a royal crown. In this way, he would perform various types of conduct. Sometimes, he benefited beings by means of numerous types of auspicious coincidences of earth, water, fire and wind.

At this time Shri Singha was invited by Resplendent Giving, the king of Li, so he went there on a six-legged white lioness, under a palanquin with three parasols of silk unfurled above, which was carried by six powerful *yaksha* youths. On the morning of the eighth day after his departure, a loud sound was heard. When Jnanasutra looked and saw the sublime master seated amidst a mass of light in the sky, he fell to the ground in a faint.

After Jnanasutra had regained his senses, he saw that the heavens were illuminated amidst a mass of light and all of the sky resounded with endless harmonies in the most melodious ways. The whole earth was quaking, trembling and shaking, and was covered with boundless heaps of flowers of gold, silver and other types. Thinking, "My guru has performed the drama of passing away," he uttered deep-felt cries of despair:

Alas, alas!
When the teacher, the light of the lamp, has faded,
Who will dispel the darkness in the world?

When he had uttered this, Shri Singha's testament, the *Seven Spikes*, fell into the palm of Jnanasutra's hand. Then he heard a voice giving this prediction, "Take out all the instructions on the *Secret Heart Essence* that are concealed within the intersecting pillars of Auspicious Ten Thousand Gates, and then go to the Bhasing charnel ground."

This happened nine hundred and eighty-four years after the Buddha's passing. And this chapter also discloses the topic on the charnel ground for forming the resolve towards supreme enlightenment.

§

Homage to the wise lord of knowledge
Who is endowed with the three kayas and five wisdoms.

Jnanasutra then thought, "I will act in accordance with the guru's instructions." He took out the secret manuscripts, wrapped them in reed-silk, and gave them to two Chinese, Limin Ganapati and Noble Spirit Wisdom Glory, to take care of while he went to the Bhasing charnel ground in India.

This charnel ground lies far to the east of the Vajra Throne. To its north is a black mountain that resembles a sleeping elephant with water flowing from its mouth. To its south is a mountain that resembles a yellow tiger standing upright, fragrant with the scent of *gorshikha* sandalwood. To its west is a cliff that looks like a lion leaping into the sky, which has the nest of a garuda bird. To the east is a *li* tree resembling the head of a *brahma* god, from which all possible needs and wants appear.

In the center of this charnel ground is the Stupa of Perfect Merit cast from precious copper and iron. Its life-pillar is made from *snake-essence* sandalwood and its top is a parasol looking like the bud of a multicolored lotus flower. On the ledges are painted layered wheels of azurite gemstones. At the base are interlinked lotus-hearts on the surface of its ledges. On the last ledge are *singha,* the king of trees, extending into all directions. The interwoven branches of these trees are connected by garlands and pendants resembling turquoise cords. On all the lower ledges are numerous creatures of the charnel ground. Above them countless divine maidens make circumambulations. Above them scores of nuns holding cymbals circumambulate. Above them circle emanated birds of many types.

Half a league directly south is a crystal mansion, a shrine for mundane gods embellished with portals. Here dwells the black-colored Time-Line Lord of the Dead, tossing her mane, clenching her fangs. With a huge belly and heaven-turned eyes, she is surrounded by a thousand mundane *mamos.*

Above there dwells Dhari the Divine Maiden, the one who sets the world in motion. She is red, naked and riding a donkey. Her bloody braids cover the earth and smoke pours from her eyes. Flames spring from her mouth and her right hand brandishes a trident stacked with human corpses. Holding a vase in her left hand, she is surrounded by a retinue of eight hundred *maras.* She sucks the blood of the living and slays samaya violators.

This is the charnel ground of never-ending heaps of corpses, both old and new, piled one top of the other in untold numbers. The creatures dwelling in this charnel ground enjoy a boundless variety of fruits and have no interest in flesh and blood.

In the cardinal and intermediate directions are houses made of fresh human heads. In the east is the dark brown Learned Splendid Wisdom with five faces who rides a garuda and travels throughout the three realms. Her braided hair coiling upwards is fully enclosed in garlands of skulls. Her ten hands hold a wheel, lotus flower, spear, small corpse, and a bow with arrow. Her left hold a monk, lion, jackal, banner, bow and so forth. She wears the attire of the charnel ground and is surrounded by a retinue of one thousand pacifying dakinis.

To the south is the dakini Protective Mind of yellow color. With one face and two arms, she rides a *ganapati.* Her terrifying, naked form has wings of turquoise and sapphire. Her right hand has a skull filled with Varahi's wine while her left holds the form of accomplishment. Mouth agape, she glares with bulging eyes, and is surrounded by a thousand enriching dakinis.

Furthermore, to the west is the Great Blaze who is red and naked, with captivating hair. Her right hand holds a vajra and her left extends a lasso. She rides an antelope and is surrounded by a retinue of one thousand dakinis of the magnetizing family.

To the north is Ever-Excellent of green color, with free-flowing hair. Her right hand holds an owl and her left raises a falcon. She rides a wolf surrounded by one thousand dakinis of the karma family.

The narration continues with a much more lengthy, colorful description of the various inhabitants of the charnel ground.

§

Amidst all of these, Jnanasutra remained seated while teaching all the dakinis the definitive secret teachings of the Secret Heart Essence.

At this time, Vimalamitra was living in the Smaller charnel ground, engaging in the courageous conduct, riding a blue buffalo, a shading parasol in hand, and wearing his robe over his right shoulder. From the sky he heard the voice of the dakini Splendid Wisdom giving this prediction, "Listen, fortunate one! If you wish to receive the instruction of the Heart Essence, even more profound than the previous cycles, go to the great Bhasing charnel ground."

Since Vimalamitra had exceedingly deep perseverance, he immediately proceeded to Bhasing charnel ground where, as stated above, the learned Jnanasutra resided. By merely meeting him, he felt an extraordinary devotion so that—even though they had formerly been peers and disciples of the same master—he bowed down and made circumambulations, with no regard for his own stature.

"Pay heed, sublime one," he said. "You now possess an instruction that is unlike what I received in the past, so please accept me as your disciple." He accompanied this request with a bow of his head, and upon doing so the master emitted rays of light from the curl of hair between his eyes, extending nine hundred and ninety-five fathoms. Vimalamitra was struck with amazement. The master then said, "There is nothing amazing about things like this." Turning his gaze to the sky, he conjured forth sambhogakaya realms filling the expanse of space and declared, "These sublime buddha emanations with countless different instructions have no material forms and are utterly beyond samsara. They possess nothing but wonderful instructions you have never received. So, noble son, you must complete the four empowerments with the utmost devotion and yearning."

Right there, he conferred the entire elaborate empowerment. As the sign of having received it, the curl of hair between Vimalamitra's eyes shone with a brilliant glow. For a year following this, Vimalamitra was given the unelaborate empowerment within a divine mansion. As the sign of having received it, smoke-like vapor rose from every pore of his body.

Then, for a duration of six months on the peak of Mount Brilliant, Vimalamitra completed the practices for separating samsara and nirvana. He was then bestowed the very unelaborate empowerment in full and gave rise to extraordinary experiences. As the sign of having received this empowerment, a white A appeared at the tip of his nose, hanging like a drop about to fall. For six months after this, he was given the extremely unelaborate empowerment in completeness and through this he perceived the nature of mind unimpededly. By then, the two learned masters were one hundred and three years old.

When receiving the first empowerment, he was given the instructions and scriptures for the three cycles. During the second, he was given the scriptures of the Secret Unexcelled Cycle and at the third empowerment he was also given the oral instructions. At the fourth, he was given all the concise key points for the Heart Essence teachings without anything left out. For fourteen years he resolved the instructions definitively.

It was then nine hundred and ninety-four years since the Buddha's passing beyond the wretched world, at which time Jnanasutra dissolved his material body and displayed the manner of transcending the world of woes, departing with no physical remains left behind, and the sky filled with lights.

In a faint, Vimalamitra fell to the ground. When regaining his senses, he looked up and saw that in the sky, amidst a mass of light, the master was seated, the sky filled with parasols, victory banners and standards, all of divine raiment, and the ground was thronged with various kinds of devas and human beings. In deep sorrow, he cried out,

Alas, alas, oh my!

When the teacher, the lamp, is gone,
Who is there to dispel the world's darkness!

As soon as he had uttered these lines, the master Jnanasutra extended his right arm, and dropped a jewel casket in the palm of Vimalamitra's right hand. By merely receiving this casket studded with five types of jewels, he received the instruction known as the *Fourfold Means of Settling*. Through this Vimalamitra's understanding was complete—free from omissions or duplications in words and free from misunderstandings in the meaning—just like a vase filled to the brim from another. To bring his unripened understanding to maturity, he proceeded to open up the charnel ground abodes.

ITHI

🅢

Guru Tashi Tobgyal further mentions: At some point, Vimalamitra remained as the teacher and object of veneration for King Dharmapala in the city of Bhirya to the west. Later he engaged in the courageous conduct of total victory, living in the great charnel ground known as Brilliant while teaching the Dharma to ferocious beings.

Vimalamitra made three copies of the manuscripts of the supreme secrets: one set he concealed on the island Covered with Golden Sand, in the land of Uddiyana, one set within the craggy cave known as Suvarnadvipa in Kashmir, and one set he placed in that charnel ground to serve as an object of veneration for the dakinis.

In the scripture Vimalamitra continues to explain the definite numbers of charnel grounds in this world.

🅢

I shall now reveal the wondrous story of the *hearing transmission of sublime individuals*.

In this regard *individuals* are of three types: individuals who are magical emanations, individuals who master the path and aspiring individuals. The magically emanated individuals included the precious king, ministers and so forth who are truly enlightened buddhas that only magically appear in the form of ordinary people. Individuals with mastery of the path are those who have attained accomplishment. Aspiring individuals are those who wish to attain accomplishment. The word *individuals* (*gang zag*) literally means those whose tainted (*zag*) physical body is filled (*gang*) with full-fledged sublime wisdom so that through the unmistaken oral lineage this materiality vanishes and they awaken to enlightenment; by doing so, all the taints, the emotions and so forth, are brought to exhaustion.

The word *hearing* refers to the flawless faculty of hearing so that there is an understanding of words articulated free from omissions and duplications and that their meaning is conclusively verified by the individual. The meaning of *transmission* is that—from the dharmakaya teacher, the truly and completely awakened buddha down to me, the present yogi—the words are free from omissions and duplications, they are articulated flawlessly, without additions or deletions by ordinary people. From the very first, the words have been transmitted from one person to the next in exactly the same quantity, just like a gold ingot of highest quality passing through many people's hands, so that it arrives in the last person's hand without being added to or subtracted from. In the same way, the oral lineage has remained unaltered. Like a perfect vase filled to the brim from another perfect vase contains the exact same quantity as the first vase, the fact that the meaning has remained the same from the buddhas down until this present yogi—with neither omissions nor duplications—and can withstand scrutiny is the sign of the utterly profound instructions.

Now, to whom were these instructions, the Definitive Great Secret, transmitted? It was around that time that a religious king known as Indrabhuti the Younger, an emanation of Lord Maitreya, lived in the Indian city of Kapilavastu, with five hundred panditas as his officiating priests. Among them was the learned and accomplished Vimalamitra, who had manifested the body of transformation, and who presided as the foremost priest for a period of sixty years.

About the same time, in the country of Tibet, the king called Trisong Deutsen, who was an emanation of the bodhisattva Manjushri, had constructed the temples of glorious Samye, the spontaneously fulfillment of

King Indrabhuti

boundless wishes, and so caused the sacred Dharma to spread and flourish. Tingdzin Zangpo of Nyang, his court priest, was able to remain seven years and seven months in a state of one-pointed shamatha, and could see the four continents simultaneously with the purity of his physical eyes. The great monk of Nyang gave the king the following advice, "Listen here, Your Majesty. In the Indian city of Kapilavastu lives the king Indrabhuti with five hundred panditas as his court priests. If you invite one of them who is learned in Secret Mantra, it will cause the Secret Mantra teachings to spread and flourish in Tibet."

Deeply delighted, the king pronounced "This I will do!"

In the whole country of Tibet at this time the sharpest minds belonged to Kawa Paltsek—the son of Kawa Lotsen and Lady Dorjecham of Dro from the Kawapa area of Phen in central Tibet—and Chokro Lui Gyaltsen—the son of Chokro Gyaljung and Lady Dzema of Dro from the Dargong region of Rulag Shab. Having summoned them to his court they were treated with drinks of *ligarda* and given helmets adorned with precious gems to wear. Then the king spoke:

> "Listen to me, noble lads, you two have achieved the mastery of the miraculous tongue. In order to make the extremely profound teachings belonging to the resultant Secret Mantra spread and flourish here in our Tibetan kingdom, you must go to India, to the city of Kapilavastu where King Indrabhuti lives with five hundred panditas as his court priests. Present him with these seven gold ingots, as well as these nine *drey*[45] of gold dust as a gift from the king of Tibet, and ask that in return he sends one learned pandita, especially one who is adept in the Secret Mantra teachings."

Having spoken these words the king ordered them to start their journey. Since they had received the king's command, the two translators traveled to India where they paid their respects to King Indrabhuti. Presenting him with their king's gold dust and ingots, they conveyed his message as well. This greatly pleased the monarch and he said, "You two Tibetan bodhisattvas, stay here in this cool pavilion."

When the panditas arrived for lunch, the king announced, "Listen to me, great scholars. The king of Tibet has sent me a most valuable gift and in return has requested me to send a learned pandita, one who is especially adept in the resultant teachings of Secret Mantra."

The master Buddhaguhya said, "Where are the messengers who carried the gift. Let them be brought here." The king had the two translators led in and upon seeing Vimalamitra's physical presence the two felt deep devotion.

ᠪ

The story continues with Vimalamitra arriving in Tibet at the request of King Trisong Deutsen. These details are found in the chapter "The Written Narration: Tibet."

The songs received by Nyang Ral Nyima Özer, in his vision of journeying to Sukhavati and other buddhafields, are found in his inner life story. The version used here was included by Kyungtrul Kargyam in his collection of songs from the Nyingma lineage masters.

Songs from the Buddhas and Bodhisattvas of Sukhavati

Once in a vision Nyima Özer, king of Nyang, the monarch of all tertön siddhas, journeyed to the Blissful Realm where Buddha Amitabha, mighty Lotus-Eyed, addressed him in these words:

> Emaho.
> Desire unrejected is the lotus family;
> And this desire intensifies your bliss.
> As greatest bliss the essence of your mind abides,
> And since the nature of desire is mainly bliss,
> Uncontrived, let mind-essence be filled with fourfold joy.
>
> Hard it is to shun one's yearning passion,
> So never part it from the mood of empty bliss.
> Desire, unrejected, then dissolves within itself,
> Dissolves into the nature of discriminating wisdom.

Thus this buddha pointed out the emotion of desire as the ground, bliss as the path and discriminating wisdom as the fruition. Moreover, the King of Nyang also met the buddhas Vajra Akshobhya, Ratnasambhava, Vairochana and Amoghasiddhi who pointed out the emotions of aggression, conceit, close-mindedness and envy as ground; compassion, loving kindness, luminosity and impartiality as path; and the wisdoms of the mirror-like, equality, dharmadhatu and persevering action as the fruition.[46]

Then Avalokiteshvara spoke to him in verse:

> Emaho.
> With the arsenal of bodhichitta sever
> The six causes of confusion at their root.
> Gaze into the uncontrived, space-like state of mind,
> And free of both extremes, the Middle Way you find.

Guru Padma sang:

> Emaho.
> Unconstructed mind-essence, primordially pure,
> Is the realization of the buddhas of the triple times.
> When let alone and uncontrived, a lucid wakefulness will dawn.
> While training do not craft, let be and stay without distraction.

Glorious Hayagriva sang:

> Emaho.
> One horse-neigh, emptiness devoid of constructs,
> Outshines two sidetracks: that of nothing, that eternal.
> One horse-neigh, bliss and emptiness nondual,
> Swallows up the failings of the path, of indolence and dullness.
> One horse-neigh, spontaneity unbridled,
> Cuts asunder judgment's clinging web.

Arya Tara spoke in these words:

> Emaho.
> Not some other thing, therefore samsara cannot be rejected.
> Just your mind itself, therefore nirvana cannot be achieved.
> Like ice and water, nondual are samsara and nirvana.
> And so remain in the nondual state of greatest bliss composed.

Dharmevajra spoke:

Emaho.
Within the sky-like vastness of your empty mind
Uncontrived the clouds of thoughts and of emotions vanish.
And while the great sun shines—a lucid wakefulness—
Stay settled loosely in this changeless, brilliant state.

From an untold number of bodhisattvas and awakened ones, the King of Nyang received amazing blessings and predictions, but here only how the conquerors in Sukhavati and their offspring bestowed their instructions upon him is included.

ઉ

The Heart Essence of the Dakinis, the Khandro Nyingtig, consists—in Padmasambhava's words—"of the Dakini Tantra of the Sun of the Brilliant Expanse and the Seventeen Tantras that Shri Singha entrusted to him." Then, at the Upper Cave of the Slate Mountain he practiced and attained the vidyadhara level of longevity and the rainbow body of the great transformation that is beyond birth and death.

To quote Dilgo Khyentse Rinpoche's succinct words: "The precious master Padmasambhava—the embodiment of all buddhas who possesses an immortal form of indestructible wakefulness—received all the ripening and liberating instructions, tantras and statements of the luminous Great Perfection from the knowledge-holder Shri Singha. Having performed the play of attaining the vidyadhara level at which the five kayas are spontaneously accomplished, he proceeded to Tibet, and there, in the Tidro Cave at Upper Zho where dakinis gather to feast, Padmasambhava bestowed these teachings upon Yeshe Tsogyal, the queen of wisdom dakinis, and one hundred thousand other dakinis.

"Later, when Princess Pema Sal, the daughter of the Dharma-king, was about to pass away, Padmasambhava entrusted her with the small chest containing the manuscripts of the profound Heart Essence of the Dakinis before it was concealed as a terma treasure. Princess Pema Sal's reincarnation as Pema Ledrel Tsal revealed the terma in the Tramo Cave at Danglung in the fourteenth century after which the Omniscient Dharma-king (Longchenpa) received its mandate."

Shri Singha Confers the Eighteen Dzogchen Tantras

Padmasambhava then received this prophecy from Vajra Varahi:

> Worthy One, the true teaching on fruition within a single
>   lifetime
> Is unique and not realized by everyone.
> It abides in the vajra heart of Shri Singha.
> In Rugged Grove you shall attain the realization!

Thus she spoke and through his miraculous power, Padmasambhava arrived at the marvelous charnel ground Rugged Grove in a single moment. There he bowed down before the great master Shri Singha, circumambulated him and begged to be accepted as his disciple.

Consenting, Shri Singha then taught the Lotus-Born master the complete Cycles of Mind, Space, and Instruction, including the *Tantra of the Great Perfection that is Equal to Space*. In particular, upon having received all the Outer, Inner and Secret Cycles of the Sphere without exception, Padmasambhava asked, "Great master, I beseech you to grant an instruction that enables the material body to disappear within this very lifetime, brings forth the vision of the sambhogakaya realms, and awakens one to buddhahood in the realm of dharmakaya."

Shri Singha replied:

"Excellent, noble son! I have an instruction that is the pinnacle of all teachings, the innermost of all views. It transcends all the vehicles, is the heart essence of all dakinis, the subject of extreme secrecy more secret than ordinary secrets. It is the great vehicle of the Luminous Vajra Essence, beyond thinking, devoid of conceptual mind, and outside the domain of dualistic cognitions. It does not lie within the confines of what is and what is not, and transcends the ranges of view and meditation, development and completion. It is the mother of all the victorious ones of the three times, the short path of all the great vidyadharas, the ultimate and unexcelled instruction through which one can attain the enlightenment of the buddhas within three years. I shall teach it to you!"

Shri Singha then bestowed upon him the empowerments of the *Great Perfection's Heart Essence of the Dakinis,* numerous scriptures of instructions on its application, and, as supportive teachings, these *Eighteen Dzogchen Tantras: Dra Talgyur Root Tantra, the Tantra Beyond Letters* as the basis, the *Tantra of Shining Relics* on signs, the *Tantra of Self-existing Perfection* on empowerment, the *Tantra of Pointing-Out Instructions,* the *Blazing Lamp Tantra,* the *Tantra of Self-Manifest Awareness,* the *Tantra of the Mind Mirror of Vajrasattva,* the *Tantra of Piled Gems,* the *Tantra of the Union of the Sun and Moon,* the *Tantra of Studded Jewels,* the *Tantra of Self-Liberated Awareness,* the *Pearl Garland Tantra,* the *Tantra of the Heart Mirror of Samantabhadra,* the *Tantra of Graceful Auspiciousness,* the *Tantra of the Perfected Lion,* the *Tantra of the Six Spheres,* and the *Tantra of Samantabhadri's Sun of the Brilliant Expanse.*

After Shri Singha taught these in their entirety and entrusted him with the teachings, Padmasambhava remained for twenty-five years studying and reflecting upon the instructions. Following that he went to the great charnel ground of Sosadvipa, and after practicing for three years, he attained the bodily form beyond birth and death that is like a reflection of the moon in water. Through his miraculous powers he brought benefit to an incredible number of human and nonhuman beings in a variety of places. In particular,

Padmasambhava

he remained as the object of worship of the Indian king Dharmapala during the day while at night he went to the great charnel grounds Cool Grove, Sosadvipa, the Brilliant, Enchanting, Bhasing, the Little, the Terrifying and so forth, where together with cloudbanks of dakinis he abided in the conduct of Secret Mantra.

๖

Later on, Padmasambhava was invited to Tibet by King Trisong Deutsen, the details of which can be found in The Lotus-Born.

The Heart Essence
of the Dakinis

ཁྲག་འཐུང༔

Homage to all the sublime masters.

In order to create trust and authenticate the source, here I shall briefly mention the succession of the lineage masters. To quote the *Tantra of the Union of the Sun and Moon*:

> Without explaining the meaning of the history,
> The blemish of mistrust may then arise
> Towards the teachings of the *Certain Greatest Secret*.

As for the history of how this transmission occurred, this same tantra continues:

> Through blessings the teacher Samantabhadra with consort
> Entrusted the sovereign,
> Who was Sattva, a recipient not separate from himself,
> So that all dharmas were liberated by knowing one,
> Beyond the confines of bondage and liberation.

> Through the blessings of Vajrasattva
> They arose in the mind of the self-appeared Prahevajra,
> Who entrusted the tantras to Shri Singha.
> The *Tantras that Liberate through Wearing*, the utterly perfect
>   fruition,

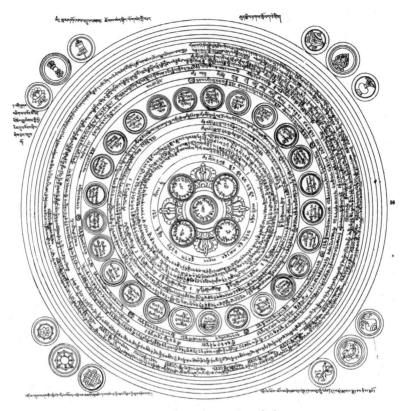

Liberation Through Wearing Chakra

He entrusted to Padma of Uddiyana.
Reveal the fivefold to the disciples.

Thus it was said.

To explain in more details, in the dharmadhatu palace of Akanishtha which is utterly pure space, the glorious conqueror Samantabhadra with consort is the dharmakaya beyond defilement which is not made out of any concrete entity whatsoever and yet manifests in a form with face and arms. From within this unconstructed state of dharmakaya, in the realm of Akanishtha, he taught glorious Vajrasattva by means of natural blessings.

Glorious Vajrasattva, the sambhogakaya adorned with the major and minor marks, in the celestial palace of the Blazing Fire Mountain charnel ground, taught—with few words—the emanation Prahevajra, the one who though remaining in the world of men is equal to the buddhas in realization. Prahevajra taught the master Shri Singha in the charnel ground of Wild Jungle by establishing the actuality in Shri Singha himself. In the great charnel ground of Sosadvipa, Shri Singha then taught the great vidyadhara known as Padma Tötreng Tsal, the one whose vajra-like body is beyond birth and death, passing and transmigration, by revealing the natural state free of assumptions.

In the Tidro Cave at Upper Zho, Padma Tötreng Tsal then taught Tsogyal, the Lady of Kharchen, the one who received the prophecy from all the dakinis, by divesting her of deluded meditation, assumptions and mental darkness, and revealing the fivefold wisdom essence by establishing it as a self-luminous actuality.

I, the Lady of Kharchen, then acted as the compiler and gave my blessings that these teachings may be transmitted to the minds of those in the future who are endowed with a karmic link. Thus I entrusted them to the dakinis and concealed them as a precious earth treasure. May they meet with the destined one in the future!

SAMAYA. SEAL, SEAL, SEAL.

ᧈ

In The Narration of the Precious Revelation of the Terma Treasures from the cycle the Quintessence of the Dakinis (Khandro Yangtig), Longchen Rabjam continues with a more detailed description of how Padmasambhava transmitted the Heart Essence of the Dakinis in Tibet:

During this time, at the borderland of Chokro Dri, Tökar-Lek of Mangje and his wife Lady Gyalmo Tso of Ru, were joined in marriage. After they had established a home, Gyalmo Tso dreamt that a blue-colored woman in the middle of the sky threw a radiant star which then entered her. When nine months and ten days had passed she gave birth to an extremely beautiful girl who had the design of a vajra-cross on her forehead and issued the scent of a blue lotus flower. They named her Tsogyal, Lake of Victory.

When she grew up she was accepted by the king as a queen, and due to her deep devotion to the Lotus-Born master and her disenchantment with samsaric aims, she asked the king to be allowed to practice the Dharma and received his permission. The master then took her as his consort and she served him, following him wherever he went. Having attended him and practiced one-pointedly, she attained accomplishment and acquired the supreme and common siddhis.

Later, when the master and his consort were practicing in the Tidro Cave at Upper Zho, the wisdom dakinis all directed Lady Tsogyal in these words, "In the heart of the incarnated great master dwells the profound pith instruction of the *Heart Essence in Actuality,* the teaching on awakening to enlightenment within three years so that in this very lifetime the material body vanishes. You must beseech him to give it." Thus she received the direction of the dakinis.

Yeshe Tsogyal then presented a lavish feast offering and said, "Great master, please bestow the sublime pith instruction of the *Heart Essence in Actuality,* the teaching on awakening to enlightenment so that in this very lifetime the material body vanishes."

As she made this supplication accompanied by innumerable prostrations and circumambulations, the great master replied:

Tsogyal, it is extremely excellent that you make this request. It is an instruction unlike any I have given in the past, the summit that transcends all the nine gradual vehicles. By seeing its vital point, conceptually created views and meditations are shattered; the paths and levels are perfected with no need for struggle; and disturbing emotions are liberated into their natural state without any need for correction or remedy. This instruction brings one to realization, the fruition of which is not produced by causes. It instantly brings forth the spontaneously present realization; liberates the material body of flesh and blood into the luminous sambhogakaya within this very lifetime; and enables you to capture—within three years—the permanent abode, the precious dharmakaya realm of spontaneous presence, in the domain of Akanishtha. I possess such an instruction and I shall teach it to you!

Having spoken these words Padmasambhava unfolded the mandala of the peaceful and wrathful ones in the great assembly hall and conferred the empowerment upon one hundred thousand dakinis headed by Yeshe Tsogyal. Having given the teachings in completeness, he taught the *Seventeen Tantras* and the *Tantra of the Sun of the Brilliant Expanse,* as the eighteenth, and numerous pith instructions for these texts as well.

Following this, he separated all the pith instructions for the extensive tantras into one category and the Kusulu Cycle written by the master himself into another. These were separately written down by the master and Tsogyal and entered into a list of contents.

Around this time, at the invitation of the king, the master, the king, his queens and offspring, all went up to Chimpu and participated in one hundred and eight feast offerings. At this time Princess Pema Sal, the daughter of the late queen Lady Jangchub Men of Dro, who was eight years of age, passed away. When the king saw her dead body he fell to the ground and wept.

Tsogyal took a white silken cloth and sprinkled him with saffron water. When the king had regained his senses, the master spoke:

> Listen your majesty.
> In general all mundane pursuits are like dreams.
> The mark of composite things is that they are like magical
> illusions.
> Your kingdom is like last night's dream.
> Your wealth and your subjects are like dew drops on a blade of
> grass.
> This fleeting life is like bubbles upon water.
> All composite things will perish.
> Meeting ends in separation.
> All composite things are like this.
> There is not a single thing that is stable and lasts.
> Do not cling to the impermanent as being permanent.
> Train in the nonarising nature of dharmakaya.

Thus he spoke.

༄

The king made many prostrations and circumambulations and then said, "Great master, since samsaric pursuits are futile, please give an instruction for being content in this life, happy in the following and ultimately awakening to enlightenment."

Again the master spoke to the king:

Emaho,
Your majesty, great king, listen once more!
Since samsaric things have no essence,
To continue endlessly spinning about brings further and further
    suffering,
So capture the royal stronghold of dharmakaya.

As your true homeland, keep to the nonarising dharmadhatu.
As your true dwelling, adhere to forest retreats and remote
    places.
As your true retreat, look into the empty and luminous
    dharmata.
As your true house, remain in your original mind nature.

As your true bounty, keep attentive and mindful.
As your true treasury, form the resolve of the twofold awakened
    mind.
As your true wealth, keep to the two accumulations.
As your true farming, endeavor in the ten virtuous practices.

As your true fatherhood, embrace all beings with compassion.
As your true motherhood, sustain the natural state of emptiness.
As your true offspring, practice development and completion
    indivisibly.
As your true spouse; train in bliss, clarity and nonthought.

As your true companion, read the scriptures of the sugatas.
As your true farm land, cultivate unshakable faith.
As your true food, eat the nonarising nectar of dharmata.

As your true beverage, drink the nectar of oral instructions.

As your true clothing, wear the garment of modesty and
decorum.

As your true retinue, preserve the dakinis and protectors.

As your true enjoyment, engage in spiritual practice.

As your true spectacle, look into your own mind.

As your true diversion, engage in elaborate spiritual pursuits.

As your true entertainment, train in emanating and absorbing
the development stage.

As your true close friend, keep to the empowerments and
samayas.

As your true prejudice, use the five poisons for training.

As your true ornament, study and reflect free from partiality.

As your true activity, have the profound scriptures copied.

As your true caller, be generous without bound.

As your true pursuit, direct your innermost aim to the Dharma.

As your true court chaplain, venerate the Three Jewels.

As your true objects of respect, treat your parents with reverence.

As your true object of honor, respect your vajra master.

As your true samaya, keep your mind free from hypocrisy

As your true precept, give up all evil.

As your true temple, keep the three precepts purely.

As your true mandala, look into the unchanging luminosity.

As your true instruction, tame your own mind.

As your true view; look into the changeless, empty cognizance.

As your true meditation, let your mind nature be as it is.

As your true conduct, let the delusion of dualistic fixation
collapse.

As your true fruition, don't seek the result that is spontaneously
present.

If you practice like this you will be content in this life, joyful in
    the next,
And soon attain complete enlightenment.

On hearing this song the king was delighted and made many prostrations
and circumambulations.

Following this, Padmasambhava placed the pith instructions and the
brocade cloak that had belonged to the princess inside a brown chest of
rhinoceros hide and concealed it as a terma treasure with the wish that the
princess meet with it again. The master then wrote the syllable NRI with the
vermilion of knowledge on the heart center of the princess, summoned her
consciousness back so that she began to breathe and could speak. Then he
bestowed upon her the empowerment of the *Heart Essence of the Dakinis* and
gave her the secret name Pema Ledrel Tsal. Holding the chest of rhinoceros
hide at the crown of her head, the girl made this wish, "At some time in the
future, may I meet again with this teaching and bring benefit to beings!"

The master then explained that when the karma of the former life of the
princess re-awakens she will meet again with her father, brothers and the
master himself. He then allowed her spirit to pass on and acted as if performing the funeral ceremony at that same place, but in order to purify her obscurations he brought the dead body in an instant to Uddiyana and performed a
feast offering. In an instant he returned and said, "Tsogyal, write these events
down in a narration. Conceal them together with the profound terma treasure. By doing so, when she meets it in the future she will believe in it."

So Lady Tsogyal committed this to writing, then asked the master,
"Should these instructions on the *Secret Heart Essence* be propagated or concealed?" The master replied:

The time has not yet come for them to be propagated so they should
be concealed as a terma treasure. The princess made an aspiration
when I placed the casket with the text at the crown of her head and
therefore the teachings will be her heritage. Some years from now
the great master Vimalamitra will arrive and, since the time will have
come for his disciples, the teachings of the *Heart Essence* will flourish.

Pema Lingpa the Treasure Revealer

When the early translations have become corrupted so that they are close to perishing and the Buddhadharma is about to disappear, these teachings of my *Heart Essence of the Dakinis* will manifest widely and forcefully, but briefly, just like the flame of a butter lamp flares up before burning out.

In general the teachings of the Old School will be widespread but short-lived, and among them the terma teachings especially will flourish at the same time as the terma door unfolds. They will for the most part subside when the destined owner of the terma remains no longer, therefore conceal these teachings.

After he had spoken, the entire Kusulu Cycle was concealed in the Overhanging Cave at the Multicolored Cliff of Dakpo Danglung. The extensive tantras and instructions of the Learned Pandita Cycle were concealed at the Lion-like Cliff in Lower Bumtang.[47] Padmasambhava then entrusted the teachings to the Rahula, Mamo, Mara[48] and numerous dakinis in charge of termas, with the command that they be entrusted to the worthy destined one when the middle-age of a human life is fifty years.

§

And so it was that Padmasambhava clearly predicted the future incarnations of Princess Pema Sal as Pema Ledrel Tsal, Longchenpa and Pema Lingpa who were to reveal, codify and propagate the Heart Essence of the Dakinis.

As Prahevajra described the Tantra of the Single Child:

This tantra is the primordial essence extracted
From the pure realized minds of one billion awakened ones.

The tantras that grant liberation through wearing, known as takdröl, *have been revealed by all the major tertöns. The following belongs to a collection of six such tantras within the* Heart Essence of the Dakinis. *The basic meaning of takdröl is that it "voids samsara when it's worn and kept"—worn on one's body close to one heart, or while the meaning is kept alive in the center of one's heart. Best of course is to do both.*

The Essence Tantra of Liberation Through Wearing

In the language of Uddiyana: PRADDHAKANIRA.
In the language of Tibet: *btags grol stong gsal ti la math' dubs brawl.*[49]
In the English language: *The Essence Tantra of Liberation Through Wearing.*

Empty luminous *tila* without center or edge,
Homage to the self-existing basic space.

The teacher, Ever-Excellent and consort,
Amidst the brilliant expanse of dharmadhatu,
Spoke this tantra of the self-occurring self-existence:

Ema, listen retinues of self-existing knowing.
Clinging to identity, the root of all existence,
Explore its outside and its inside;
Such identity primordially is empty and is freed.
Open up the door for the empty, lucid fivefold radiance,
The luminous and empty *tila*, free of limitations.
Leave it free of circumstance, free of effort, and in naturalness.

Essence, nature and capacity—this triad
Is awakened and in liberation through this wearing.

This quintessence of the tantras, in these seven lines,
Voids samsara when it's kept as that which liberates through
    wearing.[50]

This completes the *Essence Tantra in Seven Lines that Liberates
through Wearing*
That naturally arose from the expanse of Samantabhadra and his
    consort.

It has the seal of body, ༔ seal of speech, ༔ and seal of mind. ༔

ཕ༔ཁ༔ གེ༔ཚ༔ ཉེ༔རྨད་པ༔

SAMAYA. SEAL, SEAL, SEAL. ༔ ITHI ༔

ༀ

The following excerpt is from the Great Single Cut of Complete Liberation *(Chigchö Kündröl Chenpo). It includes an excellent piece on the mind transmission of the conquerors and was revealed by Rinchen Lingpa (1295-1375). He was the reincarnation of the Indian pandita Prajnakara—known for his* Ornament of Pramanavartika *and for an explanation of the difficult points in* The Way of the Bodhisattva (Bodhicharyavatara). *This lineage goes from Prahevajra to Shri Singha who bestowed it as a hearing lineage upon Padmasambhava. When the great Lotus-Born master arrived in Tibet he gave it to only a few destined disciples to use in their personal practice. Yeshe Tsogyal and other recipients encoded these precious instructions in the secret sign script of the dakinis and concealed them at Kharatira Black Turtle Boulder, which is situated to the north of the Vajra Throne at Bodhgaya in India. Centuries later, the master tertön Rinchen Lingpa made the journey to India to recover the hidden treasure and brought an untold number of beings to maturation and liberation. In later times, though the scriptures still existed, its transmission had disappeared and so Jamyang Khyentse Wangpo revived the lineage after receiving it from the tertön in his wisdom body.*

The Great Single Cut of Complete Liberation

Historical Framework for
the Great Perfection

ཉེ་བར་འགྲོ་ལ་འཇེ་རྐྱ་ཐིམ་ཐ་ཤ་སྟོ་སྒྲ་གི་གོ༔

Homage to the exalted Shri Samantabhadra, the perfection of all dharmas.

ལུབ་སྒྲིག་ག །སྲི་ཟྦོ་ཐར་སུ་ཅ༔

This *Great Single Cut of Complete Liberation,* the utmost secret of the Great Perfection—which is the realization of all conquerors, ultimate of all teachings, source of all statements, pinnacle of all vehicles, mirror of all meanings, essence of all instructions—is explained by using the framework of a synopsis in the following six essential points.

In order to inspire trust in the person who is about to enter this supreme vehicle, first comes an explanation of the history of how the teachings originated.

First, about the history, a tantra says:

Without teaching the history, people may feel no trust.

Accordingly I shall describe the history of the transmission lineage to instill trust in the practitioners and authenticate its source; beginning with the mind transmission of the conquerors, followed by the symbolic transmission of the vidyadharas and concluding with the hearing transmission of sublime individuals.

First, the mind transmission of the conquerors.

The place is dharmadhatu, the immense equality that defies every conceptual construct. The teacher is Samantabhadra, the all-pervasive dharmakaya that is not confined to any category. His indivisible retinue, in no way different from himself, is the buddhas of the five families. The time is the equality of the three times and timelessness. The teaching, self-existing and not composed by anyone, is this *Tantra of the Great Single Cut of Complete Liberation,* which they spontaneously understood through his blessings. Just like the sun rising in the sky appears on the surface of water even though it never descends into the water, likewise there is an understanding through blessings even though the dharmakaya does not explain.

From there, the sambhogakayas who are blessed by dharmakaya, in the place known as the pure Densely Arrayed realm of Akanishtha, the teacher Vajradhara, in the wisdom body of sambhogakaya, taught the assemblies of male and female bodhisattvas who are the retinues of their respective five families, during the time when personal experience is pure within the mind, the self-existing sections of the *Tantra of the Great Single Cut,* which they understood through the teacher's specific identity. Even though the sambhogakaya uses no words to explain—just like a crystal's colors are understood by simply showing it without a need for words—there is an understanding of this identity by simply being shown the major and minor marks of sambhogakaya.

From this time forth nirmanakayas have appeared—from the sambhogakaya's continuum and in the places of unpredictable realms—to the retinues of inconceivably myriad types of pure and impure beings, at the time which is whenever they attain sincere interest. By means of his body the teacher Vajrasattva emanates as the six Munis for the sake of the six classes of beings, appearing in any necessary way to guide and benefit whoever is in need, including in the guise of eminent universal rulers—whether peaceful or wrathful—to tame those who are otherwise incorrigible. By means of his speech, he benefits beings by teaching the eighty-four thousand entrances to the Dharma including Sutra, Vinaya and Abhidharma and the six paramitas of the philosophical vehicles, Kriya, Upa and Yoga, as well as the secret tantras

Vajrasattva

of Maha, Anu and Ati. By means of his mind, with his wisdom that perceives the three times of past, present and future as well as the time of equality, he benefits disciples by ensuring that each of them gains understanding.

All these emanations, the activities of their body, the utterances of their speech and the effortlessness of their mind are just like the wish-granting gem that holds no concepts and yet fulfills every wish of individual sentient beings—whatever they may desire. These nirmanakayas hold no conceptual intentions and yet bring forth understanding by appearing to manifest in whatever way is necessary for disciples to be guided.

In particular, the sections of the *Tantra of the Great Single Cut* were bestowed upon Prahevajra in the realm of Braided Ones by the teacher Vajrasattva—not by hand and not articulated in words, but rather syllables of lapis lazuli spontaneously appeared in the unconditioned sky of personal perception and the scripture appeared in this sky. Then, within the jeweled mansion in the sky, Prahevajra let his reflection emerge as the nirmanakayas of the body, speech and mind of the buddhas that guide beings.

Without using words or letters they all bring understanding of the Dharma's meaning through blessings thus this is known as the mind transmission of the conquers.

The lineage of the symbolic transmission of the vidyadharas.

It was after the teaching of Shakyamuni that the emanation Prahevajra enacted the deeds of taking birth from Princess Radiant Lamp, a nun who was the daughter of a secular king[51] in the fragrant valley of Dhanakosha in Uddiyana. When he reached the age of eight, he knew all of the Dharma without having even studied, and was recognized as a nirmanakaya. The king, his ministers and all the subjects rejoiced, and named him Prahevajra—Delightful Vajra.

After this emanation and knowledge-holder of Vajrasattva had stamped out every evil attack from Mara, extremist philosophers and the like, he proceeded to the Vajra Throne and resided under the bodhi tree of enlightenment. It was then that the bodily form of Vajrasattva appeared like a rainbow in the sky, accompanied by sounds and lights, and exclaimed, "Noble

son, look into the unconditioned sky of personal perception!" Prahevajra
looked and saw all the teachings of the Great Perfection come down before
him like an immense shower of spontaneously appearing scriptures.

Next, Prahevajra, together with the dakinis Serene Purna and Conch of
Brahma's Voice, catalogued and recorded in volumes of scripture the collections of teachings given earlier by the Buddha, as well as these teachings of the Great Perfection. These were placed within the Freedom Cave
of Dakinis where they were worshipped by the dakinis. When Vajrasattva
departed Prahevajra prayed to him with deep-felt yearning, and Vajrasattva
reappeared in midair within a sphere of light.

> Alas, vidyadhara son of Vajrasattva!
> Within sambhogakaya, from the dharmakaya
> The nirmanakaya that is Vajrasattva's form
> Nowhere does it dwell, yet it dissolves into the dharmakaya.
> So capture the omniscient state!

Having uttered this, a box one inch in size with this tantra of Ati's innermost nature, written with self-appearing letters of lapis gems landed on the
crown of Prahevajra's head. Simply through this, Prahevajra attained the
confidence of realization. Vajrasattva then disappeared.

Prahevajra now understood these teachings to consist of three aspects—
tantras, statements and instructions. The tantras and statements he concealed at the Vajra Throne, while he retained the instructions within his
heart. He then proceeded to the Cool Grove charnel ground where, his
back to the glorious stupa Descended from Heavenly Realms, he remained
in samadhi and was worshipped by the dakinis.

ॐ

*The descriptions of the twelve sugatas of the Great Perfection are found mainly in the
terma revelations of Vimalamitra and Padmasambhava. These twelve buddhas—from
Youth of Inconceivable Sublime Light down to Buddha Shakyamuni—are all emanations
of Samantabhadra. The twelve buddhas (or "Mahasandhi Sugatas"—Sugatas of Great
Peace—as they are referred to in Chokgyur Lingpa's termas) belong to the conqueror's*

mind transmission. This is because the single realized intent of Vajradhara's mind is transmitted through these teachers.

In explaining how nirmanakaya appears in the specific Dzogchen context of the conqueror's mind transmission, Longchenpa speaks of two types of major emanations:

"The supreme emanations of blessings" are renowned as the Three Sources of the Doctrine. They are also known as the great self-existing emanations of enlightened body, speech and mind.

"The sublime emanations of wisdom" are the twelve Dzogchen buddhas. This chapter briefly mentions each by name. The following chapters will then give more details of how these primordial beings of great peace taught the Great Perfection and the other eight vehicles in various worlds.

The supreme emanations of blessings appear simultaneously with the twelve buddhas, and in the same twelve worlds, to benefit beings. They appear in the form of three miraculous phenomena that deserve special attention in that they serve as sources for the Dzogchen teachings in our kalpa. To paraphrase Gyurmey Tsewang Chokdrub's Great Drum of the Gods:

The vajra of dharmata spontaneously appeared from the blessings of the Great Perfection, the true source of the dharmakaya doctrine on this Jambu continent, and is made from one hundred precious substances.

The scripture spontaneously appeared from the blessings of the Self-Existing Single Child of the Doctrine, the true source of the sambhogakaya teachings, also made from one hundred precious substances, is a volume four fingers widths wide and emits the natural sound of dharmata.

The statue spontaneously appeared from the blessings of the twelve nirmanakaya teachers and is also made from one hundred precious substances.

These three supreme emanations of blessings are formed spontaneously, transcend birth and death, and possess boundless miraculous power and virtues that ensure that every person who encounters their sight, sound or touch will be liberated, and their material body will vanish. For every nirmanakaya buddha who has appeared, now appears and will appear, these three emanations form the support for the doctrines of their body, speech and mind.

Longchenpa begins his narration with, "This history of the vehicle of the Luminous Vajra Essence, the Secret Heart Essence of the Great Perfection, has three aspects: the mind transmission of conquerors, the symbolic transmission of vidyadharas and the transmission that came orally through sublime individuals. Of these, I will now explain the first."

The Jewel Garland Records

Our teacher, the conqueror, the glorious Samantabhadra awakened to true enlightenment within the primordial space of the ground and remains unmoved from the state of realization in which the kayas and wisdoms are indivisible. This is the way in which, at the time of the inner brilliance of dharmakaya, the three aspects of essence, nature and capacity—which are the three kayas of basic space—remain uninvolved in objects and therefore the omniscient wakefulness which is awake by nature.[52]

In the perfect place, the dharmakaya realm, and in the perfect time, the changeless time of dharmata, it is Samantabhadra, the perfect teacher, who lucidly manifests the perfect teaching—the natural Great Perfection, the spontaneous presence, a possession most intrinsic—to the perfect retinue, the ocean-like assembly of timeless wakefulness.

While unmoved from that state, here is the way in which he naturally unfolds sambhogakayas that are self-display. There is the Densely Arrayed realms of perfect bliss, which all appear as natural radiance of the five wisdoms; they have no up or down, no cardinal or intermediate directions, and within the palaces of light, the exquisitely decorated jewel mansions, reside the buddhas of the five families, each surrounded by hundreds of thousands of their own mandalas of countless clusters. None is a teacher with disciples, but rather a natural radiance of mastery over the self-display as a spontaneous presence.

It is from the manifest aspect of this that an inconceivable number of the buddhas of the five families are emanated and appear, all of which are exquisitely decorated, like mansions of unfurled brocade and shine with the lights of the five colors; while from the six syllables in the mandalas of their mouths and tongues unending rays of light spontaneously appear.

This is the situation in which at the perfect place that is the Densely Arrayed realms of self-display,[53] the perfect teachers, who are the buddhas of the five families, reveal to the perfect retinue of infinite buddha mandalas surrounding them the perfect teaching, which is the realized state of luminous wakefulness, at the perfect time, which is the inconceivable time of dharmata, in the way in which the natural state of luminosity is an intrinsic possession that defies description.

Here is how the nirmanakayas are fully emanated from this state. Due to the incidence of those to be guided, emanated lights naturally manifest, just like the moon reflected in water. During this time, each of the six types of beings above and below, in the cardinal and intermediate directions, undergo their manifold individual kinds of painful and pleasant experiences due to the power of their delusion and so are caught up in their minds' mistaken perceptions. This is the time when the natural nirmanakaya buddhas of the five families individually manifest to the bodhisattvas from the first to the tenth level, in the realms of the ten directions, and when countless perfect buddhas all turn the wheels of the Dharma and accomplish the welfare of the six classes of beings in their various realms.

Here, for instance, is how emanations manifest in this Saha world. From the Densely Arrayed realms of self-display two types of major emanations manifest.

THE SUPREME EMANATIONS OF BLESSINGS are of three types. The first is a bodily form made from one hundred and one precious substances, equal in size to the body of any of the six classes of beings who share a similar lifespan, from which innumerable miraculous displays manifest to liberate beings. The next is the great scripture known as the *Single Child of the Doctrine* that naturally appeared from precious substances, and acts to benefit beings through spontaneously resounding an indescribable number of teachings. Third is the vajra of dharmata that fits in the hand of the first human beings, and acts to liberate beings by showering down a rain of

Vajra the Dharmata

Youth of Inconceivable Sublime Light

teachings and articles to guide whoever needs in whichever way is necessary. The letters are also in various languages and resound in whichever language is required. All these emanate rays of light throughout the ten directions of the six realms and perform the activity of spontaneously and effortlessly liberating countless beings. They are also known as the great self-existing emanations of enlightened body, speech and mind.

THE SUBLIME EMANATIONS OF WISDOM, the other type, act for the welfare of beings by manifesting as their individual chief figure. That is to say, the great Vajradhara—who is naturally manifest from the inexhaustible adornment-wheels of the body, speech and mind of all the conquerors of the Densely Arrayed realms of self-display—spontaneously appeared in the attire of a sambhogakaya on a lotus flower in the first eon of this realm known as Abundant Delight. Here he communicated to Vajrasattva and Vajrapani the teaching of the natural Great Perfection beyond words and letters, so it was naturally present through his intention.

At this time Vajradhara himself spontaneously appeared as the perfect teacher known as Youth of Inconceivable Sublime Light, and to the perfect retinue who were the thousand buddhas of the Good Eon, he taught, in the way of natural display, the perfect teaching, which was the *Seventeen Tantras*

Lovingly Playful Wisdom

of Innermost Luminosity including the *Dra Talgyur Root Tantra* and so forth, in the perfect time of self-manifest original wakefulness.

In this case, the teacher and retinue are no different, but they appeared separately out of the intention to guide beings. How is that? In this eon the buddhas appear with different names, in different periods and with different teachings. Therefore they appeared separately, in sequence, out of the intention to guide beings. In this context, the transmission is said to originate from Vajradhara who taught Vajrasattva and Vajrapani. Here is how these nirmanakayas were emanated:

After the teacher Youth of Inconceivable Sublime Light had appeared in Abundant Delight during the first eon, the teacher Youth of Immutable Light appeared in the realm of the Saha world.

Following that the teacher Protector Against Fear appeared in the place known as the Mass of Light.

In the place Manifest Womb of Passionate Elements appeared the teacher Youth Playful Grace.

In the place Healing Garden of Youth on the southern part of Mount Sumeru appeared the teacher Vajradhara.

In the charnel ground Delighting in the Great Secret appeared the teacher Powerful Warrior Youth.

In the place Raksha Sound of Rulu appeared the teacher Wrathful Sage King.

At Vulture Peak Mountain appeared the teacher Sublime Golden Light.

In the land of Turquoise-Browed Sogpos appeared the teacher Lovingly Playful Wisdom.

At Vulture Peak appeared the teacher Kashyapa the Elder.

At the Vajra Throne appeared the teacher Truly Perfected King.

In the place Kapilavastu appeared the teacher Shakyamuni.

From the time when lifespans were unfathomable down until they were one hundred years, nirmanakayas spontaneously appeared as sublime guides of all beings. Likewise, the steersmen of all beings will manifest in succession from the time when Maitreya appears in the future until Buddha Aspiration appears in the kalpa's end. All these conquerors appear naturally from the single identity of Samantabhadra in their respective eras. Thus, since they appear in succession without moving from the nature of the realized state they are known as "the lineage transmitted through the intention of the conquerors."

ᕒ

The rest of the story continues with how the lineage was transmitted through the symbolism of the vidyadharas. There is mention of Vajrapani who taught the dakinis, siddhas and vidyadharas in the Blazing Fire Mountain charnel ground situated on the northern part of Mount Sumeru. Later on the teachings are brought to the human world, where the story begins in the country of Uddiyana where people wear their hair in top-knots, to the west of the Vajra Throne, King Uparaja and his Queen Radiant Light had a daughter by the name Sudharma who was a nun and later gave birth to Prahevajra.[54] The Turquoise Scripture *in the* Vima Nyingtig *cycle mentions that this took place three hundred and sixty years after Buddha Shakyamuni's passing.*

Another fabulous history of the universe and the Dharma in India and Tibet by Longchenpa is Illuminating Sunlight. *This text was regarded by many later masters as authentic enough to plagiarize shamelessly, an action which in Tibet was considered a virtue. Longchenpa himself gathered this text from the many sources available in the fourteenth century, primarily the* Great Image *and the termas contained in the* Four Branches of Heart Essence. *His chapter about Padmasambhava's arrival in Tibet is almost identical with the* Sanglingma *version revealed by the King of Nyang (Nyang Ral Nyima Özer) in the twelfth century.*

The following chapter from Illuminating Sunlight *describes how Ananda Garbha—a young god living at the summit of Mount Sumeru—had four special dreams that set a whole series of events in motion resulting in him receiving the entire transmission of the Great Perfection from Vajrapani. It is this god Ananda Garbha who then incarnates into the human realm and becomes the famous Prahevajra, the first master in the Dzogchen lineage. Also included is how he passes on the lineage of teachings to his chief disciple, Manjushrimitra.*

The wonderful exchange between Prahevajra and Manjushrimitra in poetic song is also found in Terdak Lingpa's revelation Ati Zabdön Nyingpo *from the seventeenth century. I took the liberty to mention the differences between the two versions in endnotes since the great master of Mindrolling's terma treasure is so recent and could be more reliable.*

Illuminating Sunlight

Illuminating Sunlight to
Reveal the Treasury of the Precious Dharma History

The following story recounts the origin of the effortless Great Perfection—the most secret among secrets, the innermost and wondrous, the topmost view of Vajrayana, the quintessence of the minds of all the buddhas in the three times—that universally reveals the basic nature of things as self-liberation in actuality.

This account includes the way in which the Great Perfection was transmitted through the mind of the conquerors, how it was transmitted through the insight of the knowledge-holders, how it was transmitted orally by sublime individuals, and how it was proclaimed in the realms of gods and men.[55]

First, mind transmission through the conquerors.

The Dharma of the conquerors in their four kayas appeared in Akanishtha and other realms when the Svabhavikakaya Buddha taught by revealing natural luminosity,[56] when the Dharmakaya Buddha taught the natural liberation in actuality through inspired resplendence, when the Sambhogakaya Buddha taught through his own identity, and when the Guhyakaya Buddha taught by the method of great bliss.

Then the teacher, in the form of the Lord of Secrets, empowered the nirmanakaya Prahevajra to be the holder of all these teachings and to proclaim them throughout the realms of gods and men. The history of how the nirmanakaya Prahevajra taught by means of excellent composition and how he proclaimed and transmitted the teachings is found in detail in *The Great Image.*

Concerning the story to be told here, the teachings of the effortless Ati Yoga came to pass when these sixfold omens for the Secret Mantra occurred:

> When negative emotions swell, and faith declines;
> When karmic life-span wanes, and the meaning of the words is lost;
> When harmful views distort the Buddhadharma;
> When remedies are ineffective, perseverance faint—
> This is when the principle of *rigpa* dawns.

Thus, the quotation describes the time when emotions swell, when the power of faith and devotion has grown weak, when the karmic life-span is shorter, when only the literal sense of the Buddha's words is regarded as the meaning, when unwholesome beliefs degenerate the Buddhadharma, when the remedies are ineffective and perseverance becomes faint—that is the time for the advent of the Ati Yoga that reveals distinguishing, resolving and self-liberation in actuality.

It was during such a time that the deva Bhadrapala, on the plateau of the Thirty-Three Gods, had five hundred and one sons, the eldest bearing the name Ananda Garbha. Though he was superior to his peers in both sports and intelligence, while the other young gods would enjoy themselves with songs and dances, playing music and games, taking baths and composing poetry in their delightful gardens, Ananda Garbha preferred the solitude of his meditation hut, chanting the vajra recitation. The king of the gods therefore gave him the name Noble Spirit.

Now it happened that during the Great Miracle month in the year of the female Water Ox, this young god had dreams with four omens. First he dreamt that rays of light from all the buddhas radiated into the ten directions after which the light rays and the six Munis encircled Noble Spirit and finally dissolved into the crown of his head. Next he dreamt that he swallowed Brahma, Vishnu and Pashupati in one gulp. Third Noble Spirit dreamt that the sun and moon rose in the sky, and he took them both in his hands and illuminated all worlds with their light. Fourth he dreamt that nectar showered down from the cloud-covered sky which nourished all the greenery and forests so that sprouts, flowers and jewel-like fruits simultaneously ripened.

In the morning he related these dreams to the king of the gods who delightedly exclaimed these words of praise:

> Emaho![57]
> The time has come for the authentic essence of the teachings to appear.
> Those perfectly awakened in the triple times have sent an emanation
> To dispel the darkness of the worlds, uplifting times of gloom.
> What wonder that my noble son will be the glory of the Jambu Isle.

His father continued with these words:

> The first omen in the dream is a sign that you shall gain the realization of all the buddhas of the three times and be the regent of all awakened ones. The second is a sign that you shall bring all demonic forces under your command and cut the three poisons at their root without rejecting them, so that you awaken to true and complete enlightenment. The third is a sign that with the vehicle beyond cause and effect you shall dispel the darkness of disciples and be the lamp of the Buddhadharma. The fourth is a sign that with the self-existing nectar of pith instructions you shall forever dispel the torment of negative emotions so that the effortless fruition is spontaneously present.

The king delightedly turned to face each of the four directions and addressed all the conquerors of the three times with this invocation:

Having mastered the enlightened voice,
You taught the yanas needing effort, to perfection,
But not the vehicle requiring none.
Has your great compassion vanished, lords?
Since there are fortunate disciples now,
Teach, I pray, the yana on spontaneous presence.

When he had made this supplication, all the buddhas of the ten directions and three times gathered, like cloud banks in the sky, and with a single voice they invoked Vajrasattva in these words:

You are the nature that is compassion
Of all the buddhas in the triple times,
Please manifest as their enlightened deeds.

Since you are the wisdom nature
Of all the lords of the enlightened speech,
Please manifest as their awakened mind.

Gifted with the essence of enlightened body
Of all sugatas, not excepting one,
Please manifest as their displays of form.

Perfect lord of countless meanings from a single word
Show the essence-gate of precious magic
To the ones endowed with proper fortune.

Thus they entreated him by means of praising his five aspects of body, speech, mind, qualities and activities. They also requested him, saying, "Teach the effortless vehicle in accordance with their individual mental capacities."

And continued with this request:

With skillful means of precious magic
Bestow upon them riches beyond effort.
Fitting their respective inclinations.

After these words were spoken, Lord Vajrasattva emanated Vajrapani from his own heart center who raised a wheel of self-radiating jewels in his hand and gave this instruction:[58]

To the assembled gathering you shall reveal
The straight and greatest middle way,
The secret nature of nondual wakefulness,
Undivided, effortless—the timeless buddhahood.

Having been given this mandate, Vajra Being pledged to teach:[59]

Vajrasattva, spacious vastness
Lies beyond the reach of spoken words,
And so I must toil to describe it.
To indicate through words to those who do not understand,
According to the situation I shall now explain
That they too may gain this understanding.

With this pledge to teach, Vajrapani—in order to be in harmony with the realization of all the buddhas of the three times and since all these buddhas abide as the identity of the five families—set out to resolve his doubts about the nature of ground and fruition by raising questions to these buddhas.

In the eastern buddhafield known as Perfectly Subjugating Vajra, he went before Tathagata Vajra Secret and his retinue, indivisible from him, and inquired in these words:[60]

If mind's nature is like a vajra,
Why does it appear to rise and cease?

In response to this question, the Tathagata, the truly and completely awakened Vajra Secret spoke in these words:

Mind's nature, the unchanging vajra,
It neither arises nor does it cease.
Ceasing and arising both occur within conceptual mind.

Then, in the southern realm of Jewel Light, the Tathagata Ratnapada was seated upon a throne of self-radiating jewels, teaching his retinue the reality of Secret Mantra. Vajra Being inquired of him in these words:

When the nature of awakened mind
Is not produced through effort nor through causes and
    conditions,

Vajra Bearer

How can the qualities, the fruit, appear?

The tathagata Ratnapada responded in these words:

Like the ornament of *dagshaka*
Causation is perfected, complete within the ground.
But when you realize, by using secret methods,
The fruition, the supreme and self-existing essence,
Manifests like daylight from the sun.[61]

Then Vajra Being went to Lotus Mound, the western realm where the conqueror Lotus Light was seated on the throne of an immaculate lotus teaching his retinue the reality of Secret Mantra. Vajra Being inquired of him in these words:

When mind's nature is pure just like a lotus flower,
How does the flaw of dualistic clinging come about?

The conqueror Lotus Light replied in these words:

The lotus flower growing in the swamp
Remains untainted by the muddy soil.
The essence of awakened mind
Is never muddied by samsaric states.[62]
Samsara comes about due to conceptual mind.

Then he went to Perfect Accomplishment, the northern buddhafield where the tathagata Perfected Brilliance was seated upon a throne while teaching his retinue the reality of Secret Mantra. Vajra Being asked him in these words:

When mind's nature is effortless,
How do the deeds to benefit others come about?

The tathagata Perfected Brilliance replied in these words:

When finally you realize the self-existing wisdom,
The actions of enlightened deeds spontaneously appear.

Then, in the Boundless, the central realm, the very moment Vajrapani arrived in the presence of Tathagata Vairochana, the buddha spoke these words of welcome:

> Retinue assembled, all of you
> Must realize the secret wisdom's nature,
> The heart essence of all the conquerors!

Upon hearing this Vajrapani rose from his seat and addressed the tathagata Vairochana in these words:

> You are the lion of enlightened speech,
> Teach us, please, the secret wisdom's nature.

In response Vairochana spoke:

> Vajra Being, please pay heed!
> The nature of this secret wisdom
> Is that buddhas and beings are not two.
> Just like the sky is all-pervasive,
> Ignorance and wisdom are not separate things,
> But, whether knowing or unknowing, simply one.

> The essence of this secret wisdom
> Is that lucid, natural knowing is entirely pure
> And thoughts are in themselves wisdom pristine.
> This natural jewel treasury, intrinsic to the ground,
> Is self-existing, unsought and pristinely pure.

> The outward form of secret wisdom
> Is the host of all appearances, without a thing to grasp.
> The view is when you are forever clear about
> This indefinable and magical spontaneous presence.

In this way Vajrapani received from all the buddhas the quintessence of their realized state—the wondrous essence of the doctrine, the realization of self-existing and effortless Ati, the teachings beyond cause and effect, in sum all the teachings on Ati Yoga.

Vajrapani then went to the plateau of the Thirty-Three Gods, to the top floor of the Palace of Victory, into the principal hall that holds the life-pillar made of a nine-pronged vajra, and appeared before Noble Spirit.

A throne of shining jewels was arranged upon the life-pillar of the nine-pronged vajra, and a canopy made of various gems was unfurled. Here Vajrapani took seat and conferred upon Noble Spirit the empowerment of the *Perfect Royal Vase* and gave the instruction on the *Ten Miraculous Statements*.

Having conferred the empowerment of the *Threefold Spontaneous Presence*, he gave the instruction on *Encountering the Three Kayas*. Having conferred the empowerment of the *Great Sphere*, he imparted the instruction on *Unchanging Mind Essence*. Having conferred the empowerment of *Changeless Steadiness*, he gave the instruction on *Insight during Daily Activities*.

Having conferred the empowerment of *Immediacy of Awareness*, he gave the instruction on *Identifying Original Wakefulness*. Having conferred the empowerment on *Nondual Mingling*, he gave the instruction the *Great Seal*. Having conferred the empowerment of the *Vajra Statement*, he gave the instruction on the *Regent Nomination*.

Furthermore, within a single moment of the finality of time, Vajrapani completely entrusted Noble Spirit with numerous empowerments, pith instructions and tantras, and empowered him to be his regent with these words:

> This wondrous essence of the doctrine,
> Proclaimed throughout the triple deva realms,
> Must now be spread across the Jambu Isle
> By heart sons and by many emanations!

Having said this, the teachings flourished throughout the three divine realms.

ॐ

Rajahasti the Senior Prince

Now follows the story of how the effortless doctrine
emerged in the human world.

It was during the declining Age of Strife that Shakyamuni appeared and among his three modes of influence—namely body, speech and mind—his influence through body was the actual period the Buddha was alive. The influence through speech was while Ananda and others wrote down his teachings. The influence through mind was more than a hundred years after the Buddha had passed away, and it seems evident that this was the time the doctrine of the effortless Ati Yoga appeared.

Why is that? It is because the teachings containing the instructions of the Great Perfection had not arrived in the human world prior to the appearance of Prahevajra, the incarnated teacher, because Prahevajra's mother was the daughter of King Ashoka, and because it was one hundred and ten years after the Buddha's passing that the king Dharma Ashoka arranged the second council for compiling the Buddha's Words by an assembly of seven hundred arhats, including Hunchback, Peaceful and others. This was the time when the entire Dharma was committed to writing, and King Ashoka was the benefactor for this event. According to the sutras, this is the king who in both the *Sutra on the Wise and the Foolish* and in the *Sutra on the*

White Lotus of Compassion is the Dharma-king Ashoka predicted to appear one hundred years after the Buddha's passing.

Here is the story about how the master Prahevajra appeared. It was in the land of Uddiyana, situated outside India to the west, in the area of Dhanakosha, (the name of which means Treasure-house of Generosity), on the banks of Lake Kutra near the Vajra Haven Cave. Here lived the caste known as the Virtuous and Dhahena Talo was the king. His eldest son was Rajahasti and he had a daughter named Parani as well, a most beautiful and gifted maiden, whose virtuous attitude and yearning for enlightenment were deep and vast and free of faults. She had renounced all mundane aims and turned away from every worldly fickleness, and now observed with utmost purity the disciplines of a fully ordained nun. She lived among her retinue of five hundred nuns and where the company of men was banned.

It happened during dawn, on the eighth day of the autumn's final month. It was the female wood ox year, that the princess had this dream. She dreamt that rays of light shone forth from all the tathagatas and that the light transformed into a sun and moon. The sun dissolved within her, down through the crown of her head, and then the moon as well dissolved up through the soles of both her feet. In the morning she awoke, incredulous, in wonder, and then set out to bathe along Lake Kutra's banks.

While facing east she saw a golden swan, the king of birds, who in fact was Vajrapani, having magically transformed, and who came with Noble Spirit drawn within the letter HUNG. The swan came flying through the sky accompanied by four other swans. They landed, bathed, and four of the enchanting birds again took flight, but one, the bird the Lord of Secrets had miraculously created, touched his beak three times to the princess' heart. She saw a syllable, a shining HUNG, and it dissolved within her heart. The swan took flight and soon was lost from sight.

The princess was amazed at this and narrated to her father and his retinue this dream, as well as the story of the swan. Her father was astonished, and then was filled with joy and said, "Could it be that an emanation of a buddha may appear?" He gave her many guards, and the rituals to protect her were performed.

Within a year the term was full. A nine-pronged vajra set with an assort-
ment of the finest gemstones now emerged out from the princess' heart, and
everyone was struck with wonder. Right there the vajra by itself disinte-
grated and became a boy-child beautified with all the major and the minor
marks. His right hand held a vajra and his left a jeweled staff, and to the joy
of all he uttered many verse lines such as "Vajrasattva, great expanse."[63] They
took him to a brahmin trained in omens who, amazed, exclaimed, "This is
an incarnated buddha who will become the lord of Dharma and the vehicle
supreme." Prahevajra, the Delightful Vajra, was the name he then received.

From early childhood he excelled in games and sports and every other
field. Quite soon his education was concluded and he was ready to be
crowned as king. Right then it was that Vajrapani came, in person, and conferred upon him the empowerments, the *Perfect Royal Vase* and many more.
Then Vajrapani summoned the three bearers of the Putra[64] name, who came
from Damshö Haven charnel ground to the southwest, and he empowered
them and bound them under oath. Then, in a single moment, the finality of time,[65] he entrusted them with all the tantras in completeness—the
Twenty Thousand Sections of the Ninefold Space, and also with empowerments
and pith instructions.[66] Prahevajra he empowered to be the doctrine's lamp.
The oath-bound were entrusted with assisting yogis and to be the teaching
guardians.

It was right there and then, within a single moment, the finality of time,
that Prahevajra, the nirmanakaya, awakened truly and completely to the
level of the effortless and Great Perfection so that his state of realization
became one with that of all the buddhas of the threefold times. Without
exception, he had comprehended both the general causal and resultant
teachings. In particular, he realized the meaning of the countless tantras
and the fourfold kayas of the conquerors—including all the basic tantras of
the effortless and Great Perfection, which are the *Twenty Thousand Sections
of the Ninefold Space,* Samantabhadra's lore, the branch tantras expounded
by the fivefold families of the victorious ones and by the Lord of Secrets, as
well as the explanatory tantras and subsidiary tantras too. The pith instructions of the conquerors' words that reveal in actuality the natural liberation,
the *Royal Vase* empowerment, the river of empowerments of the fourfold

Prehevajra the Nirmanakaya

kayas of the conquerors and many more—all these were perfectly contained within his mind.

And thus he, Prahevajra, now remained, while propagating teachings of the effortless and self-existing Great Perfection to his retinue of numerous exceptional disciples.

2. The Symbolic Transmission of the Vidyadharas

Now it happened that an emanation of noble Manjushri, the foremost in knowledge, was born to the brahmin Glorious Sustainer of Bliss as the father and the brahmini Kuhana as the mother. The boy-child had the most excellent characteristics and was highly intelligent. He was named Siddhigarbha the Brahmin, as well as Samvaragarbha. He became a monk skilled in the five topics of knowledge and extremely learned in the teachings on cause and effect after which he remained as the supreme among five hundred panditas.

During this time, all the panditas heard that there was a nirmanakaya, Prahevajra, who was proclaiming something superior to all the teachings on cause and effect, a wondrous essence of the doctrine, a teaching known as the effortless Great Perfection transcending cause and effect. This was the time when Siddhigarbha the Brahmin received this prophecy from Manjushri:

In the land of Uddiyana to the west, in the area of Dhanakosha, on the banks of Lake Kutra, neighboring the great charnel ground Golden Sanctuary of Expanding Delight, in the cave known as Vajra Haven, is the son-like emanation of Vajrasattva whom all the buddhas have empowered to be the lamp of the effortless doctrine. He is the nirmanakaya Prahevajra and he has the wondrous essence of the doctrine known as Ati Yoga which effortlessly brings enlightenment in a single moment. Receive it and become the nirmanakaya's compiler!

This was the prediction he received. All the other panditas found the news that there should be something superior to the teachings on cause and effect utterly unfounded and they made plans to refute it. Siddhigarbha the

Brahmin knowingly joined their plans for a refutation, in order to reveal the nirmanakaya's greatness.

The panditas next discussed who should go. The land of Uddiyana was far away and the journey arduous since none of the others could go, it was Siddhigarbha, the senior prince Rajahasti and some others, seven in all, who were sent off.

The seven of them arrived at the Vajra Haven Cave where they met the nirmanakaya Prahevajra. In order to put him to a test they debated the truth where they extolled the greatness of the vehicles of cause and effect. At first they discussed the Three Collections (the *Tripitaka*) of the causal teachings and they couldn't best Prahevajra. Next they discussed both the outer and inner Mantra of the resultant teachings and again they couldn't outdo Prahevajra.

Now they held a debate with the panditas taking the position of the vehicles of cause and effect, while the incarnated Prahevajra took the position of Ati beyond cause and effect. Again the seven panditas couldn't defeat him.

In a calculated way Siddhigarbha then acted as if conferring with the other panditas about whether or not they should request a teaching beyond cause and effect from the nirmanakaya Prahevajra. Some of them said, "It would be wrong of us."[67] The senior prince Rajahasti and others wanted to request it, but said, "We have disparaged him, so I don't dare request it."

Then Siddhigarbha and the others discussed how to apologize to the nirmanakaya Prahevajra. Some of them paid respect by prostrating themselves and made circumambulations. Some of them wept and shed tears. Siddhigarbha[68] bowed down with tear-filled eyes and prepared to cut off his own tongue as an atonement. The nirmanakaya Prahevajra saw this and, in the melodious voice of purity, spoke these words:

> Emaho,
> Unconfined equality, spontaneous perfection, greatest bliss,
> This is the very essence, the awakened state of all,[69]
> And yet, the sixfold beings grip their objects and by clinging
>   they are bound.

The extremists all misconstrue the nil and the eternal by fixating
    on extremes.

Clinging to what is and what is not, the eight vehicles remain
    within duality;
With bias and ambition, they cling to basic space as having
    sides.[70]
The nature of equality is split into divisions;
Ignoring what they have, they seek it somewhere else.
Through effort they pursue a spontaneous presence,
And in a distant life they hope to reach the buddha of their
    minds.

Equality is never realized by such narrow views of longing.
I pity all these views, so wearisome and boastful.

Be therefore free from bias, cut the horns of clinging,
And embrace the blissful path of unconfined equality![71]

Having sung this, Prahevajra continued, "Siddhigarbha, cutting off your
tongue does not purify misdeeds. Compose a teaching that is superior to the
teachings on cause and effect. Through that you will be purified."

Those among the panditas without the karmic fortune then returned.
Siddhigarbha attained realization in a single instant by simply being shown
a symbol. But, even though he had realization, he was conferred the empowerment of the *Royal Vase* in order to fully perfect the teachings. Having been
entrusted with all the tantras and pith instructions in their entirety, including the *Twenty Thousand Sections of the Ninefold Space,* Siddhigarbha was
given the name Manjushrimitra, Kinsman of Manjushri.

Prahevajra then condensed the meaning with these words, spoken in the
melodious voice of purity:

The nature of your mind is the primordial buddha,
Beyond rising, beyond ceasing, this mind is like the sky.
Once you realize that dharmas neither rise nor cease,[72]
The training, then, is to let be within this nature free of seeking.

Takshaka the Naga King

At this, Manjushrimitra understood the nature of realization. He had perfected the essence of the teachings and then expressed his realization in these words:

> I am known as Kinsman of Manjushri;
> I attained the siddhi of the Slayer of the Lord of Death.
> I realized samsara and nirvana as a great equality,
> And everything now dawns as wisdom-knowledge.

Manjushrimitra then composed the *Pure Golden Ore of Awakened Mind*, as his act of contrition, and functioned as the compiler of the nirmanakaya's teachings.

King Dhahena Talo, the senior prince Rajahasti, Princess Parani,[73] Takshaka the naga king, Bodhi the Yakshini, Kukkuraja the elder, and others, all met Prahevajra in person, received his teachings and were part of his close retinue.

᧞

From Manjushrimitra, King Dhahena Talo, Buddhaguhya, Shri Singha, Padmasambhava, Lalitavajra, and down to Vimalamitra, there are many lineages, for example those transmitted through twenty-five or twenty-one successors, transmitted through the seven or five heart sons, transmitted through three or through just one lineage-holder. These successors do not have any fixed order, so that each transmitted teaching has its own lineage.[74]

In his Ocean of Wondrous Sayings, the great historian Guru Tashi Tobgyal mentions that Prahevajra's heart son Manjushrimitra is pivotal in the transmission, whether the lineage goes through three, seven or twenty-one masters. Moreover, there are several other lineage traditions when specifying the teachings: the Brahmin's Cycle for distinguishing, the King's Cycle for resolving and the Instruction Cycle for revealing self-liberation in actuality.

PART III
Revelations of Samantabhadra's Mind

In future times some fortunate people endowed with the karmic readiness will discover the teachings I have given here and they will all awaken to buddhahood.

—*Padmasambhava*

Rigdzin Godem the Treasure Revealer

The treasure cycle Gongpa Zangtal—which is a Tibetan abbreviation for Direct Revelation of Samantabhadra's Mind—deserves its own section for several reasons: little of it has been made available in English, the lineage is intact and is still given widely, and its incredibly profound termas consist of the combined efforts of Vimalamitra, Padmasambhava and Vairotsana. All Kagyu and Nyingma practitioners recite its most famous text, the renowned "Aspiration of Samantabhadra," from memory.

The Gongpa Zangtal scriptures fill five volumes together with Kadag Rangjung Rangshar, the Tantra on the Self-Arising Self-Existence. These termas were revealed by Rigdzin Gödem, the master whose termas form the foundation for the Jangter tradition of the Nyingma School.

Rigdzin Gödem, alias Ngödrub Gyaltsen lived from 1337-1408. When he was twelve years old three white tufts of hair resembling vulture feathers grew on his head, and five more when he was twenty-four; hence his name which means "the Vidyadhara with the Vulture Feathers." He passed away at the age of seventy-one amidst miraculous signs.

In the following narration we hear how the dharmakaya buddha teaches Vajrasattva, Vajradhara, Vajrapani and others.

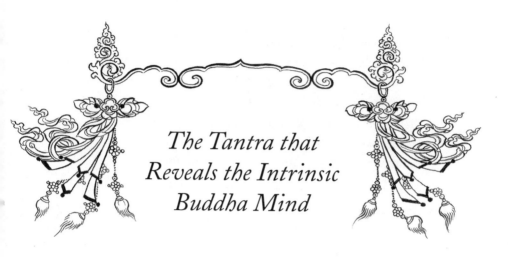

The Tantra that Reveals the Intrinsic Buddha Mind

The pith instructions on the Great Perfection

༈ རྫོགས་པ་ཆེན་པོ༔

In the language of India: BUDDHA SAMAYA TIRO MAHA DHARMA TANTRA NAMA

In the language of Tibet: *sangs rgyas kyi dgongs pa rang chas su bstan pa'i rgyud*

In the English language: *The Tantra that Reveals the Intrinsic Buddha Mind*

Homage to the transcendent perfect conqueror, the dharmakaya Changeless Light.

These are the words that I once taught:

It was within the dharmadhatu realm of Akanishtha—the pure and unconditioned nature that does not rise or cease throughout the triple times—that Buddha Changeless Light, the one who shows awareness beyond all things composed of matter, resided in the sphere of precious secrets, indivisible from his retinue, the realization of his self-display.

It was at this time, in the sambhogakaya realm known as the Radiant Displays of Wisdom, that Changeless Light, the great primordial awakened one, spoke these words to Vajrasattva, who was the natural radiance of his awareness:

Self-knowing wakefulness, when realized,
Is known as Self-Existing Vajrasattva.
Within the realms of the sambhogakayas,
Now you, my heart-son Vajrasattva,
Shall open up the door of dharmakaya's treasury.
And for samsaric beings of the six mind-streams
Simultaneously reveal the means of liberation!

As soon as this was spoken, many hundreds of billions of members of the vajra family came together from the pure sambhogakaya realms to the realm of dharmakaya. In the presence of the dharmakaya Samantabhadra, the one who shows awareness beyond all things of matter was Vajradhara the Great Sixth, and Vajrapani the Compiler, as well as the three emanated bodhisattvas together with their retinues. Having taken seat they made this request:

O wondrous Buddha Mass of Light, a perfect freedom,
Please bestow upon your heart-sons of awareness,
The assemblies belonging to the vajra family,
The teaching on perceiving dharmata directly,
The pointing-out instruction to the truest meaning.

Victorious One, please give the prophecy
Declaring with precision all the masters
Who reveal for the six classes of samsaric beings
The realization of the state of dharmakaya.

And at that moment, while awareness remained vividly present as a radiance of five-colored wisdom lights, Samantabhadra taught these eleven thousand five hundred seeds of the self-existing dharmakaya—tantras that spontaneously flowed from the vastness of his mind.

Specifically, in order to guide sentient beings in conformity with their deluded attitudes, Samantabhadra taught three thousand tantras of self-liberated mind essence that establish the nature of the ground. Since dualistic mind does not perceive dharmakaya, he taught three thousand tantras to establish the nature that reveals awareness as being self-cognizant. From among the tantras that reveal original wakefulness through the perfection of awareness, he taught four thousand tantras that fully reveal the fruition. In order to unravel the hidden and mend any incompleteness in the pith instructions of these tantras, he taught one thousand five hundred tantras that are like lamps for eyes to see. Then Samantabhadra spoke these words of entrustment:

> Emanations most sublime, all of the vajra family,
> Retain this treasury, the secrets of my heart.
> From now and lasting for one hundred twenty thousand years,
> At certain times there will be suitable disciples
> For incarnations in the worlds of gods and men.
> Entrust the tantras of the Great Perfection of Instruction
> To those who are endowed with karmic links.

> Display of the Ever-Excellent's awareness,
> Child of Dharmadhatu Mamo's heart,
> Black Wrathful Mother, guard this teaching!
> JNANA PANCHA CHAKSHU BHIDYA

These were the words he spoke.

After the realm of Akanishtha, now in sambhogakaya's buddhafield, Samantabhadra remained for sixty-one years, measured within the time frame of his own magical creation, in the state in which the knowing of original wakefulness is a vivid presence.

Samantabhadra then appeared on the plateau of the Thirty-Three Gods, upon the Amolika Rock, together with the three members of the vajra family and their retinues, and remained for twenty-four magical years. Then, in the god realm at the summit of existence, he taught the nirmanakaya Prahevajra, the perfect king of the gods Shakra and the teaching guardian Black Wrathful Mother, in the manner of entrusting the symbolic meaning.

After that, he taught the god king Shakra in order to liberate the bodily forms of the gods in the abode of Radiant Light.[75] He taught the condensed meaning to Prahevajra in order to liberate fortunate human beings. He taught the entrustment to Black Wrathful Mother because of the weighty nature of the teachings of the Great Perfection.

This is the entrustment he gave to Prahevajra:

Delightful Vajra, incarnated being,
For twenty-one and hundred human years
Your work shall be to benefit the beings on the Jambu Isle.

When seven times five hundred years have passed,
Teach noble Gentle Splendor's wondrous son
Who will appear while bearing the name Manjushri;
Entrust him with the Great Perfection that is Renowned as
Body.

Three heart-like people will concurrently appear,
The incarnated sons of Lokeshvara;
Teach them the Great Perfection that is Renowned as Speech.

A son of Vajrapani's mind will come,
A bearer of the name Resplendent Lion;
Teach him the Great Perfection that Liberates as Mind.

Thus he spoke.

This was the first chapter, on the entrustment of the conqueror's mind transmission.

SAMAYA. ⁝ SEAL, SEAL, SEAL. ⁝ COMPLETED. ⁝

ⓢ

The nirmanakaya Prahevajra then went to the southern Jambu continent where he entrusted the entire Great Perfection Renowned as Body to Manjushrimitra. The entire Great Perfection that Clarifies the Essence Distinguished as Speech he entrusted to the three sons of the king, the minister and the brahmin. The entire Great Perfection that Liberates as Mind he entrusted to the learned Shri Singha.

These entrusted vidyadharas he taught like a child running to its mother's lap or a mother going to her child.

Following this Prahevajra spoke these words of entrustment to his heart-son Shri Singha:

Son of noble family, listen here to me.
Resplendent subjugator, Shri Singha, bearer of the Lion name,
Upon the Jambu continent you must remain three thousand
   human years.
I trust you with this essence of the teachings of the sacred
   Dharma,
And all the pith instructions of the Great Perfection.

In future times three heart sons you will have.
The body vidyadhara will come from Tibet's land.
Entrust him with the Great Perfection that is Renowned as
   Body.

The speech vidyadhara will come from Uddiyana.
Entrust him, in entirety, with the Great Perfection that the
   Essence Clarifies.

The mind vidyadhara will come from India.
Entrust him, in completeness, with the Great Perfection of the
   Liberated Mind.

Having spoken in this way, he departed for the realm of Akanishtha.

Following that, the great vidyadhara Shri Singha remained for five hundred human years in the nature of the Great Perfection within the Indian jungles of Magadha. Then the learned Indian Vimalamitra arrived. Seeing that a suitable recipient for the Great Perfection of Mind had arrived, Shri Singha taught him and gave him the seal of entrustment.

One hundred and twenty-one years after this Padmasambhava, the master of Uddiyana, came. Seeing that a suitable recipient for the Great Perfection that Clarifies the Essence had arrived, Shri Singha taught him and gave him the seal of entrustment.

Following this, after one hundred and twenty-one years had passed, the Tibetan Vairotsana came. Seeing that a suitable recipient for the Great Perfection renowned as Edict had arrived, Shri Singha taught him and gave him the seal of entrustment.

Shri Singha then spoke these words of entrustment to his three heart sons:

> Listen Flawless Kinsman, learned one.
> You are the son of Vajrasattva's mind.
> In future times, in India you will have
> More than three hundred thousand heart sons.
>
> And in Tibet one hundred thousand there will be.
> All these are heart sons of the essence.
> Make them undivided from the Vajra Being.
> Condensed, entrust them with the tantras of awakened mind.
>
> Nine heart sons there will be in India's land.
> Teach them the Great Perfection that liberates with tantras.
> And in Tibet three heart sons there will be,
> Who only reach the freedom through instructions.
>
> Teach Tibetans the instructions from the triple sections;
> Teach the early ones through your identity;[76]
> And for the later, conceal in terma treasures.
> Entrust the Hearing Lineage to the son appearing at this era's
>   end.

Shri Singha spoke these words to Padmasambhava:

> Lotus-Born of Uddiyana,
> You are the son of Amitabha's mind.
> A vessel suited for the Great Perfection's essence,
> I entrust you with the Great Perfection that Clarifies the
>   Essence.
>
> Two times ten and one will be your heart sons
> Appearing in succession on this Jambu Isle,
> And in Tibet you will have seven worthy heirs.
> Teach them, while condensing key points to the most profound.
>
> In India you will find seven worthy vessels;
> Teach them while instructing in minutest detail.

Vimalamitra

Your seven worthy heirs in Kashmir and in Uddiyana
Should be taught in full the inner and the outer cycles.

Teach the early ones through your identity.
And for the future, you shall hide your terma treasures.
Entrust the Hearing Lineage to the son appearing at this era's
end.

Shri Singha spoke these words to Vairotsana:

Vairotsana from the clan of Pagor,
You are the son of Vairochana's body,
A suitable receiver of the Mahasandhi tantras;
I entrust you now with all that is Renowned as Great Perfection.

Five heart sons you will have, appearing in the future.
These heart sons will be found in Tibet's land.
Teach the early ones through your identity,
And for the later, you shall hide your terma treasures.
Entrust the Hearing Lineage to the son endowed with five
qualifications.

Having spoken this, Shri Singha remained in the state of the Great Perfection, the unimpeded wakefulness in which the five-colored light is vividly present.

This completes the second chapter, on the entrustment of the vidyadhara's transmission of insight.

SAMAYA. ⅜ SEAL, SEAL, SEAL. ⅜

ᠪ

At this time and on the same occasion, all the Great Perfection's teachings
on the Unexcelled Fruition dissolved into the hearts of the three incarnated
vidyadharas, like the sun gathering back its rays of light.[77] The five hundred
panditas and other incarnated masters concealed the Indian manuscripts, in
a compact fashion, within the eastern side of the Vajra Throne.

Formerly, when the truly and completely enlightened Shakyamuni let his bodily form pass from this wretched world, his head faced north under a bodhi tree, while he made pure aspirations for Tibet. As the times for these aspirations ripen, all his deepest teachings will flourish in the land of Tibet to the north. Moreover, all the profound teachings of Secret Mantra, the realization of the Buddha's mind, will be translated into Tibetan. The essence of the entire Dharma, all the teachings of the Unexcelled Great Perfection, were retained within the hearts of the three vidyadharas; and then came to the Snowy Land of Tibet.

Among them, Vairotsana, the great vidyadhara of Body, taught through his identity the Outer Mind Section Cycle of the Great Perfection to the three destined Tibetans: King Trisong Deutsen, Jnana Kumara of Nyak and Yudra Nyingpo, the king of Gyalmo Tsawey Rong.

To Yudra Nyingpo and Mipham Gönpo he taught, through his identity, the Inner Space Section Cycle. All of the Instruction Cycle of the Great Perfection he concealed as terma treasures in the temple at Paro Gyerchu and at the Caves of Yerpa at Lhasa. He made the prophecy that two people with the name Ney and Nyingpo would reveal them at future times through the power of their aspirations.

The three incarnated vidyadharas held a discussion about Vairotsana's *Hearing Lineage on Distinguishing Mind and Awareness* and they agreed that it should be concealed as a terma treasure for the sake of someone with sixteen major signs on his body in the age of the five rampant degenerations. It was to be concealed at the Divine Cliff of Zangzang, to the northwest of glorious Samye, beyond the distance of eight leagues, where there is a mountain resembling a king seated on his throne.

This completes the third chapter, on the occasion of Vairotsana's entrustment.

SAMAYA. ꣸ SEAL, SEAL, SEAL. ꣸

ᰒ

In the meantime, the lotus vidyadhara of eminent speech known as the master Padmasambhava, who had realized the nature of the sacred Great

Jnana Kumara of Nyak

Perfection, had come to the Snowy Land of Tibet. There he taught through his identity to these three: the Dharma-king Trisong Deutsen, the dakini Yeshe Tsogyal and Namkhai Nyingpo who was a vidyadhara of Mahamudra. For the sake of future generations he concealed terma treasures in these five places: the triple-styled central temple of Samye,[78] Kharchu in Lhodrak, Bumtang in Mön (Bhutan), Kongpo to the east, and in the Ogre's Fortress of Nyaljar. He made the aspiration that in future times five incarnated masters would use them to benefit beings. All these teachings of the Great Perfection which Padmasambhava of Uddiyana taught and concealed belonged to the Innermost Unexcelled Cycle.

Padmasambhava concealed his Hearing Lineage on Establishing the Meditation and Post-Meditation and the Cycle on Establishing the Visions in Actuality as terma treasures at the slope of the cliff that resembles a cluster of poisonous serpents. They were concealed for the sake of someone marked with a self-appeared OM, in the age of the five rampant degenerations, who is a suitable recipient for the Great Perfection and who will reside eight leagues beyond glorious Samye to the north-west near a mountain that resembles a queen with a child on her lap.

At the same time there will be someone with the face of a lion in the Indian jungles of Magadha for the sake of whom he concealed the teachings to the east of the Vajra Throne. In the land of Uddiyana someone will come with a face like the sun and moon and for the sake of whom he concealed the teachings beneath the triple-roofed self-appeared stupa.

This completes the fourth chapter, on Padmasambhava of Uddiyana's entrustment.

SAMAYA. ⅗ SEAL, SEAL, SEAL. ⅗

ⓢ

Eventually the great learned Vimalamitra came to Tibet. He entrusted King Trisong Deutsen with the Great Perfection Renowned as Edict. To Tingdzin Zangpo of Nyang he entrusted the Great Perfection of Profound Instructions. These he taught personally through his identity.

Vimalamitra concealed the Innermost Unexcelled Great Perfection in the Subjugating Stupa of Exposition resembling an imprint on white rock at Samye Chimpu and in the Crystal Cave of Yangdzong. He made the aspiration that in future times these teachings would be utilized by his four lineage-holding heart sons.

Vimalamitra possessed the *Hearing Lineage on Freely Resting Mind Essence,* as well as the *Self-Luminous Wakefulness.* Eight leagues beyond glorious Samye to the northwest there was a mountain resembling a victory banner raised into the sky. In the age of the five rampant degenerations, there will appear someone marked with the mole of subjugating the three poisons for the sake of whom he concealed these teachings as a terma treasure within an awesome triple-peaked cliff.

This completes the fifth chapter, on Vimalamitra of Kashmir's entrustment.

SAMAYA. ⁑ SEAL, SEAL, SEAL. ⁑

⟳

In the cavern of Samye Chimpu, the three incarnated vidyadharas then opened up the gateway for the mansion of the spontaneously present nature of the Great Perfection, bestowed the empowerments of both symbols and meaning, and conferred the essential readings and entrustments.

OM AH HUNG SVA HA

Then follows their predictions of Rigdzin Gödem as the revealer of the Gongpa Zangtal and of his disciples. There is also an entrustment of the seal of samaya to the guardians of the teachings. The text concludes with:

Among the three sets of *Hearing Lineage for the Innermost Unexcelled Great Perfection,* all these—the *Direct Revelation of Samantabhadra's Mind,* the *Expanse of Vajrasattva's Heart,* the six tantras that establish mind, awareness and original wakefulness, the twofold hearing lineage of the learned great Vimalamitra, the twofold hearing lineage of Vairotsana, the twofold hearing lineage of Padmasambhava, and the hearing lineage that predicts the destined recipients—these six basic sets of tantric teachings are combined into one single set known as the *Hearing Lineage on the Self-Liberated Awareness of the Great Perfection.*

May these six instructions of the three vidyadharas—which, when combined, are known as the *Hearing Lineage on the Self-Liberation of the Great Perfection*—meet with the fortunate people of future generations!

This completes the eighth chapter on stating the combined name of the *Threefold Hearing Lineage of the Great Perfection.*

SAMAYA. ⁞ SEAL, SEAL, SEAL. ⁞

This was revealed from a terma treasure by Rigdzin Gökyi Demtruchen (Rigdzin Gödem) at the slope of the cliff that resembles a cluster of poisonous serpents.

Sarva mangalam.

ᦠ

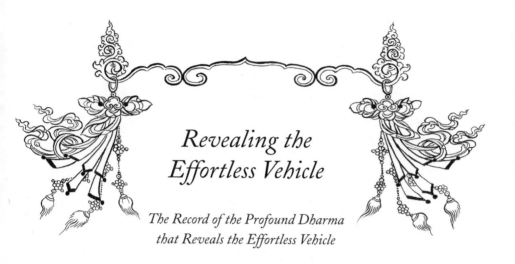

Revealing the Effortless Vehicle

The Record of the Profound Dharma that Reveals the Effortless Vehicle

Homage to the primordial buddha Changeless Light.

It was while the great conqueror Changeless Light resided in the unshakable samadhi of equality in Akanishtha's mansion of spontaneous presence, within the celestial palace Wakefulness of Self-Display, that the Great Vajradhara, his wisdom emanation and heart son, arose and addressed him in these words:

> Pay heed, great Changeless Light, primordial awakened one. Though your capacity is such that you perceive the triple times, to clear the darkness of the world's delusion, please open up the doorway of your heart's self-knowing wakefulness and reveal the most sublime empowerment of awareness display.

Then the great sovereign arose from the unshakable samadhi of great equality, opened the doorway of his heart's self-knowing wakefulness and, in order to dispel the darkness of samsara all at the same time, declared:

> Listen, heart sons of awareness.
> Just as Vajradhara has requested,
> I shall open up the secret treasury of wisdom,
> Present it from the tip of this, my perfect tongue,
> And reveal it to the retinue of wisdom emanations.

Karmeshvari the Dakini

As soon as he had spoken, the entire realm of Akanishtha was invoked by the sounds of empowerment, and Vajradhara was conferred the empowerment of awareness display.

Considering the welfare of beings, and in order to dispel the world's darkness, Vajradhara then appeared on the divine plateau of the Thirty-Three Gods where he conferred the empowerment upon the Lord of Secrets and a large retinue of other members of the vajra family.

Soon after, the Lord of Secrets gave this prophecy to the dakini Karmeshvari and the nirmanakaya Prahevajra:

Supreme within the secret treasury of conquerors,
This empowerment of awareness display
Will dispel samsara's darkness,
Upon the Jambu Isle, south of the world.

Send two emanations—means and knowledge—
In order to complete the aim of beings,
Let them fly forth on the shiny path of wisdom.

Not everyone is ready to receive such teaching,
But when a worthy one or two receive it,
They will dispel the darkness in the world.
They will reign as regents who uproot samsara;
Ensuring ceaseless streams of heart sons of the conquerors.
Therefore expand the massive strength of wakefulness!

Having spoken in this way, the Lord of Secrets gave the prophecy and permission for the empowerment. Entrusted with the *Three Tantras* and the *Four Signs,* a wisdom pathway appeared in the sky and the two emanations of means and knowledge went to the island of Dhanakosha.

After considering a worthy recipient, Prahevajra saw that the master Manjushrimitra who resided in the jungle of Singala possessed the pure karmic continuity and conferred the empowerment upon him.

Manjushrimitra saw that the master Shri Singha, living in the Magadha region of India, possessed the pure karmic continuity and bestowed the empowerment upon him. Shri Singha successively conferred the empowerment upon the master of Uddiyana known as Padmasambhava, the master from Kashmir known as Vimalamitra and others.

When the master Padmasambhava was invited by the Tibetan king Trisong Deutsen, he tamed all the malicious gods and demons, built the temples of Samye, the Spontaneously Accomplished Boundless Wishes, and made the Buddha's teachings spread and flourish in the Snowy Land of Tibet.

Once while Padmasambhava resided at the upper retreat of Samye Chimpu, the Dharma-upholding king Trisong Deutsen and the dakini Yeshe Tsogyal presented him with a mandala offering of five kinds of precious articles. They arranged a throne with silk and brocade, offered a variety of food and drink, and then made this request:

> Pay heed, master of the triple kayas, protector of all beings.
> Your perfect wisdom body is free of any signs of flaws.
> Compassionate, your strength achieves the aim of every being.
> Like a wishfulfilling gem, your form dispels the darkness in
>   Tibet.
> Son of Amitayus, transcending birth and death,
> Wondrous and amazing one, we earnestly salute you.

They offered many such praises and prostrations, and then they continued with this request:

> Please pay heed, great master. You are the emanation of all the buddhas of the three times. As your wisdom body beyond birth and death is no different from the Buddha in person, it is a great kindness to us Tibetans that you have come to this snowy land.
>
> Indeed it is so that all the buddhas, out of their immense compassion and skillful means, teach beings the Dharma in accordance with their individual needs. Nevertheless, as you, Guru, are an emanation of Buddha Amitabha and the son of Maha Heruka, we beg you to bestow upon us a teaching that does not necessitate purifying misdeeds and obscurations, which does not require the toil of meditating and sad-

hana practice, but rather a teaching that by simply being spoken by you, Guru, we may awaken to enlightenment by merely understanding and realizing it, merely through seeing, hearing or touching.

Guru Padmasambhava replied:

Listen King and Tsogyal, such a teaching rarely appears in the world. The buddhas are compassionate, but sentient beings lack the karmic readiness. In the past, it was not taught by the former buddhas. It has not been taught by Shakyamuni, the present buddha. It will not be taught by the buddhas of the future including Maitreya. Why? Because beings do not possess the karmic readiness. This is not, however, because the buddhas do not know such a teaching but because it is difficult for it to appear in the world.

Formerly, during the completion of Buddha Kashyapa's teachings, when the demon Matram Rudra misconstrued the instructions and brought the world to the brink of destruction, the capacity of all buddhas was summoned from Akanishtha and thus the activity of enlightened body subjugated this dark Rudra demon, the activity of enlightened speech showered down a rain of Dharma as volumes of scripture, and the intent of enlightened mind taught the effortless vehicle of original wakefulness.

At first this vehicle appeared in the abode of Akanishtha followed by the divine plateau of the Thirty-Three Gods. Then, out of the heaven of the utterly pure sky, a nirmanakaya appeared and landed on the island of Dhanakosha. This vehicle was subsequently transmitted through three knowledge-holders who had attained the vidya-dhara level of Mahamudra beyond birth and death, and was kept within the ninefold pagoda at the Vajra Throne in India. Since then, only I, Padmasambhava, and the great Indian pandita Vimalamitra have taught it. Due to former aspirations Vimalamitra will come if Your Majesty invites him. He has the mandate to teach the effortless vehicle, so invite him and request it.

Thus he spoke. Once more, the king and Lady Tsogyal asked:

Please heed us, great master. According to your command, we beg you to send someone to invite Vimalamitra from India. But for us there can be no awakened one superior to you. So we insist and beseech you to bestow this profound, sublime teaching upon us.

As they persisted in requesting in this way, Padmasambhava spoke:

Listen here, King and Tsogyal. When giving others a profound teaching treasured more dearly than one's own heart, one must examine the recipient. The testing of the recipient requires the sacrifice of strong resolve, the giving of what is extremely difficult to part with, and the ability to keep the bond of secrecy. Are you capable of those three?

His Majesty the King replied:

As for resolve, I am willing to follow you even if you tell me to cut off my arms, legs and head and place them before you. As for an offering, I have willed one third of my kingdom and wealth to my sons and people, but I offer you the other two thirds. As for secrecy, I will obey whatever you command.

Having said this, he proceeded to present an offering of a jewel-studded cup filled with gold, a cloak made of nine layers of brocade, and then undid his personal turquoise necklace and gave it as well. Then Lady Tsogyal of Kharchen spoke:

Precious master, as for resolve, even if you were to ask me to cut open my own chest and give you my heart I would do so. As for an offering, since we women are attached to clothes and jewelry, I offer you eleven garments of the finest Chinese silken brocade including my splendid multicolored dress, twenty-one Tibetan costumes including my dress of dark blue gown, my multicolored coat of golden-hued Tajik lamb, my magnificent fur coat from Drugu, my fabulous embroidered dress, the Roaring Red Dragon and thirty other turquoise ornaments, eighteen large chunks of turquoise such as Brilliant Star, seven trays of gold, and seven garlands as well as my shining amulet box. I offer you these and many other precious possessions. As for the bond of secrecy, even though like most women I am usually unable to keep secrets, I will not break your command. By all means, I beseech you to please bestow the profound teaching upon us.

Having said this, she offered her necklace with seven pieces of turquoise. Guru Padmasambhava then said:

Your Majesty the King and Lady Tsogyal of Kharchen, you have auspiciously passed the test to be recipients. There is no need to offer me two thirds of your royal wealth; instead use it on virtuous deeds. Thoroughly restore the Khönting Temple at Lhodrak, conceal your choicest wealth in terma treasures, and bury the Lady of Kharchen's garments and jewelry for the benefit of future generations in the rock face of the Long Cave at Nadün Lhodrak.

As for the bond of secrecy, do not let it be heard—not even by the wind—that Padmasambhava is teaching this profound Dharma. Why? Because these teachings are the treasury of my heart and therefore rare is the appropriate recipient to whom they may be taught.

The teachings of sadhana practice are currently being established in Tibet, like planting the never-lowered banner of victory, but if anyone hears or sees a Dharma as profound as this, these present sadhana teachings will fade—like the metaphor of seeing other gems as earth and stones once one has seen a wish-fulfilling jewel. The vehicles of effort are for the sake of testing worthy recipients for the Unexcelled Secret.

As for your different karmic links, Your Majesty, you are connected with Vimalamitra from former aspirations, but you, Lady of Kharchen, do not possess this link, therefore I shall teach you.

For eighteen months, from the beginning of the Year of the Dragon through half of the Year of the Snake, the three of them, master and disciples, remained practicing meditation, and unnoticed by anyone Padmasambhava taught the entire Innermost Unexcelled Effortless Vehicle.

During this time, the manuscripts were written down in Tibetan by three people—Acharya Yeshe Yang, Denma Tsemang and the Lady of Kharchen. The original manuscripts were written in seven kinds of script of precious substance: the deva script written with gold letters, the rakshasa script written with copper letters, the bodhisattva script written in refined lapis, the yaksha script written with conch letters, the Sogdian script with the turquoise letters, the Akanishtha script with *tra* letters and the naga script with azurite letters. Thus they were written down in seven particular types of script.

The originals written with Indian characters and those scriptures that had been translated into the language of Tibet, fully complete and in immense detail, were then concealed in the Lion Cave of Bumtang in Bhutan. The abbreviated and condensed version was concealed in the Spangled Cave of Danglung. The concise but inclusive version was concealed at the Divine Cliff of Zangzang. The version with the principal intent in harmony with the effortless was concealed in the Naga Demon's Belly of Lhodrak. A version with the complete method for someone to be liberated was concealed in the Bear's Nest of Sha-uk. He neither taught nor concealed any other versions of this terma.

Having concealed these profound teachings as terma treasures and sealed the places of concealment with his command, Padmasambhava spoke these words:

> Your Majesty, for three lifetimes you have perfected the activities of a bodhisattva, so there is no fear that you will fall into the abyss of the three lower realms. By practicing the profound teachings of Secret Mantra in this life, after a couple more lives you will arrive at the vidyadhara level of mahamudra. You have now received these profound teachings of mine and they are teachings for awakening to buddhahood without any physical remainder. Since you are a king and have many distractions, you will not perfect the training and awaken to enlightenment within this lifetime. For many lives you will be reborn in a special body in the higher realms while bringing the activities of

emanations to perfection. Following that you will go to the Lotus-Endowed Realm and finally awaken to buddhahood in Akanishtha.

Tsogyal, remain in the Splendid Long Cave of Lhodrak and, after seven years of flawless practice, your material body will disappear and you will attain the stage of the miraculous powers of the daki-nis. Abiding for a long time as a dakini emanation in the Palace of Lotus Light, you will finally awaken to buddhahood in the sphere of Akanishtha.

In future times some fortunate people endowed with the karmic readiness will discover the teachings I have given here and they will all awaken to buddhahood. Their lineage holders as well will be of the type destined to be liberated, so everyone who encounters them will attain enlightenment.

Once more the king and the Lady of Kharchen asked, "Guru Nir-manakaya, please heed us. When these profound teachings are applied in practice, how many Dharma sections with complete key points are there to these teachings that liberate by simply seeing, hearing or touching?"

Padmasambhava replied:

Listen here, King and Tsogyal. When teaching this Effortless Vehi-cle while distilling its key points, it is like this:

The awakening through hearing is the experience of basic space and wisdom. Look for it in the *Tantra of the Great Total Perfection*!

The awakening through practice is the experience of intrinsic pri-mordial purity. Look for it in the *Tantra that Directly Reveals the Intrinsic Mind*!

The awakening through seeing is the experience of original wake-fulness. Look for it in the *Tantra of the Utterly Perfect Great Wakeful-ness*!

The awakening through touch is the seed of the protector Changeless Light. Look for it in the *Tantra of the Single Child of the Buddhas*!

All these are the teachings of the mind transmission of the con-querors.

In order to open up the doorway to these teachings, there is the *Great Empowerment of Awareness Display* for training, the *Manual of Key Points* for establishing certainty and the *Manual of Signs* to reach perfection and the *Manual of Degrees of Progress.* All these are verified by means of the Hearing Lineage of vidyadharas and dakinis who have attained the paths and levels.

The one who practices these teachings in their entirety will be a disciple of Vajradhara and awaken to buddhahood without any doubt.

Then His Majesty the King and the dakini Yeshe Tsogyal presented a mandala offering of seven types of precious substances, respectfully bowed down and offered this praise:

> Such a marvel, precious master!
> Heart son of the buddha Boundless Light,
> Born from the bed of a lotus flower.
>
> Heart son of the Vajra Heruka,
> Subjugator of all cruel, worldly forces.
>
> Child of Vajrasattva's heart,
> Revealer of the buddha-mind, the effortless.
>
> Daka form, defeater of the fourfold demons,
> Attainer of the knowledge-holder's level of immortal life.
>
> Upholder of the doctrine, scion of the conquerors,
> You are the perfect form of greatest wisdom.
> Sincerely, we salute and praise you, noble being.

Having offered such praises, they committed these questions and answers to writing. This completes the *Record of the Profound Teachings.*

SAMAYA. ₿ SEAL, SEAL, SEAL. ₿

This was revealed by Rigdzin Gökyi Demtruchen (Rigdzin Gödem) from the northern slope of the Divine Cliff of Zangzang. Sarva mangalam!

☙

The Great General Background for the History of the Authentic Lineage has some precious details that must be included since they describe how to request the Dzogchen teachings in royal style:

When the Dharma-king Trisong Deutsen, the ruler of Tibet, the land known as Purgyal, had begun the construction of his temple he was prevented from completing it by various gods and demons. After consulting divinations and astrology, he saw that his aim would be fulfilled if he invited Padmasambhava, the master of Uddiyana, to Tibet. So he dispatched Dorje Dudjom of Nanam, Palgyi Senge of Shubu and Shakya Prabha of Chim, furnishing each with a *drey* of gold.

After Padmasambhava of Uddiyana had bound all the malicious gods and demons of Tibet under oath, he was requested to reside at Glorious Samye, the great temple of Spontaneously Accomplished Boundless Wishes where he extensively turned the wheels of the Dharma. During this time, magical dakinis gave the Dharma-king this prediction in a dream:

> Trisong Deutsen, Dharma-king, pay heed.
> If you wish a teaching, which by simply meeting will suffice,[79]
> Request then from the Lotus-Born of Uddiyana
> The quintessential, profound instruction of the Hearing
>   Lineage,
> Known as the Bindu Cycle of the Buddhas' Mind.

Upon hearing this prophecy, Trisong Deutsen awoke and went to the top of Mount Hepori. There he had silken streamers and a large throne set up. He requested Guru Padma to assume his seat and presented him with thirteen mandala plates of gold and silver adorned with sixty-five thousand pieces of turquoise.

The king had arranged a mansion of brocade with three consecutive walls, lined with twenty-five pennants, and encircled by the numerous types of food and drink common in his kingdom. There was *chang* made from rice and dried grapes served in *tramen* vessels filled to the brim, and Hepori was surrounded by five hundred vessels of aromatic powder, suspended to waft their fragrance into the air. Moreover, thirteen cauldrons were filled with five hundred bags of clarified butter.

King Trisong Deutsen

The Lady of Kharchen and the princess[80] were adorned with the finest jewelry and velvety silks, and the king offered them as companions. Having made innumerable prostrations and circumambulations, the king made this request:

> Please heed me, you whose mind can clearly see the triple times
>   throughout this world,
> Your splendid voice, the Dharma ocean guiding gods and men,
> Your form, the wisdom lamp dispelling darkness of unknowing,
> Steersman for all beings, we offer you sincere salute.
>
> Bestow upon us a teaching most sublime, the deepest,
> The final vehicle, the quintessence of Ati,
> The Dharma that awakens in the evening or in a single
>   morning,
> Which overflowed from the vastness of Samantabhadra's heart.

Requested thus, Uddiyana bestowed the following teaching cycles upon the king. In general, he taught many exposition tantras of the Innermost Ati Cycle. He also gave the entire Unwritten Cycle of the Hearing Lineage.

Among Ati Yoga's Refined Bindu Cycle of the Secret Edict , the essence of precious treasures, the *Six Dharma Sections of the Great Perfection that Reveal the Innate Nature in Actuality,* he instructed the king and the Lady of Kharchen in the one that is profound and contains the condensed extract of all the essences: the entire mother and child cycles of the *Tantra that Directly Reveals Samantabhadra's Mind.* By receiving this, their realization and liberation were simultaneous.

🙵

The special feature of this next text—*Vairotsana's Profound Mind Tantra*—is Shri Singha's remarks about the demise of Buddhism in India, his prophetic dream about Padmasambhava, Vimalamitra and especially Vairotsana, to whom he explains the dream. Here I would like to repeat a succinct summary of Vairotsana's life by the nineteenth century master Jamgön Kongtrül:[81]

As the first major translator of Tibet, Vairotsana was sent to India by the great Dharma-king Trisong Deutsen. He journeyed to Dhanakosha's cooling forest of sandalwood and it was there, inside a nine-storied pagoda, that he met the master Shri Singha. After requesting the master to teach the "vehicle beyond effort", this great knowledge-holder Shri Singha revealed the quintessence of his heart and bestowed upon Vairotsana all the empowerments and instructions for the Mind Section of the Great Perfection in eighteen parts and sixty tantras, as well as the White, Black and Multicolored aspects of the Space Section.

Fearing royal persecution unless this transmission was kept extremely secret, Vairotsana studied the Dharma of general philosophy during the day, while at night he received the Dzogchen teachings by using a quick-witted subterfuge.

During his journeys that were wrought with dangers—he underwent fifty major hardships—Vairotsana met the twenty-one learned ones [of the Mind Section]. He even met Prahevajra in the great charnel ground Smoldering Domain and received the ultimate transmission from the six million four hundred thousand segments of the Great Perfection. At that very moment Vairotsana attained the siddhi of liberation that occurs simultaneously with realization.

Vairotsana then learned the art of "swift walking" and based on his accomplishment he was able to reach Tibet. Here he taught the king in secret and rendered into Tibetan the Five Early Translations. Due to a false accusation, Vairotsana was exiled to Tsawa Rong in the Gyalmo area where he taught Yudra Nyingpo, Yeshe Lama the Sangtön, and Sangye Gönpo the mendicant of Pang. After his return to Tibet, Vairotsana taught Jnana Kumara of Nyak as well as Sherab Drönma, the Queen of Li. These are known as the five recipients of Vairotsana's teachings on the Great Perfection and it is through them, as well as Mipham Gönpo the mendicant of Pang, that his lineage gradually flourished so that the instruction on Mind Section and Space Section produced countless Samantabhadra kingdoms.

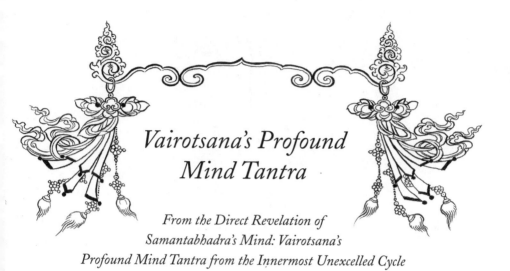

Vairotsana's Profound Mind Tantra

From the Direct Revelation of
Samantabhadra's Mind: Vairotsana's
Profound Mind Tantra from the Innermost Unexcelled Cycle

Homage to Glorious Vajrasattva.

The great knowledge-holder Shri Singha had achieved the vidyadhara level beyond birth and death, was the chief among the seven later Indian vidyadharas, and had been empowered in actuality by Buddha Vairochana. He resided in the land of India within the nine-walled Buddha Palace.

The Tibetan translator Vairotsana asked him:

"Pay heed, great master. It is a profound kindness that the great master has bestowed upon me the essence of all teachings—the precious threefold Hearing Lineage that you cherish more than even your own heart—among the outer, inner and secret teachings of the sacred Great Perfection.

"Now the master will depart to the realm of Akanishtha through the pathway of the five vidyadhara levels. I too must leave, for in the Snowy Land of Tibet disciples remain for me to guide.

"In general, all the teachings have extensive, concise versions, as well as a version condensed to the most profound. This sacred teaching of the Great Perfection does not reach the ears of the shravakas and pratyekabuddhas. It does not fit within the understanding of the followers of the three sections of Kriya and Yoga. It is not comprehended by the three aspects of development and completion. Its high view, its vast teachings and its practice

**Vairotsana
the Translator**

contained in the key points are like the heart within the body of a sentient being. Since it is extremely difficult to realize, please give me that which is superior to even the Hearing Lineage, the practice that you embody within your *Mind Tantra*."

He made this request while offering one hundred and eight ingots of gold and making a thousand prostrations and circumambulations.

At this time the great vidyadhara Shri Singha spoke in these words:

"Listen, Vairotsana of Pagor. You have been empowered by Buddha Vairochana and you are a bodhisattva in his last rebirth, so from now on you need not fear the lower realms. Your benefit to beings will be boundless. Seven lives after this you will awaken to enlightenment.

"The teachings of the sacred Great Perfection are like the sun shining in the sky; their meaning is vast and profound. The teachings of the nine gradual vehicles are like the walking staff for a blind man, like the foundation of a castle, like the hem on a garment, like the limbs of the body—they are indispensable. Though they are required, they are not the true essence.

"The sacred Great Perfection is like giving the blind man eyes: after getting his eyesight he has no need of a cane. It is like the owner of a castle: when he has taken charge of the center of the castle the foundation is naturally included. It is like having the heart in the body: the limbs naturally follow.

"You are the only Tibetan who has come to receive the sacred Great Perfection. In any case, Tibetans will not comprehend the sacred Great Perfection as they descend from a thoughtless creature.[82]

"Vairotsana of Pagor, at one point the king and his ministers will persecute you and reduce you to a commoner's standing. You will be banished to a borderland. Yet there is only you, the monk from Pagor, who can comprehend my teachings on the Great Perfection.

"All the teachings of the sacred Great Perfection that have been heard in the human realm have been passed down to me—without a single exception. If they were to be written down, there would be seven hundred thousand *shlokas.*

"I have concealed the three hundred thousand belonging to the Outer Cycle to the east of the Vajra Throne; and one thousand are in the pagoda's eastern side. Two hundred thousand belonging to the Inner Cycle are in the first pagoda, and five hundred are in the southern pagoda. One hundred thousand belonging to the Secret Cycle are concealed in the northern part of the first pagoda, and five hundred are in the middle pagoda. One thousand belonging to the Innermost Unexcelled Cycle are in the center of the lower pagoda.

"There are five hundred thousand shlokas of the Hearing Lineage, twenty thousand shlokas of the *Mind Tantra* and three thousand of the extremely precious, the most profound of the most profound, like the life-force.

"Now in the land of India they must remain concealed as terma treasures in a number that equals the stars in the sky. The magical emanation Prahevajra said, 'When Buddha Shakyamuni's teachings have passed their peak, conceal all the teachings of the Great Perfection as terma treasures! The future sentient beings there do not have the fortune to practice the teachings of the Great Perfection. Tromo Rakdongma, be the guardian of these teachings!' So he proclaimed.

"From now until that time, there are no more than two hundred and fifty human years.[83] The Great Perfection will not remain long in the central part of India. To the east, the west and in the land of Uddiyana, they will flourish from now until five hundred years hence. After that they will all be concealed as terma treasures.

"Listen to my prophecy about what will be your fate back in Tibet. At dawn on the eleventh day of the previous month, three suns simultaneously rose from my heart center: one went to the forest of Magadha, one went to the western part of India, and one went to Tibet. After that all three went to Tibet. There one became dimmed by the dust-whirls of Tibet so that it became a brilliant white, like the moon. The other two increased in brilliance and dissolved into the side of a cliff. Then again their brilliance increased; and again they dissolved into a cliff. After this happened seven times, the two suns vanished into the sky accompanied by lights.

"Now I will explain the meaning of this dream. Vairotsana of Pagor, you will propagate the teachings of the Great Perfection and make them flourish in Tibet. You will also liberate numerous people with the karmic link.

"But there will come a time in the future when various practitioners with broken vows have their hearts seduced by the *gongpo* demon.[84] They will distort the sacred Great Perfection. Disparaging true teachings while exaggerating falsehoods, they will bring many people to ruin.

"Your Tibetan people are also gullible and therefore indecisive, so there will come a time when these teachings of the Great Perfection are no more than the 'scent lingering in an empty box.'[85]

"Padmasambhava of Uddiyana and the learned Vimalamitra are both holders of my lineage, as well as accomplished in the meaning of the Great Perfection. At present they are working for the benefit of India. At some point in time they will go to Tibet and their teachings will be utilized by a few destined people here and there. Sometimes my teachings will be concealed as terma treasures and then again later be utilized by some destined ones. At the end of this having happened seven times, all of them—the teachings and the pith instructions, the masters and the destined disciples—will go to dharmadhatu.

"Vairotsana of Pagor, your effort in pursuing the teachings of the Great Perfection has been unflagging, so I will teach you my profound and all-inclusive *Mind Tantra*. Besides this present one, you will not take any further rebirth, but your emanations will be unceasing. During the last five hundred year period, you will, through the power of your aspirations, take one rebirth in the manner of an emanation. Following that you will be truly perfected and thus awaken to enlightenment."

Thus Shri Singha spoke. This completes the historical narration of the Great Perfection on the condensed realization and imparting the pith instructions.

SAMAYA. ⅜ SEAL, SEAL, SEAL. ⅜

᧚

Homage to the three kayas' expanse of wakefulness.

"The incarnated teacher Prahevajra has placed the quintessence of his pith instructions, the profound and all-inclusive teachings that overflowed from the expanse of his mind, within a golden casket that lies in the middle of the pagoda. I have asked Dorje Tromo Rakdongma, the guardian of the teachings, to undo the seal so at sunrise tomorrow I will teach you."

Having said this, Shri Singha went up on the upper roof of the palace. That night Vairotsana dreamt that a dark-blue woman appeared and spoke to him in these words:

Vairotsana from the clan of Pagor,
If you want the teachings Innermost and Unexcelled,
The *Mind Tantra* exists in three known types,
One is outer, one is inner and the last is secret.

The outer *Mind Tantra* you must write down in gold.
Write the inner *Mind Tantra* in lapis lazuli.
It is inadmissible to write the secret down.
If a destined person comes, you must then teach it.
If you don't find a receiver, bury it as terma treasure.
The one who breaches this command will have his life-vein cut.

Having said this she vanished into the side of a huge cliff. At sunrise the following morning, a woman appeared dressed in resplendent white and red garments holding a golden casket. The master Shri Singha arrived on a pathway of five-colored light and, taking seat in front of the palace, he advised:

"Listen, Vairotsana of Pagor. Among my one hundred and one *Mind Tantras,* pith instructions that combine their intent into one, three are within this golden casket. They are in an outer, inner and secret version. This woman is the Sun-Adorned Dakini, the consort of the seven vidyad-haras.

"Here is one parchment scroll with the outer Mind Tantra written in gold on azurite paper; take it with you concealed in your bag. This is the inner Mind Tantra written with lapis; memorize it. The secret Mind Tantra you must retain within your mind."

Thus he spoke.

SAMAYA. ៖ SEAL, SEAL, SEAL. ៖

ၭ

Here is an ancient source text outlining the structure of scriptures of the Great Perfection. Even though terma treasures differ, as they are meant for different people in different times, here we see a wonderful example of Padmasambhava's kindness in preserving a most precious teaching for future generations, the Tantra that Directly Reveals Samantabhadra's Mind. We also see how a master should not be frivolous in disseminating the Dzogchen termas and how disciples should be guided.

In the Great General Background for the History of the Authentic Lineage Padmasambhava describes Gongpa Zangtal, the Tantra that is the Direct Revelation of Samantabhadra's Mind, in these words: "The essence of all teachings, the king of all tantras, the ultimate summit of all vehicles, the conclusion of all meaning, the mirror of all dharmas, the quintessence of all instructions, the embodied intent of all victorious ones is the Ati Yoga of the Great Perfection, the single sphere of great simplicity. It has the Outer, Inner and Secret Cycles, the Innermost Unexcelled Cycle of the Precious Fruition, as well as others."

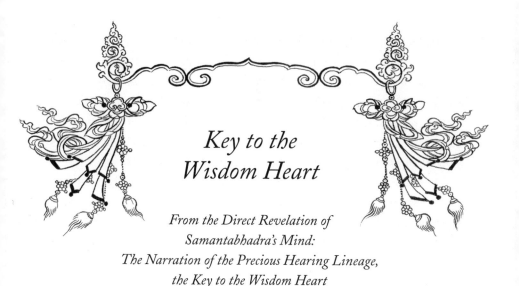

Key to the
Wisdom Heart

*From the Direct Revelation of
Samantabhadra's Mind:
The Narration of the Precious Hearing Lineage,
the Key to the Wisdom Heart*

Homage to glorious Samantabhadra, the transcendent conqueror.

The teachings of the Great Perfection appeared on the southern Jambu continent and were kept in three sections: the Extensive Outer Cycle, the Profound Inner Cycle and the Essential Unexcelled Cycle.

As the *outer*, the teachings of the Mind Section of the Great Perfection establish the view while considering the ground. As the *inner*, the cycle of the Space Section of the Great Perfection, being concerned with practice, chiefly teaches the meditation and conduct. As the *secret*, the Instruction Section of the Great Perfection contains the ultimate teachings on realizing the fruition.

The Instruction Cycle can be taught with an inconceivable number of subdivisions, but they can all be contained within these three: the Cycle on Mind for entering the path, the Cycle on View for applying it in practice, and the Cycle on Self-Existence for recognizing the essential nature.

Each of these has three aspects: the Cycle on Instruction for imparting the profound, the Cycle on Essence for transmitting the words and the Cycle on Hearing Lineage to ensure that the teachings neither disappear nor are spread unheededly.

The Hearing Lineage has two aspects: Teaching Cycle on Tantra, taking the root as witness, and Teaching Cycle on Instruction, its condensed meaning.

Thus, these teachings that *Directly Reveal Samantabhadra's Mind* are the ultimate of all teachings, the pinnacle of all vehicles, the essence of the *Three Sections of the Great Perfection*, the root of the *Sixfold Hearing Lineage*, the quintessence of the *Sixfold Expanse of Vajrasattva's Mind*, and contain the *Unwritten Hearing Lineage* in three parts that are like my heart.

These tantras of the *Direct Revelation of Samantabhadra's Mind* arose out of the expansive mind of Samantabhadra and are sealed with seven consecutive seals. Entrust them to the karmically destined one who is capable of undertaking thirteen types of hardship. Do not proclaim them to others, not even to the wind.

SAMAYA. ⁀ SEAL, SEAL, SEAL. ⁀

There is also the *Liberation Through Wearing* that arose from the precious sphere of Vajrasattva's heart and is entitled *Self-Existing Brilliance*. Entrust it to one who is capable of undertaking seven types of hardship. Do not proclaim it to others, not even as much as the sound of a finger-snap.

SAMAYA. ⁀ SEAL, SEAL, SEAL. ⁀

There is also the *Ultimate Hearing Lineage*, the condensed essence of the vidyadhara Prahevajra's heart, the pithy oral instruction of the vajra master in three chapters. Entrust it to one who is capable of undertaking the three types of hardship. Do not mention it to others, not even as much as a word.

SAMAYA. ⁀ SEAL, SEAL, SEAL. ⁀

The *Six Self-Existing Root Tantras* that arose out of the expansive mind of Samantabhadra have the profound instructions of the *Hearing Lineage in Six Chapters* as well as their profound quintessence, the *Ultimate Hearing Lineage* in three sections.

In the beginning these teachings overflowed out of Samantabhadra's expansive mind and were taught to Vajradhara, the Great Sixth. Vajradhara unlocked the treasury of his heart and taught them to the teacher Vajrasattva. Vajrasattva taught them to the emanation Prahevajra. Prahevajra taught them to the mind-vidyadhara Shri Singha. Shri Singha taught them to the great knowledge-holder Padmasambhava.

**Vajradhara
the Great Sixth**

Padmasambhava opened up the treasury of his heart and wrote down these scriptures in magical writing on the surface of Indian *karika* paper, and arranged them together with mantras and the sixfold substance as the key to disclose the teachings.

They should be taught to a worthy regent. Since the sentient beings of the Dark Age with unwholesome karma are not suitable to be taught, they are sealed with three seals of unfailing profundity.

SAMAYA. ⸭ SEAL, SEAL, SEAL. ⸭

⁖

Homage to the deities of the three kayas.

People of lesser capacity or those of inferior karmic destiny lack the merit to be taught Padmasambhava of Uddiyana's *Hearing Lineage in Six Chapters*. When those of higher and medium capacity have presented a mandala offering of precious turquoise three times, they should be given the *Profound Six Seals of Vajra Varahi* and then taught in completeness. First teach them the root texts, next teach the *Six Profound Treasuries* and lastly teach while revealing the hidden meaning.

Teach people of the highest destiny and capacity the *Sixfold Expanse of Vajrasattva's Mind*. Teach them in completeness once they have presented a mandala offering of precious gold. First, teach the method for entering, next teach the *Six Mind Tantras* and lastly confer the empowerment of the Great Perfection.

The karmically destined disciple of the most eminent among those of the highest capacity who can uphold the single lineage can be taught the Hearing *Lineage of the Vajra Masters in Six Chapters*. Teach it in completeness once this disciple has presented a precious mandala offering three times. First, teach the *Hearing Lineage on Distinguishing Mind and Wisdom*, next teach while decisively resolving the meditation state and samadhi, and lastly teach the *Ultimate Hearing Lineage* in the manner of identifying the natural state.

If at a certain point someone who has received the triple prophecy appears, teach him once he has presented a precious mandala offering thirteen times. Then teach in completeness all the instructions of the Hearing Lineage. First, teach the Cycle on Practice, next teach the Cycle on the Pointing-Out Instructions and lastly teach the *Ultimate Hearing Lineage*.

In this regard, do not give the complete instructions in one year, one month or one day out of convenience. It is only permissible to explain everything over a period of three years. Furthermore, do not teach merely for the sake of the words but for pointing out the true meaning.

It is rare that someone is a suitable recipient for being taught this threefold lineage, so it should be someone who is able to offer a mandala of precious articles either in pints or handfuls. Such a person who seeks the true meaning without even an instant of concern for the pursuits of this world is suitable to be taught the *Ultimate Hearing Lineage* for the pointing-out instruction to the awakened state of the buddhas.

After he has presented a mandala offering filled with pints of precious substances, this worthy person—who is capable of remaining in solitude in a remote mountain retreat without roaming the cities or villages of this world—is allowed to be taught the *Tantra that Directly Reveals Samantabhadra's Mind*.

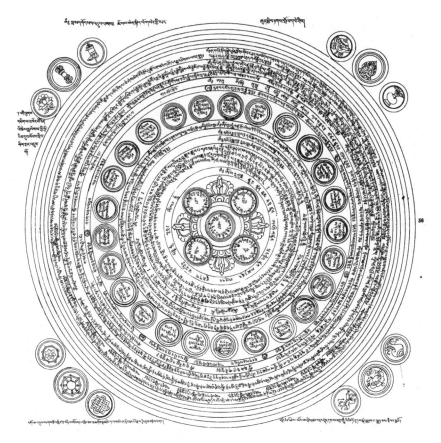

Liberation Through Wearing

After they have presented a mandala offering of precious substances equal to their own weight, it is permissible for a capable teacher to teach the *Liberation Through Wearing* to a few people who wish to be liberated.

When an upholder of the Mind Tantras of the conquerors evaluates a recipient to be a disciple, it is not appropriate to take the size of the material wealth as the final measure. Rather, from a king he should accept an amount equal to the king's own weight, from wealthy householders he should accept an amount measured in pints, from people of meager riches he should accept an amount measured in handfuls and from very poor people he should accept whatever they have of value.

It would be inappropriate for the master to take the size of a disciple's wealth as the final measure, since this attitude would be impure. It is also inappropriate if the disciple is unwilling to offer whatever possessions he has, since he would then be an unsuitable recipient.

Someone should be taught only if he or she is able to sacrifice whatever he has for the sake of these Dharma teachings and then practice for the sake of future lives.

Thus he spoke.[86]

The master Padmasambhava concealed the profound teachings of the Hearing Lineage in the Snowy Land of Tibet, at the northern slope of the Divine Cliff of Zangzang, within the central casket of brown rhinoceros hide and sealed it with thirteen consecutive seals.

Padmasambhava entrusted the teachings in the care of three mamos of the charnel ground and to Ekajati Devi. Then he made this aspiration:

Emaho!
Supreme essence of the Dharma, in completeness,
Overflowing from the conquerors' expansive minds,
For this Hearing Lineage of the Great Perfection
The time has yet to come, so conceal it as a terma treasure.

But there will be a time, that of the Buddha's teachings,
When someone with the signs of having purified the triple poisons,
And who is free from superficial fame or disrepute,
Who keeps to the courageous yogic conduct of nonclinging,
Is fierce but with a loving frame of mind,
This person, arriving from the eastern region,
Is worthy of the vehicles sublime—entrust this treasure to him.

Waste no time on empty talk; focus on your practice!
When finding the destined disciple, entrust him with the teaching!
If worthy students don't appear, conceal it as terma!

During this, the final age of Buddha's doctrine,
Whatever type of conduct or the method he displays,
My termas will serve as the regents of the Sage of Shakyas.

This yogi utilizing Secret Mantra
Will, at one point, be the life-force of Tibet.
This terma will uphold the Buddhadharma
For twenty and one hundred human years.

To all mamo dakinis as well, I say:
Guard this teaching and its followers
Against hindrances of every kind!

Thus he spoke.

This completes the *Narration of the Precious Hearing Lineage, the Key to the Wisdom Mind.*

SAMAYA. ៖ SEAL, SEAL, SEAL. ៖

Rigdzin Gökyi Demtruchen (Rigdzin Gödem) revealed this terma from inside of the brown rhino casket, at the slope of a mountain cliff that resembles a mound of poisonous vipers (Divine Cliff of Zangzang).

May it be virtuous! May it be virtuous! May it be virtuous!

The following text forms the first chapter of Vimalamitra's marvelous Yeshe Rangsal, a lengthy explanation of the Great Perfection, given to King Trisong Deutsen, also known as the "Great Commentary on the Hearing Lineage." Unlike most other transmission lineages where the three masters passed their teachings on to Tibetan disciples individually, here we see an example of the great harmony among enlightened beings as Padmasambhava, Vimalamitra and Vairotsana taught together in the Caverns of Chimpu above Samye in central Tibet.

The Six
Hearing Lineages

The timeless buddha Changeless Lord of Light,
Dharmakaya Vajradhara, who achieves the welfare of all beings,
Four knowledge-holders, who disclose the true and certain
    meaning,
Peaceful and the wrathful yidams, self-displays of wakefulness,
All dakinis, sporting in the greatest bliss,
Root gurus and all lineage masters,
I salute you with respectful body, speech and mind.

It was in the Caverns of Chimpu above Samye that King Trisong Deutsen requested the oral instructions on the innermost unexcelled meaning of the Great Perfection from the trio of the master Padmasambhava, the learned Vimalamitra and the translator Vairotsana. Thus he was taught what is known as the *Hearing Lineage of the Vajra Masters in Six Chapters.*

And so it was that Padmasambhava of Uddiyana taught the *Precious Ultimate Hearing Lineage* and the *Hearing Lineage of Pointing Out Dharmata;* Vimalamitra taught the *Hearing Lineage to be Understood through Explanation* and the *Hearing Lineage to be Liberated through Practice;* and Vairotsana taught the *Hearing Lineage on Distinguishing Mind and Wisdom* and the *Hearing Lineage of Practicing the Fivefold Meditation Method.*

All these were the condensed essence of the six million four hundred thousand tantras of the Innermost Unexcelled Great Perfection. The master

Padmasambhava taught using few words with inclusive meaning by com-bining all the major tantras. Vimalamitra taught extensively based on the twenty-one tantras. Vairotsana taught the king while neither adding to nor subtracting from the pithy instructions of the Hearing Lineage that he, himself, had received from the great vidyadhara Shri Singha when he requested the teachings of Great Perfection in India.

This completes the structure of the *Hearing Lineage of the Vajra Masters in Six Chapters.*

SAMAYA.⅜ SEAL, SEAL, SEAL.⅜

ௌ

In this segment, we learn how the king of Tibet—again in the rare presence of three great masters, Padmasambhava, Vimalamitra and Vairotsana—requests the essence of the Great Perfection based on an omen he receives in a dream. The next morning they begin the teachings at the Caverns of Chimpu high above the Samye temple.

Throughout this book, we have repeatedly heard of various cycles of Dzogchen teachings that may have blended. Here, however, we get Shri Singha's succinct explanation in simple and clear language to Vairotsana, what defines the outer, inner and secret cycles, as well as the Three Sections of the Great Perfection. We are also told of Shri Singha's four chief disciples.

In particular, Shri Singha goes through the nine gradual vehicles—outlining their specific features, how they differ in benefiting others after enlightenment, and how they differ from the teachings of the Great Perfection. The great master tells us never to reject the first eight vehicles of the Buddha, but to regard them as "entrance-ways and branches of the Dharma"—a perspective shared by all true Dzogchen teachers.

We are also introduced to the famous quotation—"The Great Perfection's effortless view of nondoing brings enlightenment in the morning when realized in the morning, and enlightenment at night when realized at night"—the truth of which is essential to distinguishing sem and rigpa. Next Vairotsana receives the Hearing Lineage for this.

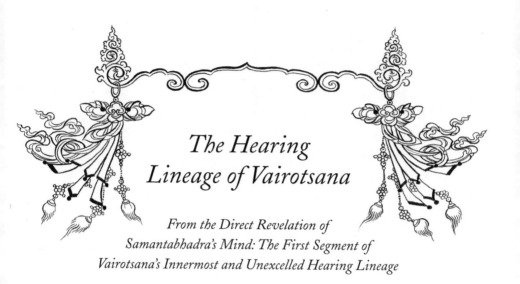

The Hearing Lineage of Vairotsana

From the Direct Revelation of
Samantabhadra's Mind: The First Segment of
Vairotsana's Innermost and Unexcelled Hearing Lineage

Once, all three masters—Padmasambhava of Uddiyana, the Indian Vimalamitra and the Tibetan Vairotsana—were composed in meditation at the Caverns of Chimpu above Samye. It then happened that Trisong Deutsen, king of the Tibetan people, was given a prophecy by seven magical dakinis, "The three vidyadharas possess—hidden in their minds—an instruction that causes awakening by simply seeing or hearing. You must ask them to bestow it."

Inspired by this guidance, the king offered each of the three masters a seat covered with an entire bolt of brocade, and a brocade cloak to wear. Having served up various kinds of food and drink from Tibet, India and China and other lands in the four directions, he made a mandala offering of gold equal to his own weight, the five precious substances and thirteen of his personal pieces of turquoise. Then he made this request, with one-pointed body, speech and mind:

Kye!
Lotus-Born, you clearly see the triple times;
Vimala, a king among the learned ones of India;
And Vairotsana, foremost of Tibet's translators—
You three, the emanations of enlightened beings,

Aspired to meet together in Tibet on this occasion.
Now kindly look upon us, the barbarian Tibetans.

You have fulfilled the noble wishes
Of I, the king of all the red-faced people of Tibet.
Now, while you three, the masters, will remain,
I, Trisong Deutsen, will not stay, but soon will die.

Pay heed to me, three eminent nirmanakayas.
How wonderful that you have taught, in whole, the Dharma
    most sublime.
The lesser and the greater vehicles all teach
That buddhahood is reached when veils are cleared.
But now, I beg, bestow a teaching that is far superior,
An instruction that condenses the essential Dharma into one,
An advice that is sufficient to just see, hear, understand.
Grant a method to awaken in a single morn or eve,
A teaching flowing from Samantabhadra's spacious mind;
Please bestow the deepest Dharma, that simply meeting will
    suffice.

I offer you my body, speech and mind in service,
And vow to never break your word.
I offer my devotion, free from all deceit.
Without a need to clear away the veils and gather merit over
    eons,
Please grant a teaching most sublime, that simply meeting will
    suffice.

When he had made this request, the three masters were of one mind and,
knowing that the right time had come, they consulted each other and then
addressed the king,

"We will give you the ultimate of all vehicles, that transcends
the hope and fear of causation, that is the realization of all buddhas, that is the essence of the Great Perfection, that is the way to
directly reveal the mind of Samantabhadra, that is the repository of

Vajrasattva's mind, and that is the extracted heart essence of the five supreme emanations. We will entrust it to you with the seal of our command."

Thus they spoke.

SAMAYA, SEAL, SEAL, SEAL. GUHYA, CHITTA, SEAL, SEAL, SEAL.

卍

At first the eight gradual vehicles were taught in India as the basis of the Dharma. These were the three outer vehicles of philosophy—each consisting of Vinaya, Sutra and Abhidharma—which are the vehicles for shravakas, pratyekabuddhas, and bodhisattvas respectively.

Within the vehicle of Secret Mantra, including both knowledge mantra and dharani mantra, first the three outer vehicles of Mantra—Kriya, Upa and Yoga—were given. Next the inner vehicles of Secret Mantra were taught: the cycle of Mahayoga tantras, the cycle of Anu Yoga scriptures and, as the ultimate, the unified view of Mahamudra.

While these vehicles were being taught, Prahevajra emanated from Shri Vajrasattva's heart, went before the five hundred panditas living in the lands of India and said, "I have a teaching that is superior to your eight vehicles; more wonderful than the unified view of Mahamudra, a teaching for awakening if realized in the morning or awakening if realized at night, which is the essence of all views, the realization of all buddhas, the summit of all vehicles; the true and ultimate teaching. It is known as the sacred Great Perfection."

The five hundred panditas did not comprehend this, but rather, they arranged a time for a debate. At the Vajra Throne they debated the nine gradual vehicles for three months. Then they began the debate on *Ati Yoga*. *Ati* is the Indian word which in Tibetan stands for *kyemey rangjung*, nonarising self-existence, and *yoga* is translated as *naljor* which means training in connecting with the real. When debating on this vehicle, the five hundred panditas were headed by the master Manjushrimitra who declared, "You other panditas will not be able to best Prahevajra now in the debate on the view. Let me debate. If I win the debate, he must be an incarnation of Mara so you shall pierce his tongue and banish him. If he wins, I shall not be able to bear having denigrated the teaching of the unexcelled fruition, so with a razor I shall cut off my tongue right in front of him as an act of atonement. In that case all of you must embrace his doctrine."

After having supplicated the Three Jewels, they entered the debate, which Prahevajra won.

Manjushrimitra then sang this apology:

> Failing to see the view to be the vast intrinsic nature,
> I claimed nondual form and emptiness, but still was bound by
>   clinging.
> For this I now apologize within the self-existing Great
>   Perfection.
>
> Failing to see that training is beyond a reference point,
> I went astray, inventing objects to be accepted or rejected.
> For this I now apologize within the state of self-occurring
>   knowing.
>
> Failing to see the conduct to be free from clinging and
>   attachment,
> I was tied by my belief in moral choices on the path.
> For this I now apologize within the unbound yogic conduct.
>
> Failing to see fruition to be the basic ground itself,
> I sought to find the wishfulfilling essence as an outer thing.
> For this I now apologize within intrinsic perfect wakefulness.
>
> Not recognizing Prahevajra as a true nirmanakaya,
> I challenged you, seeing a heretic demon.
> For this I now apologize within the triple kayas' undivided state.

Saying this he lifted a razor to his tongue, but Prahevajra took it from him and threw it away. Then Prahevajra spoke:

> Manjushrimitra, do not amputate your tongue;
> Instead you shall become a holder of my teachings.

In no way have you challenged Dzogchen's meaning,
But rather shed a light upon the view.
Continue training in the nature of the Great Perfection,
And your freedom will transcend the faults of karmic
    maturation.

Following this Prahevajra, the incarnation of Vajrasattva, transmitted the renowned Great Perfection—the root of all teachings, the summit of all vehicles, the innermost of all insights, the quintessence of all instructions. He taught the realization of Samantabhadra who awakened in the manner of the sphere of the sun and moon united, at the time of the ground—which is not made out of anything whatsoever—when the basic split occurred between samsara and nirvana, and there was a division into the three components of wind, knowing and space.[87] The sambhogakaya buddha Vajrasattva appeared, flying as swiftly as an arrow from the bow of a master archer. With his spontaneous voice, Prahevajra, like a snake shedding its skin, taught in the manner of self-manifesting magical words. He taught in two ways: the Great Perfection Renowned as Edict and the Great Perfection Renowned as Instruction.

The Great Perfection Renowned as Edict has four aspects:

THE CYCLE OF THE MIND SECTION mainly teaches the view. It consists of the tantras headed by *Extensive Tantra of Great Space,* which Prahevajra explained to Manjushrimitra. These tantras were then transmitted by the five hundred panditas. This cycle is known as the Outer Mind Section Cycle.

THE CYCLE OF THE TANTRAS that mainly teaches the expositions consists of tantras—headed by the *Kulayaraja Tantra,* the *Tantra of the All-Creating King*—which Prahevajra explained to the king's son. These tantras were then transmitted by the seven special masters. This cycle is known as the King's Developed Cycle.

Together these two comprise the Outer Cycle that resemble the body. This is the aspect of the Great Perfection that chiefly explains the terminology.

THE CYCLE OF THE SPACE SECTION mainly teaches the training. It consists of the tantras headed by the *Tantra of Secret Wisdom* and the *Tantra of the Great Perfection of Wisdom*, which Prahevajra taught to the minister's son, and were then transmitted by the seven subsequent masters. This is known as the Minister's Concise Cycle. It is the Inner Cycle that resembles the eyes. It is the Cycle of the Space Section of the Great Perfection that clearly explains the indicating words.

THE CYCLE OF INSTRUCTIONS establishes the meaning of the ground. It consists of the tantras headed by the *Tantra of Wisdom Equal to Space* and the *Tantra that Embodies the Definitive Meaning*, which Prahevajra explained to the Brahmin's son, and was then transmitted to only one worthy recipient at a time. It is known as the Brahmin's Playful Cycle. This cycle is the innermost part and resembles the heart. It is the Great Perfection's Cycle of Instruction that condenses the root to the essentials.

The teachings up to this point comprise the Great Perfection Renowned as Edict.

The Great Perfection Renowned as Instruction has three aspects: the *Profound Inner Cycle*, the *Most Profound Secret Cycle* and the *Unexcelled Mind Cycle*.

THE PROFOUND INNER CYCLE, the first of these, is the cycle for directly taking hold of meditation, and it has twenty-one sets of teachings.

THE MOST PROFOUND SECRET CYCLE has twenty-one sets of teachings headed by the *Tantra of Immaculate Jewels*.

THE UNEXCELLED MIND CYCLE has thirteen sets of teachings including *Golden Designs of Jewels* and *Solar Wheel*.

All of these, which Prahevajra taught to Manjushrimitra, were transmitted through Shri Singha and entrusted to me, Vairotsana, comprise the Great Perfection Renowned as Instruction.

These teachings that are the treasury concealed in the heart of the great master Prahevajra, the precious essence of secrets, the Great Perfection that reveals the innate nature in actuality, have six sections:

The Heart Essence of the Great Perfection (Nyingtig) are the profound and vast teachings.

The Secret Sphere of the Great Perfection (Tigle Sangwa) are the profound and pithy teachings.

The Great Perfection's Six Tantras of Liberation Through Wearing are the profound teachings with concise meaning.

The Great Perfection's Three Tantras of Liberation Through Wearing are the profound teachings with pithy power.

The Great Perfection's pith instructions, containing the *Direct Revelation of Samantabhadra's Mind,* are the profound and quintessential teachings.

The Great Perfection compatible with all the outer, inner and secret cycles, containing the *Self-Arising Self-Existence of Vajrasattva,* are the profound and comprehensive teachings.

Prahevajra taught these six profound sections of the Great Perfection—the secret and precious treasury of his mind—to his destined disciple Shri Singha who then taught them to the three incarnated vidyadharas.

These six major hearing lineages of Prahevajra epitomize the meaning of the entire Great Perfection and so they have been transmitted to only one disciple at a time. They are the great hearing lineages for separating dualistic mind and original wakefulness, *sem* and *yeshe.*

The two types of teaching that were born in Prahevajra's heart are the essence of the entire Great Perfection: the Written Cycles of the Great Perfection and the Unwritten Hearing Lineages.

Furthermore, it was, first of all, Prahevajra who taught each and every one of the above-mentioned teachings of the Great Perfection. Second, Prahevajra did not teach them twice. Third, he did not teach the Great Perfection to anyone unworthy. Fourth, the Hearing Lineages are not given to more than one person at a time. Fifth, the Unwritten has not been written down. Sixth, once one embraces the nature of the Great Perfection, awareness is not to be distracted for even an instant. It is vital to understand these six basic principles of the Great Perfection.

The master Shri Singha realized all the teachings of the Great Perfection and then entrusted them to his four heart disciples: Padmasambhava of Uddiyana was entrusted with the Innermost Unexcelled Cycle, the victorious Jnanasutra was entrusted with the Secret Cycle, the learned Vimalami-

Shri Singha

tra was entrusted with the Inner Cycle and the translator Vairotsana was entrusted with the Outer Cycle. All teachings of the Great Perfection, without exception, have passed through these four; therefore Shri Singha has shown tremendous kindness for destined people of later times.

In India the virtuous Kungamo the Eminent deliberately scrambled the order of the words in the Great Perfection teachings. They have all been gathered and concealed as a treasure at the Vajra Throne. You have no power to use them.

Shri Singha's four disciples will teach the worthy ones in present-day Tibet. But for the sake of future generations, these teachings will be concealed as terma so that many worthy beings of Tibet with a karmic link will be liberated.

This was a record of Shri Singha's words, spoken to me, Vairotsana, in the nine-storied Buddha Palace.

ꩰ

Soon after, Vairotsana raised these questions, "Pay heed to me, great master. When someone practices the nine gradual vehicles as taught by the Buddha, is there any difference in the quality of their realization at the time of attaining fruition? Do the resultant teachings taught in the four outer, inner and secret aspects of the Great Perfection differ in their nearness to buddhahood?"

Shri Singha replied, "Listen, Tibetan monk. The nine gradual vehicles were taught by the Buddha for the benefit of different beings. They do not differ in quality at the time of attaining enlightenment.

"The purpose of the lower vehicles is to direct sentient beings towards what is virtuous and, being merely seeds for rebirth in the higher realms, they are teachings for aspiring towards enlightenment.

"Following the three vehicles for shravakas, pratyekabuddhas and bodhi-sattvas require a long time to attain enlightenment. In all hopefulness they train in the path without having recognized the ground. And since they take the inhibiting of the wakeful quality as their result, enlightenment lies far away.[88]

"The three tantric sections of Kriya, Upa and Yoga—known as teachings of covert intent—are for purifying severe misdeeds. Even through them it is difficult to reach enlightenment. They take emptiness as their ground, yet take the holding of judgmental notions as their path, and due to making a superimposed emptiness their result, buddhahood lies far away.

"In this way, the three vehicles for shravakas, pratyekabuddhas and bodhisattvas, the Mind Only, the Middle Way, and the three sections of Kriya and Yoga,[89] are entrance-ways and branches of the Dharma and should therefore not be rejected. But it is a long road to expect to reach fruition through them. All of these teachings are based on the ground they do not recognize. Those who follow a path of placing their hopes in either abandoning, hampering, purifying or transforming will not capture the stronghold of fruition.

"The three tantric sections of Mahayoga, Anu Yoga, and the Mahamudra view of nondual experience and emptiness, take dharmadhatu as their ground, train in the unity of experience and emptiness as their path and experience the fruition of nonarising dharmakaya within dharmadhatu. These too are long paths by which it is difficult to arrive at the stronghold.

"In the Outer Mind Section of the Great Perfection the view is foremost. In the Inner Space Section meditation is foremost. In the Secret Instruction Section conduct is foremost. In the Innermost Unexcelled Section the fruition is foremost. There is no doubt that the being who meets with their methods for removing hindrances will instantly awaken to enlightenment.

"The ground is the universal bedrock before any name was given. The path is to separate *consciousness* and *wakefulness*.[90] The fruition is to recognize the displays of the ground and to know that whatever is experienced is self-display. Hence there is a vast difference in the length of their respective paths. After enlightenment there is a huge difference in whether or not the two kayas manifest for the benefit of sentient beings.

"As for the length of the path, the shravakas maintain that enlightenment is attained after practicing the Dharma for three incalculable eons. The pratyekabuddhas presume that they become enlightened after practicing the Dharma for one hundred eons. The followers of the Mind Only school claim that enlightenment will be attained after sixty eons. The followers of the Middle Way hold that they attain enlightenment after three eons. The

Kriya teachings maintain that one becomes enlightened after seven life-times. The Upa teachings hold that enlightenment is reached after six life-times. The Yoga teachings claim that one attains enlightenment after five lives. In this way, these seven lower vehicles that employ the causal teach-ings are vehicles for aspiring towards enlightenment but not for attaining the fruition within this very life. They are teachings bound by partiality and by the duality of good and evil.

"Through Mahayoga you attain enlightenment after seven months. Through Anu Yoga you attain enlightenment after six months. Through the Mahamudra view of nondual experience and emptiness, you attain enlight-enment after three months. But the Great Perfection's effortless view of nondoing brings enlightenment in the morning when realized in the morn-ing and enlightenment at night when realized at night.

"At the time of enlightenment there is no difference, but there is a huge difference in the benefit to beings. If you attain enlightenment through either the shravaka or pratyekabuddha teachings, you are what is known as a "single teacher buddha" and not able to send out emanations. If you attain enlightenment through either the Mind Only or the Middle Way, you are what is known as a "duplicating buddha" able to send out individual ema-nations. If you attain enlightenment through one of the three sections of Kriya, Upa and Yoga, you are a 'family-multiplying buddha' able to send out triple emanations of body, speech and mind.

"If you attain enlightenment through Mahayoga, Anu Yoga or the Maha-mudra view of nondual experience and emptiness which is their nature, you are a "sovereign of the five kayas buddha" able to send out ceaseless emana-tions of the fivefold body, speech, mind, qualities and activities.

"However, if you attain enlightenment through the Great Perfection's effortless view of nondoing, you are a 'buddha who knows the nature as it is.' You recognize the nameless ground of both samsara and nirvana. You recognize that this causal basis—the spontaneously present original wake-fulness—is the buddha. And thus recognize, as the path, that its self-dis-play—whatever is experienced and whatever may be—is the enlightenment that is spontaneously present. And you recognize, as the fruition, that every-thing is spontaneously present self-display beyond clinging.

"This awakening, through self-existing wakefulness that knows the nature as it is, is known as the 'spontaneously present enlightenment.' Clearly seeing all of samsara and nirvana is known as the 'enlightenment that perceives all possibly existing things.' Thus, knowing the nature as it is and perceiving all possibly existing things allows sambhogakaya to manifest out of dharmakaya, and one achieves the capacity to send out one hundred billion nirmanakaya emanation bodies.

"In other words, neither shravakas nor pratyekabuddhas are able to send out emanations since both attain an enlightenment that is based on realizing the nature of their respective types of emptiness. The followers of both Mind Only and Middle Way reach an enlightenment known as 'realizing the two truths' and are therefore able to send out a single emanation each eon. The followers of the three sections of Kriya, Upa and Yoga attain the enlightenment that is called 'total purification' and are therefore able to send out triple emanations each time a buddha appears.[91] The followers of the three sections of Mahayoga, Anu Yoga and Mahamudra of nondual experience and emptiness reach the 'enlightenment of perfecting the five wisdoms' and are therefore incessantly able to send out fivefold emanations of body, speech, mind, qualities and activities.[92]

"The three views—Ati Yoga's view of effortless nondoing, the Great Perfection's view of spontaneous presence and the self-existing Great Perfection's view of the innate nature in actuality—lead to what is known as 'true and complete enlightenment,' and therefore those who reach fruition through them are able, each instant, to send out one hundred billion emanations, re-emanations and re-re-emanations from the three kayas.

"*Ati Yoga* is a name for the Great Perfection's Mind Section Cycle, and the one who awakens through this can unimpededly send out emanations after fifty years.

"*Spontaneously Present Enlightenment* is a name for the Great Perfection's Space Section Cycle, and the one who awakens through this can send out emanations after seven years.

"*Great Self-Existence* is a name for the Great Perfection's Instruction Section, and if you attain enlightenment through this, you can send out emanations after five years.

"*Innate Nature in Actuality* is a name for the Great Perfection's Innermost Unexcelled Cycle, and through it you awaken immediately upon leaving the body behind;[93] and you will send out ceaseless emanations immediately upon awakening to buddhahood. This happens not just because of believing in original enlightenment.

"It is impossible to awaken to enlightenment without being free from the five disturbing emotions. The shravakas and pratyekabuddhas both (use remedies) to discard these emotions. Followers of the Mind Only and the Middle Way bring the emotions to cessation (in emptiness through the samadhis). Followers of the three sections of Kriya and Yoga purify and transform the emotions. Followers of the Mahayoga, Anu Yoga and the View of Unity make use of the emotions as the path. Followers of the Great Perfection plunge into the emotions unimpededly and free from concepts.

"It is impossible for original wakefulness to unfold without having abandoned these disturbing emotions, and wakefulness does not dawn unless emotions dissolve.

"Vairotsana, retain this Hearing Lineage of the Great Perfection, and entrust it to one worthy person in Tibet. Then conceal it as a terma for the benefit of future generations. Since you Tibetans are fickle, you have a fondness for novelties; since you are capricious, there will be sectarianism; and since you are easily influenced, the hearts of some will be possessed by demons and evil spirits.

"Dogmas bound by concepts will be masqueraded as the Great Perfection's teachings of the unexcelled fruition. Personal opinion will be claimed to be the view by people who have yet to resolve the true view. Without proper moral judgment, people will act frivolously. But unless they distinguish the all-ground and dharmakaya they will not transcend hope and fear.

"The sun of the Buddha's essential teachings will set. Demons and deceivers will rise. Disease, warfare, starvation and banditry will flourish. When that time has come this Hearing Lineage on separating *consciousness* and *wakefulness* will meet with a worthy being.

"To this worthy person I say: retain this Hearing Lineage! Apply it in practice before propagating it to others! Unravel the meaning you don't understand!

"Do not spread copies of this, since this teaching will be revealed at the end of the age by a worthy disciple who has a triple mole on his shining forehead. He should entrust it to three worthy recipients after examining them and finding them suitable. If he fails to do so, he should not spread copies but again conceal them as a terma. If he finds no chance to bury them as a treasure, he should 'offer them to the gods of fire' in front of an image of the master or while visualizing the lineage masters. If he leaves them in writing he will have broken samaya."

Thus he spoke.

This Hearing Lineage on separating *consciousness* and *wakefulness* was initially taught by glorious Samantabhadra in Akanishtha in order to remove hindrances for all yogis who practice the Great Perfection. It was received by Vajrasattva, who then transmitted it orally to the bodhisattva Manjushri the Youthful. He passed it on to Shakra, the king of the gods, who in turn transmitted it to Prahevajra, the nirmanakaya. Prahevajra then passed it on to the five hundred Indian panditas, who gave it to Shri Singha, and it was he who transmitted it to Vairotsana.

Vairotsana attained enlightenment in the manner of a drawing and a seal. He gave the transmission to Trisong Deutsen, the king of Tibet, who attained enlightenment in the manner of sounds and lights.

The king made aspirations and concealed it in three termas with this aspiration:

"May it be revealed by three emanations of body, speech and mind. May the person who discovers the three writings of the Hearing Lineage in the future attain enlightenment like a fish leaping out of the water. If the person who discovers this Hearing Lineage of body, speech and mind fails to find worthy recipients in which to entrust this, may he not spread copies of it but retain it in his heart.

"At that time many points will remain with their meaning unraveled, so may he unravel them for the sake of devoted people. At a future time there will be a person suitable to be entrusted with the Hearing

Manjushri the Youthful

Lineage, so seal it and entrust him with it. As protectors for this Hearing Lineage, may the three charnel ground mamos guard it."

Thus he spoke.

SAMAYA. ⁰ SEAL, SEAL, SEAL. ⁰

This was revealed from the northern slope of the Divine Cliff of Zangzang by the vidyadhara Rigdzin Gökyi Demtruchen (Rigdzin Gödem). Sarva mangalam.

🌀

Here is the *Middle Segment of Vairotsana's Innermost and Unexcelled Hearing Lineage* from the *Direct Revelation of Samantabhadra's Mind:*

OM AH HUNG

These are the instructions orally transmitted from the dharmakaya Samantabhadra and gradually through the sambhogakaya Vajrasattva to the nirmanakaya Manjushri, and from him to the knowledge-holder Shakra, through the nirmanakaya Prahevajra, to the five hundred siddhas who were great scholars. These instructions are the essence of all the teachings of

Secret Mantra and they are known as the Great Perfection. The way to dispel hindrances for the entirety of the Great Perfection is known as the *Triple Hearing Lineage*. It is the insight of the three later siddhas unified into a single system, the realization which the most learned Shri Singha had kept hidden within his heart.

From his fifteenth year until the age of fifty-five, the Tibetan translator Vairotsana lived in the presence of the learned Shri Singha in India, and during this time he requested and refined his understanding of all the teachings of the Great Perfection. When about to return to the land of Tibet, he prostrated himself one thousand times before his master, circumambulated him one thousand times and offered five hundred ingots of gold. Then he sang the sorrowful song of thirteen reasons why the pain of parting with one's master is unbearable, and he shed many tears. Shri Singha therefore said:

> "My destined son, in the form of a parting gift I entrust you with the Great Perfection formerly explained, as well as with these instructions of the Hearing Lineage. So you may never be apart from Samantabhadra and Vajrasattva. Do not fill your mind with sadness. Go back for the sake of Tibet. When you pass on from this life, you will uphold the Buddha's teachings for five hundred thousand great eons."

With this prophecy, Shri Singha entrusted him with the Hearing Lineage.

SAMAYA. ⸹ SEAL, SEAL, SEAL. ⸹

ᥫ

As Shri Singha began the teachings, the most subtle questions became clarified: the difference between all-ground and dharmakaya, dualistic consciousness and nondual wakefulness, and so forth.

PART IV
Later
Treasure Masters

after the 14th Century

ཿ བཀྲ་ཤིས་ཿ

Homage to glorious Samantabhadri and to your natural radiance of five dakini families who enact your activities.

Long ago, before samsara or nirvana were formed—before there was any such name or word for 'buddha' due to realizing, before there was the name or word 'sentient being' due to failing to realize—the Teacher, if a name is required, was Glorious Samantabhadri. In reality, she was an all-pervasive and wide-open sky, the expanse of the infinite womb, the basic space of aware emptiness that never arises.

Spontaneously present from the beginning, utterly without limits and not confined to any category, this basic space was incorruptible, stable, indestructible, unmistaken and unchanging. Its seal remained unbroken since there was no externalizing of the six collections. Its inner five lights, the colors of the wisdoms, were unobstructed. Facing outward the inventive forming of concepts had not begun, and within the capacity of discerning knowledge had not strayed. Thus, she remained as a body of all-pervasiveness in her natural state of original presence, teaching this unexcelled doctrine of effortlessness to her retinue of five families of dakinis, her own radiant expressions.

From Padmasambhava's History of the Brilliant Expanse,
revealed by Dorje Lingpa

Dorje Lingpa the Treasure Revealer

I would like to introduce an extraordinary notion of authorship in the context of Padmasambhava's terma teachings by quoting the nineteenth century master Jamgön Kongtrül to make clear that these are not like writings of an ordinary person. Padmasambhava's words are "tantras that manifest as the natural sound of dharmata from the Lord of the Mandala," or phrased in Padmasambhava's own voice, "the self-resounding tantras of dharmata from the luminous space of the five-colored sphere within my heart."

Jamgön Kongtrül also describes Padmasambhava succinctly in these words:

"Padmasambhava has guided countless beings through the Vajrayana teachings and in particular through the activity of the profound terma treasures. This great master was not an ordinary person on the path or just a noble being on one of the bodhisattva levels but an emanation of both Buddha Amitabha and Shakyamuni who appeared in order to guide those human beings and spirits difficult to convert. Even the great bodhisattvas are incapable of fully explaining his life example but in brief I will narrate it as follows.

"In the dharmakaya realm of the Luminous Vajra Essence he has by nature attained perfect enlightenment since the very beginning as the liberated ground of primordial purity. He is renowned as the original protector, Changeless Light.[94]

"In the self-manifest sambhogakaya realm known as the Thunder of the Drum of Purity, he spontaneously manifested as the boundless wisdom array of the five families of Buddha Immense Ocean possessing the five certainties.

"As the external manifestation of this self-appearing display, in the countless sceneries of bodily forms in buddhafields of the five families comprised of the semi-manifest natural nirmanakaya realms of Great Purity,[95] he appears to all the bodhisattvas on the ten levels. Since all these manifestations are the cloud banks of Padmasambhava's wisdom display, the 'inexhaustible wheel of adornment,' he is known as the All-Holding Lotus.

"By the power of these wisdom displays he appears in countless worlds of the ten directions as the magical apparition of nirmanakayas who guide beings. In particular, it is taught that only in this Saha world-system he illuminates fifty worlds with the lamp of the teachings of Sutra and Tantra, appearing as the eight manifestations to guide beings in the different parts of the world.

"The Dakini Yeshe Tsogyal had a vision in which she saw a manifestation of Padmasambhava called Vajra Guru Immense Ocean in the eastern direction. Each of the pores in his body held one billion realms and in each realm there were one billion world-systems. In each of these world-systems there were one billion Padmasambhavas who

each created one billion emanations. Each of these emanations carried out the activity of guiding one billion disciples. She then saw the same display in each of the other directions and in the center.

"In this world of the Jambu continent, Padmasambhava is known as just one nirmanakaya who guides beings[96] but according to the different capacities and talents of people he is perceived in various ways. The history of the Oral Transmission of Kilaya and most Indian sources explain that he was born as the son of a king or a minister in Uddiyana, while the terma treasures for the most part narrate that he was miraculously born. In some texts he is said to have appeared from a bolt of lightning at the summit of Mount Malaya. Each of these wondrous stories differ in many ways. This is indeed a topic that lies far beyond the reach of an ordinary person's intellect."

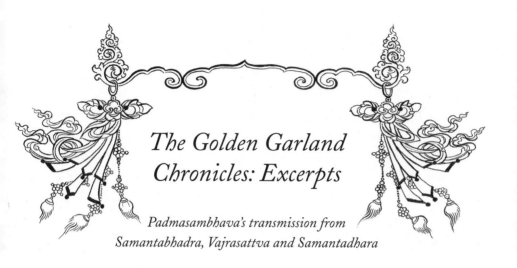

The Golden Garland Chronicles: Excerpts

*Padmasambhava's transmission from
Samantabhadra, Vajrasattva and Samantadhara*

Then Guru Nyima Özer[97] reflected, "I must seek a teaching with few words but great meaning, an instantaneous teaching the realization of which brings liberation simultaneous with arising."

In the dharmadhatu palace of Akanishtha, the dharmakaya nature known as the teacher Samantabhadra, the Ever-Excellent, whose bodily form is deep blue and unadorned, was seated on a lion throne. He was wearing the five families as his crown, his two hands were in equanimity, and all around him was alight with rainbow-colored lights. Guru Padma went before him, took a lowly seat and with his sight he gazed upon the expounder of the Dharma. With his hearing he listened unwaveringly to the voice. With his mind he retained the words and perceived the meaning. Thus he received the following teachings: *The Root Cycle of the Unconstructed Expanse of the Great Perfection* comprises the *Eighteen Marvels of Mind: Great Space, Cuckoo of Awareness, Great Soaring Garuda, Revealing Great Strength, Sixfold Meditation, Spontaneous Summit, Sky King, Jewel Studded Bliss, Perfect Comprehension, Assemblage of Vidyadharas,*[98] *Wheel of Life-Force, Awakened Mind,*[99] *All-Encompassing Bliss, Framework of Existence, Sublime King Scripture, Wishfulfilling Jewel, Sphere of Immensity,* and *Pure Golden Ore.*[100]

He was then given the secret name Unexcelled Vajra-Holder.

꩜

Padmasambhava's transmission from Vajrasattva

Then [Padmasambhava, now known as] Guru Loden Choksey went to the Utterly Pure Expanse of Immense Space, into the presence of the nirmanakaya Vajrasattva who was seated on an elephant throne. Vajrasattva's bodily form was brilliant—a color like crystal. His right hand was holding a golden vajra to his heart and his left supported a silver bell on his thigh. His head was adorned with the buddhas of the five families and his body was decorated with the six bone ornaments and various types of jewelry.

Being skilled in the Mahayoga of development, he was revealing that the nature of the entire external world is a celestial palace, that all beings within it have the nature of male and female deities, that all reverberating sounds have the nature of mantra, and that everything is the display of body, speech and mind.

When taught extensively there are five hundred thousand tantras of the Mahayoga of development, and when taught in brief the following Eighteen Tantras: the body tantras *Sarvabuddha Samayoga* and the two others proceeding from that root—*Rampant Elephant Tantra* and *Water Entering Elephant Tantra*—so that there are three including the *Sarvabuddha Samayoga* itself. The speech tantras *Secret Moon Essence* and the two others proceeding from that root—*Issuing from One Tantra* and *Mighty Lotus Tantra*—so that there are three including the *Secret Moon Essence* itself. The mind tantras *Assemblage of Secrets* and the two others proceeding from that root—*Triple Peak Junction Tantra* and *Mountain Pile*—so that there are three including the *Assemblage of Secrets* itself. The qualities tantras *Glorious Supreme Primal Tantra* and the two others proceeding from that root—*Sky Treasury Consecration Tantra* and *Nectar Sadhana Tantra*—so that there are three including the *Glorious Supreme Primal* itself. The Activity tantras *Activity Garland* and the two others proceeding from that root—the *Forty-Four Kilaya Tantra* and the *Liberating Mound Tantra*—so that there are three including the *Activity Garland* itself. The sixteenth he taught was the *Essence of Secrets* which is the general framework for all the characteristics and tantras. The seventeenth was *King of Arrangement* which is the foundation for samayas. The eighteenth was the *Skillful Lasso Tantra* which is the amendment to all activities or the conclusion to all qualities.

The view is taught as the single indivisible truth.
The meditation is to train in the three samadhis.
The conduct is to skillfully partake of the samaya substance.
The fruition is attained through the nine special qualities.

Padmasambhava became renowned under his former secret name Vajra Holder. Now renowned as Guru Loden Choksey, he then went to the Mount of Spontaneous Presence, the charnel ground in the land of Nepal.

ॐ

Padmasambhava's transmission from Samantadhara

This Guru Senge Dradrok [Padmasambhava] then went to the Palace of Spontaneously Present Arrays. It is of deep blue color and countless leagues in size. Its shape is round and amidst threefold radiating rainbows, colors and light rays is the great Samantadhara, the teacher of enlightened body. The color of his bodily form is dark blue and he is seated on a lion throne. He is wearing the eightfold charnel ground attire and the six bone ornaments and is adorned with the eightfold glorious attire and sixfold jewelry. While holding a vajra and bell across his chest, he embraces his consort. He teaches the nine general vehicles as well as all nine teachings as an indivisible oneness.

Padmasambhava went before this teacher who is skilled in Chiti Yoga, requested teachings and was taught one billion and seventy-two thousand tantras of Chiti.[101] When these are condensed there are the *Embodiment of Teachings* as the planted root tantras, the contained trunk tantras, the unfolding branch tantras, the extensive leaf tantras, and the ripened fruit tantras, as well as the condensed earth tantras. There are also the statement tantras, instruction tantras and explanatory tantras, as well as the scripture on indivisible perfect body, the scripture on unmixed perfect speech, the scripture on five wisdom gates of perfect mind, the scripture on sidetrack-cutting perfect qualities, the scripture on definite categories of perfect activities, the scripture on the steadfast root of the perfect three precepts, the scripture on continuously spinning the great wheel of the activities, and so forth. Thus he taught twenty-one special scriptures.

> The view is taught to be insubstantial and everlasting original emptiness.
> The meditation is to train in the four and five samadhis in whatever arises.
> The conduct is to be pliant in bringing the manifold into the path.
> The fruition is the eighteenfold state of the tathagatas.

Padmasambhava was then widely renowned under the secret name Maha Samantadhara.

This Guru Maha Samantadhara then proceeded to Mount Lanka, the great charnel ground in the land of Zahor.

ॐ

Prahevajra's Life Story

When the god-prince Ananda Garbha had passed on, there was, in the Indian area of Dragon Crest Jewel Ridge, a king named Ashoka and his wife Sugata Kulika. They had no sons; but their daughters were named Joyful Swastika and Radiant Lotus. Joyful Swastika had been given in marriage, but Radiant Lotus thought, "I must practice the Dharma." She then loaded a white ox with provisions and, bringing along her servant girl Virtuous Mind, she went to the Triple Fruit Forest of the Soaring Cuckoo.

While practicing meditation there she dreamt that she drank nectar poured from a precious vase. At dawn a turquoise-colored parakeet landed on her right shoulder and uttered these words: "Princess, you will give birth to a son, a teacher for gods and men who will be known as the master Prahevajra."

Having said this, the parakeet flew away. At this point the girl said to herself, "I have been practicing the sacred Dharma since I did not want any children, so why is that malicious, baleful bird saying such words?"

The following year she gave birth to a son and thought, "A fatherless child is shameful and useless. If I say it came without a father, no one will believe it. If I say it has a father, I will be counted as a vow-breaker. So, better to throw it in the ash heap."

Thinking this she made the servant girl throw it in the ash heap. In the evening of the seventh day after that she remembered her former dream and told the maid, "Last year I had this dream and this is what I was told by a turquoise-colored parakeet. I do not know if the child is some kind of nirmanakaya. Go and look."

The servant girl went to look and found that the child was not dead, but fresh and alive, sitting and playing in the middle of the ashes. Overjoyed the maid took him up on her lap, kissing him. When she gave him to his mother, she too was delighted and said, "My child has risen from the dead so he should be named Rolang Dewa, Serene Resurrected One." She then began nourishing the child and he grew up extremely fast. He grew in a single month more than others do in a whole year and in a single day more than others do in a whole month.

When he reached the age of eight he asked his mother, "Where does Shri Vajrasattva live? I am going to listen to his teachings. I want to shower the rain of the Dharma down on all sentient beings."

His mother replied, "Vajrasattva lives in an invisible realm. You can neither see him nor go there, so keep quiet."

One day the boy was missing and no matter where they looked he could not be found. He was thought to be dead for sure, but then, after some time had passed, he appeared and said, "I went to receive teachings from Vajrasattva. Whatever Vajrasattva knows I know too." His mother was astonished, so he continued, "I am going to have a discussion with the five hundred panditas."

His mother replied, "The five hundred panditas are very learned and since they are the teachers at the Dharma assembly you cannot win over them."

"Yes I can."

"Well then, since they are the officiating chaplains at my father Dharma Ashoka's court, you will have to ask permission from him."

The young boy then went to Dragon Crest Jewel Ridge and said to the king, "I am going to debate with your five hundred panditas, so please give permission for me to be formally introduced."

The king said, "You cannot win."

The boy replied, "I have no fear of losing."

The king then told the panditas, "A young boy says he wants to debate you and therefore to be given permission to be formally introduced."

The panditas replied, "We permit him to join the debate, Your Majesty, but if he loses you should punish him."

The young boy was then formally introduced and joined the debate. He defeated all the panditas so that no matter which vehicle was discussed, they could not beat him. The panditas were all amazed and exclaimed, "A la la, the Buddha has come! A la la, the Dharma has come! A la la, the Sangha has come!"

Then they gave him the name Mahasukha Bheva. Since the king was overjoyed, he named him Joyful Vajra. Since his mother laughed, she named him Laughing Vajra, and since the people of the country were overjoyed, they named him Prahevajra, Delightful Vajra.

At this same time Shri Kumara, the king of Singala, had a son known as the learned Manjushrimitra. Once, he went to refresh himself on a trip to an island. On the way back he heard rumors about a young light-skinned boy dressed in shorts of blue cotton who asserted a ninth vehicle—an Ati Yoga higher than the eight yanas—and could not be defeated by all the panditas. At this, Manjushrimitra exclaimed, "I want to defeat him!"

The master and his attendants then went to the great Dhahena assembly hall on the Dhanakosha island in Uddiyana where Prahevajra, an emanation of the Buddha, was teaching the Dharma. No matter how they debated— through scripture, reasoning or pith instructions—Manjushrimitra could not beat Prahevajra and felt remorse for having previously slandered him. In order to purify his wrongdoing, Manjushrimitra wanted to cut off his own tongue and told his servant to fetch a razor, but Prahevajra asked, "What are you about to do?"

"I have created misdeeds through slandering you, so I am going to cut my tongue off."

Prahevajra then said, "Spare your tongue. Even if you tear out your heart, it will not purify your negative action. Learn to perfection the teachings of my pith instructions. Then compose a teaching that is linked with your personal experience."

Manjushrimitra then requested all the teachings in full without a single exception. He also composed a commentary on the *Section on Awakened Mind* entitled *Pure Golden Ore.* This text's fame has spread throughout the world.

At this time, Guru Padmasambhava heard of Prahevajra's renown, felt deep faith and went to request these teachings from him: *The Seventeen Tantras of the Heart Essence of the Great Perfection,* the *Tantra of the Black Mantra Guardian* as the eighteenth, the *Subjugating Elephant Tantra* to cut through deviations, the *Royal Tantra of Resolving the View,* the *Brahmin Tantra of Distinguishing the Vehicles,* the *Twenty-one Thousand Sections of the Ninefold Space* with the threefold view.

And thus he was the guru who pointed out the mind as dharmakaya.

Nonarising self-knowing attains the three levels simultaneously.
Unceasing mind essence is the unchanging buddha.
With Prahevajra as the eminent source of the Dharma,
He knew and comprehended everything.

The view is primordial purity, the child mingling with the
mother dharmadhatu.
The meditation is uncontrived, the spontaneously present
nature.
The conduct is the awakening of disturbing emotions, without
rejecting or accepting.
The fruition is their natural liberation beyond abandonment or
attainment.

᭱

Padmasambhava meets Sukha Bhadrapala

Guru Padmasambhava then proceeded to the Divine Mound charnel ground in the land of Uddiyana. ... There he became known by his secret name Senge Dradrok, Roaring Lion.

Now Guru Senge Dradrok went to the city of Gathered Black Clouds. There lived an emanation of Vajrapani known as Kulika Sukha Bhadrapala who had accomplished a body of rainbow light beyond material substance. He was naked with free-flowing hair, his lower body wrapped in blue cotton cloth, and in his right and left hands he held a golden vajra and bell. Padmasambhava asked for teachings and was given these *Anu Yoga Tantras of Completion:* the *Tantra that Embodies the Complete Meaning of Unexcelled Secret Mantra* with its *Nine General Tantras, Fifteen Special Tantras,* and *One Hundred and One Particular Tantras;* the *Eight Sections of Magical Net* including the *Essence of Secrets* that states the magical display of mind, the *Magical Net of the Goddess* that describes the display, the *Eightfold Magical Net* that perfects the mandala, the *Fortyfold Magical Net* that reveals the activities in their completeness, the *Unsurpassable Magical Net* that is the self-manifest wakefulness, the *Eightyfold Magical Net* that perfects the qualities, the *Leulag Magical Net* that eminently demonstrates sacred commitments, and the *Magical Net (of Manjushri)* that encompasses the entirety of the Collections.[102] He received them all in full and understood their meaning to perfection.

Guru Senge Dradrok (Padmasambhava) then proceeded to the Lotus Mound charnel ground in the land of Li. ... Here he became known by his secret name Dorje Drollö.

※

Padmasambhava meets Kungamo

[Padmasambhava, now known as] Guru Dorje Drollö reflected, "I must accomplish the *naljor* teachings of Yoga."[103] Intending to primarily realize the Yoga vidyadhara level of longevity and the vidyadhara level of the great seal that is the supreme accomplishment, he went before Manjushrimitra who lived on Mount Malaya and presented his request. The master replied, "The time has not arrived for me to guide you. In the Sandalwood Forest charnel ground lives a wisdom dakini, a virtuous being by the name of Kungamo, who is skilled in conferring the outer, inner and innermost empowerments. She has great blessings, so go there and request the empowerments."

Thus he was given the direction. Dorje Drollö then went to the supreme abode of celestial vidyadharas, the charnel ground of the Intersecting Secret Path of Great Bliss in the Sandalwood Forest. The dakini by the name of Sun and Moon Siddhi—also known as Guhya Jnana, the chief of wisdom dakinis, as Kunga Mönlam the Virtuous, and as the dakini Karmeshvari—lived there. Arriving at her mansion, a celestial palace made of piled skulls, he found the gate closed and no other way in.

After a while he met the servant girl, Kumari, who was on her way back from fetching water and gave her a message for the dakini that he was to be given the outer, inner and innermost empowerments, but he received no reply. When she again came to fetch water and gave no reply he asked her if she had delivered the message, but she simply continued filling her crystal jug. He asked, "Shall I carry the water?"

She placed the jug on the rim of the well and was about to carry it away, when the master concentrated on making the jug stick to the rim. Unable to lift it even after several attempts, she dropped the rope attached to the jug and approached the master. From her girdle she then produced a curved crystal knife and cut open her chest to reveal the forty-two peaceful deities of vajradhatu in her upper torso and the fifty-eight wrathful deities of flaming herukas in the lower torso, all vividly present. Then she said, "You are also a capable *mantrika* but are these deities of mine not more impressive than yours?"

After paying homage and circumambulating her, he asked, "Please bestow the higher supreme empowerments upon me." She replied, "I am just the servant. If you want empowerment, then go inside."

He went inside and met the virtuous being. She was seated on a throne of sun and moon, with an unfolded sun and moon umbrella above her, wearing six sun and moon ornaments on her body. In her hands she held

a small hand drum and a kapala, and she was presiding over a feast surrounded by thirty-two dakinis. Padmasambhava presented a mandala
offering, paid homage and circumambulated her. After offering her a
golden wheel with one thousand spokes as a gift, he requested to be given
the outer, inner and innermost empowerments. Right then all the peaceful and wrathful deities appeared vividly in the sky before him and the
virtuous being said, "Worthy son, now receive empowerment." At this he
replied with these verses:

> Before there was a guru
> There was not even the word 'buddha.'
> Even the thousand buddhas of this eon
> Appeared by following a guru.

> Glorious guru, ocean of qualities,
> Fully disclose the mandala of your presence,
> And kindly accept me as your disciple.
> I will request the empowerment from the guru herself.

The nun replied, "You understand how to receive empowerment."

Then she drew all the deities back into her heart center and transformed
Dorje Drollö into the syllable HUNG which she put into her mouth and gave
the following empowerments within the mandala of her body.

First, by swallowing and consecrating in the mouth, she empowered Padmasambhava in the outer way to be Buddha Amitabha, so that he received
the empowerment to realize the vidyadhara level of longevity. By arriving
within her torso and being consecrated there, she empowered him in the
inner way to be the mighty Avalokiteshvara, so that he received the hidden
empowerment of Mahamudra. By arriving in the secret lotus and being consecrated there, she purified the conceptual obscuration of his body, speech
and mind, and empowered him in the secret way to be the glorious Hayagriva, so that he received all the empowerments for binding the haughty
gods and demons under oath.

ॐ

Padmasambhava meets Kuñjara

Following this Guru Dorje Drollö went to the densely arrayed and spontaneously present dharmadhatu palace of Akanishtha where the regent of the entire ocean of victorious ones entitled Knowledge-Holder Dharmevajra, also known as Vajra Garbhadhara, and as Kuñjara the king of vidyadharas. His bodily form had the color of conch coated with vermilion. He was surrounded by numerous male and female divine beings, lights in rainbow colors and was accompanied by manifold types of melodious sounds. In that same moment he conferred all these teachings and empowerments in their entirety:

> The upadaya empowerment of the spiritual teacher
> He conferred with the outer eightfold attire as the nirmanakaya.
>
> The scripture empowerment of the entrustment of the Dharma
> teachings
> He conferred with the inner eightfold attire as the
> sambhogakaya.
>
> The yidam deity empowerment of the manifest expression of
> awareness
> He conferred with the secret eightfold attire as dharmakaya.
>
> The supreme empowerment of Mahamudra in completeness
> He conferred with the majestic tenfold attire as the unchanging
> vajrakaya.
>
> The vajra-bearing master empowerment of the sovereign of the
> five kayas
> He conferred with the embracing consort as the all-
> encompassing view in actuality.

Following this he conferred the five hidden empowerments: the domain empowerment of jewels, the wealth empowerment of Jambhala, the treasure empowerment of the Brahmins, the life-force empowerment of the haughty ones, and the assemblage empowerment of magnetizing. It was then that he gave Dorje Drollö this prediction:

In the Cave of Solitude on India's Suvarnadvipa district
Lives the son of the Indian king Virtuous Victory
Known by the name Shri Singha.
You shall focus on the essential pointing-out instruction
For training in the indivisible unity of all things.
Samaya.

Then Guru Dorje Drollö went before the master Shri Singha and asked, "Pay heed, great master. Please bestow upon me the essential pointing-out instruction for the ultimate indivisibility of all things." Shri Singha showed the gesture of pointing a finger at the sky and then said:

Do not cling to whatever appears.
Do not cling to whatever appears.
No arising, no arising.
Arising, arising.
No clinging to the arising, no clinging to the arising.
Arising and liberation are simultaneous.
Empty, empty.
Not empty, not empty.
Unceasing, unceasing.
Ceasing, ceasing.
Primordially empty, fully empty and utterly empty—
This arising, devoid of cardinal or intermediate directions, above
    or below,
Shri Singha declares to be the ultimate key point.
Focus on this view and meditation, then the undivided nature
    will spontaneously manifest.

At this, Padmasambhava's mind was liberated into the state of nonarising. Padmasambhava further asked, "Great master, what is the nature of the mind of buddhas and sentient beings?"
Shri Singha replied:

"The nature of the mind of buddhas and sentient beings does not consist of any entity whatsoever. Yet, while not being a real entity, I

Dharmevajra the King of Vidyadharas

have not found it to be nor can I determine it to be in any one absolute way. Failing to find any reference point in the mind, anything to identify, concepts are liberated in themselves; there is no demon who can harm the mind. That is called 'cutting through outer misconceptions.'

"This is the way to cut through inner misconceptions: this aware self-existing wakefulness cannot be found to have arisen from a particular cause, to have been produced from certain conditions or to possess such and such an identity. Even I, Shri Singha, have not discovered any mind that could be described as being such and such. So, Padmasambhava, I also have no mind to show you as being in any one absolute way."

Having spoken in this way, he dissolved into vajra-like space.

After this Dorje Drollö proceeded to the great charnel ground Delighting in the Great Secret in the country of Sala.

🌀

Padmasambhava receives Ati, Chiti and Yangti Yoga with Tögal from Shri Singha

Then Padma of Uddiyana reflected, "I must go to the Vajra Throne in India and benefit the Buddhadharma." He went to the Vajra Throne and invited Guru Shri Singha who unfolded the expansive section of Ati Yoga with the mandala of 'similar words with superior meaning,' the Chiti Yoga with the symbolic mandala, and the Yangti Yoga with the Tögal mind essence, the mandala of the sun and moon.

When resolving all the vehicles in their entirety to be the perfect essence of supreme enlightenment, Uddiyana's body dissolved into the sky. He displayed the miracles of it being pure like space, of innumerable bodily forms gathering like rainbow clouds and filling the entire sky.

On a small hill at the Vajra Throne he erected a stupa of the great awakening with twenty-one tiers of various types of precious substances and made of crystal up to the vase. At the time of consecration the panditas of India assembled, including the twenty-one learned ones, and offered this praise to Guru Padma:

> O hear us!
> In Dhanakosha on the jeweled isle,
> Your emanated form was an immaculate conception.
> Replete with qualities you have perfected every benefit for
> beings.
> Achiever of supreme enlightenment, we praise you and salute
> you!

Perceiving that Guru Padma had the most eminent learnedness in exposition, debate and composition, they requested him saying "You must compose treatises such as commentaries on all the Buddha's Words—the sutras, tantras, statements and instructions—and also compose sadhanas, empowerment manuals and pith instructions."

ॐ

The Single Golden Letter of the Black Quintessence—popularly known as the Yangti Nagpo cycle of teachings—belongs to the most esoteric section of Ati Yoga. It is defined as "revealing the extraordinary hearing lineage of the innermost cycle." Besides practices of guru sadhana and the hundred peaceful and wrathful deities, its three profound volumes contain teachings on all aspects of the Great Perfection, including detailed instructions for retreat in complete darkness.

The short lineage comes through the conqueror Samantabhadra, Vajradhara, Vajrasattva, glorious Padma--the great master of Uddiyana--and from him to Yeshe Tsogyal and then to the treasure revealer Dungtso Repa. The longer lineage comes through Samantabhadra, Vajradhara, Vajrasattva, Prahevajra, Shri Singha, Uddiyana and his consort, Vimalamitra, Vairotsana, and so forth.[104]

Dungtso Repa "the Later" lived in the beginning of the fifteenth century, received teachings from both Kagyu and Nyima masters and became the lineage holder of the female guru Jetsunma Kunga Bum. He meditated in remote mountain retreats and received visions of Padmasambhava.

In his Ocean of Wondrous Sayings, Guru Tashi Tobgyal mentions that Dungtso Repa recovered the teaching cycles on The Single Golden Letter of the Black Quintessence beneath a boulder that resembles an upside-down turtle on the bank of the Black Mandala Lake that lies behind Mount Gampo. He propagated it to worthy recipients, many of whom attained the body of light. The transmission of the empowerment and instructions is still unbroken thanks to the kindness of Kyabje Trulshik Rinpoche.

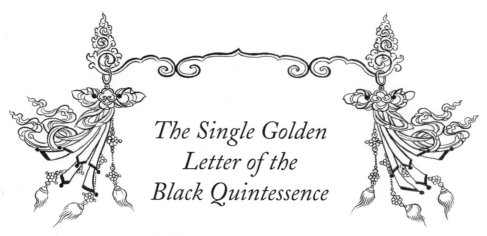

The Single Golden
Letter of the
Black Quintessence

*The History of the Great Perfection
from the Single Golden Letter of the Black Quintessence*

To teach the prelude, at the beginning of the *Self-Liberated State of Dharmata,* a tantra is quoted:

> Without explaining the meaning of the history,
> The blemish of mistrust may then arise
> Towards the teachings of the *Certain Greatest Secret.*

So it is said and accordingly we begin here with the story of the lineage masters.

While I, Uddiyana, remained in meditation in the great charnel ground Cool Grove, one evening glorious Samantabhadra appeared and spoke to me, Uddiyana, in these words, "Noble child. If you wish to abide in the profound nature of dharmata, look here!" With these words I was entrusted with a self-appeared casket of gold one inch in size. Upon opening it, I saw the entire cycle of the *Self-Liberated Dharmata.*

At midnight, glorious Vajradhara appeared in person and said, "Noble child. If you wish to abide in the state of meditation, look here!" And having spoken, a thumb-sized crystal casket naturally appeared. I opened it and saw the entire cycle of the *Self-Liberated State.*

As I continued supplicating at early dawn glorious Vajrasattva appeared. As I received a silver casket enveloped in lights of five colors, he said, "Noble child. If you wish to abide in the ground of dharmata, look here!" Opening it I saw the entire cycle of the *Complete Peaceful and Wrathful Ones*.

I continued supplicating, and at sunrise glorious Samantabhadra encircled by the five families of conquerors appeared in person and said, "Noble child. If you wish to abide in self-liberated dharmata, look here!" With these words they entrusted me with a self-appeared casket made of manifold precious substances. Opening it, I saw the entire cycle of the *Self-Manifest Nature*.

Thus, all these teachings presently being taught here are superior in being root statements of major importance. They are the extracted essence of Samantabhadra's heart, the mirror of Vajradhara's mind, the innermost treasury of Vajrasattva's secrets, the gems from the treasury of Prahevajra's mind, the heart essence of Padmasambhava, the blood from the hearts of all the wisdom dakinis, all of which have not been grammatically and linguistically dissected by translators. If the Indians obtain these teachings, it will be their fulfillment. If the Chinese obtain them, it will be their fulfillment. If the Tibetans obtain them, it will be their fulfillment.

These teachings are the rinsing water that washes away evil karma, the razor that shaves off misdeeds and obscurations, the guide who leads on the path of liberation, the escort for traversing the bardo, the mirror for beholding the buddhafields. They will be a wish-fulfilling jewel for whoever obtains them,.

These teachings are superior in ten ways. In other teachings you must pray to go to a buddhafield, but these teachings are superior since you see the buddhafields in actuality right now. In other teachings you imagine the deity after receiving empowerment, but these are superior since you receive the empowerment from the yidam deity in actuality. In other teachings you put your hopes in familiarization, but these are superior since you realize the view right now. In other teachings you visualize deities, but these are superior since you see the buddhas in actuality. In other teachings having been told that your body is the mandala of conquerors you imagine that it is so, but these are superior since you see the body as a mandala of deities in actuality. In other teachings though told that the five poisons are the five wisdoms you do not recognize them to be so, but these are superior since you see the five wisdoms in actuality. In other teachings you are told that the bardo exists even though you are given no more than words, but these are superior since you verify the bardo in actuality right now. In other teachings you must train for months and years, but these are superior since you recognize the unconditioned nature in seven days. In other teachings there is daytime phenomena and nocturnal phenomena, but these are superior since you see the buddhafields of luminosity beyond day and night. In other teachings you see your body as flesh and blood, but these are superior since you see it as a body of light. The qualities are inconceivable!

If a father has obtained these teachings it is only right that he would give them to his son as heart advice. If a son has obtained these teachings it is only right that he would give them to his mother as heart advice. If a mother has obtained these teachings it is only right that she would give them to all sentient beings as heart advice. These teachings are to be kept by fortunate people endowed with the proper karmic destiny. For those without the right fortune they are only wasted or cause wrong views.

Being too profound, the precious great guru did not reveal this, the ultimate of vehicles, to anyone. It is meant for the beings of the dark age of decline who have no leisure in their lives and yet spend their days in boredom. Three years after arriving in Tibet, he bestowed this teaching upon the king, the princes and the royal consort, Lady Tsogyal. Tsogyal then concealed it as a profound treasure.

ᔕ

The Tantra of the Sun of the Brilliant Expanse was taught by the female buddha Samantabhadri to the dakinis of the five families. After she taught this, the dakini Karmeshvari retained its hundred and forty chapters, wrote it down with golden ink on lapis parchment and placed it within a crystal casket. This tantra was kept in the dakini mandala in the mystical charnel ground Blazing Fire Mountain, within the uppermost part of a jeweled stupa with one hundred and eight tiers standing at the roof of a pagoda made of five precious metals. And here it remained until the lineage was passed to Hayagriva and Vajra Varahi, and from them to Padmasambhava.

Among the several versions of the Tantra of the Brilliant Expanse, this dakini lineage is recorded in the revelations of the fourteenth century tertön Dorje Lingpa who received this terma at the early age of fifteen but "kept it secret until forty-two, when he had practiced, received its blessings and attained the signs and confidence of accomplishment."

The following excerpts are from the terma treasures of Ratna Lingpa.

Transmitting the
Brilliant Expanse

ཧྲཱིཿ རྫོགས་ཆེན་ཀློང་གསལ་ཉི་མ།

I, known as the Lotus-Born,
Traveled far and wide through India,
From east to west, and all the points between them.
Abhishekas and instructions I pursued,
Like a thirsty man who drank but salty water.

I learnt, reflected, meditated and resolved the view.
The yidam deities I beheld, as clear as daylight.
Now I've gained the perfect insight of all buddhas
And attained the knowledge-holder's siddhi of longevity.

By the power of a karmic link created in the past
I have met in person Splendid Lion,
Who bestowed the tantras, all the seventeen,
The explanations, with advice and the activities.

But chiefly he bestowed the *Tantra of Samantabhadri's Sun of the Brilliant Expanse*
Together with its explanation, the *Lamp for the Brilliant Expanse,*
And the complete advice for the activities.
I then requested the empowerments, the precepts and entrustments.

For the sake of trust I had them written down,

And especially, the *Tantra of Samantabhadri's Sun of the Brilliant Expanse,*
Since it is the insight of the Ever-Excellent, the Mother,
It is the sacred essence of the tantras, all the seventeen.

The lucid explanation of its meaning, replete in every aspect of the Dharma,
Is sublime, the most exalted, unexcelled.
For the benefit of all the worthy ones in future generations
I shall elucidate the history of masters most sublime.

Mandarava, you must put this down in writing. Samaya!
May it meet the destined one with worthy karma!
This has seals of body, speech and mind. Samaya. ༔
SEAL, SEAL, SEAL. ༔

ཀཊཐྃༀཿ ཀྱུརྂཧཝཿ ཧྲཱིཀཐཔཀཎཾཿ ༀཿ ཨརྒྱཧྃ༎ཿ

In the Indian language: DAKINI CHITTAMAKRI ༔
In the language of Tibet: *kun tu bzang mo klong gsal 'bar ma nyi ma'i lo rgyus zhes bya ba* ༔
In the English language: *The History of the Tantra of Samantabhadri's Blazing Sun of the Brilliant Expanse*

Samantabhadri, spacious vastness of nondoing,
Lucid wakefulness, self-knowing dharmakaya,
In Samantabhadri, in the Mother's vastness, I pay homage.

It is in order to instill confidence and authenticate the source that I give here the history of the lineage masters for these innermost instructions on how to realize the greatest secret, the instructions that place buddhahood in the palm of one's hand and lead to awakening within this same body and life.

It was in the dharmadhatu palace of Akanishtha, a realm of unconditioned purity, that awareness while in the formless form of Samantabhadri's single sphere, not yet cast in any image, arose into a form with face and arms—the form of the female buddha Samantabhadri.

And so it was that, from the dharmakaya's unconstructed sphere, she

Vajradhara
the Buddha

taught the glorious sambhogakaya, Vajradhara, the Great Sixth, who was ornamented with the major and the minor marks in the form of blessings that occurred in naturalness.

Then Great Vajradhara—in the Akanishtha realm known as the Densely Arrayed, in the mansion of the multi-layered lotus, in the palace of the purity of space—taught the glorious nirmanakaya, Vajrasattva, through his own identity, utilizing all the major and the minor marks.

And it was Vajrasattva who then taught, by using spoken words, the incarnated Prahevajra, who lived within the human realm though his mind could match the state of any buddha.

Then in the incarnated Prahevajra's mansion, staged as the charnel ground of Sosadvipa, Prahevajra taught the great pandita Shri Singha. And in Uddiyana's charnel ground known as Putrid Corpses, it was this learned Splendid Lion who then taught me, the Lotus-Born.

And from the land of Uddiyana I proceeded to stay in the Upper Cave of the Slate Mountain where I trained in the quintessence of the *Seventeen Tantras* and the *Brilliant Expanse.* The conditioned body made of flesh and blood dissolved and was an unconditioned form like an illusion—visible yet inconcrete, transcending birth and death. Thus I had attained the knowledge-holder's level of longevity. This was written down on parchment within that Upper Cave of the Slate Mountain in order to assist those who are inclined toward simplicity so that they may transcend this world of sorrow:

> When coming to Tibet to benefit all beings,
> I brought along these tantras and instructions.
> There have been many worthy ones and numerous disciples,
> The ruler of Tibet and all his ministers,
> But since Vimalamitra, the most learned, is arriving
> The time has come for him to teach the Great Perfection.
> The time has come for me to tame the gods and demons.
> The time to teach this Great Perfection has not come;[105]
> It should not be mentioned, even to the wind.
> Instead, I give the Lady of Kharchen the transmission
> For all the cycles of instruction and the first two manuscripts.
>
> I and Tsogyal, the two of us together,
> Shall practice it within the Tidro Cave at Upper Zho.
> When Jomo has completed her compiling,
> Compared and verified, all discussions settled,
> We shall conceal the seventeen, the very heart of all the tantras,
> And chiefly the quintessence of the *Sun of the Brilliant Expanse,*
> The *Blazing Lamp,* and so forth, together with the tantric statements,
> And the pouring forth of Uddiyana's personal experiences,
> Condensed into the *Heart Essence of the Dakinis*—
> All these shall be concealed at the upper part of Danglung
> For the benefit of future generations.
>
> In particular, the secondary copy of the manuscripts
> Shall be concealed at Bhutan's Lion Snout in Bumtang.
> While this shall be concealed within the Sky Plain's Lion Fortress
> With the aspiration that it meets the one who has the karmic link.
>
> Until they reached the hands of Padma
> They have never once been written down.

But for the sake of people in the future
I have had these teachings written down on parchment.
May they reconnect with the worthy one who has the karmic link!

This was the record of the lineage masters. It bears the seal of body, speech and mind.

SAMAYA. ⁞ SEAL, SEAL, SEAL. ⁞

卐

Ratna Lingpa the Treasure Revealer

The Great History

Transmitting the Lineage of the
Precious Teachings

ཀྵེ ༈ རྒྱ་གར་སྐད་དུ་ཆེན་པོ་རྫ་མ་སོ་སྭཿ

Homage to the lineage masters of the teachings of the three kayas, and to the yidams and dakinis.

This lineage history of the instructions of the Innermost Unexcelled Great Perfection, too wonderful for words, the Ultimate Cycle of the Precious Fruition, has three points:

How conquerors transmitted the instructions through their intent,
How vidyadharas transmitted the instructions through symbols,
How sublime individuals transmitted the instructions orally.[106]

The teachings may belong to the definitive meaning but will be flawed unless I explain how they were transmitted intentionally by the conquerors. They will not be the unexcelled definitive meaning unless I explain how they were transmitted symbolically by the vidyadharas. Also, the instructions will not be considered a trustworthy source unless I explain how they were transmitted orally by the sublime individuals connecting India and Tibet. This being so, the *Essence of Statements from the Oral Lineage* mentions:

When the conquerors appear within the worlds,
All the noble statements they assert
Will be opposed by hostile disbelievers,
So the authentic history of lineage is essential.

The *Tantra of the Magical Storehouse* also states:

> Without explaining the meaning of the history,
> The blemish of mistrust may then arise
> Towards this certain teaching of the *Greatest Secret*.

So it is taught and therefore it is of utmost importance to begin with the history.

FIRST, HOW THE CONQUERORS' INTENT WAS TRANSMITTED:
It was within the realm of dharmakaya—the basic space of natural purity, the consort's space of greatest secret—known as the perfect buddhafield of Densely Arrayed. The time transcended a beginning and an end within the triple times. The teacher was Samantabhadra, the primordial victorious one, also known as the King of Natural Knowing.

From his nature, not yet cast in any image, he appeared as means and knowledge indivisible—a self-existing body in a form with face and arms—and transmitted to his retinue, the sugatas of the five families that were no different from him, in these two ways: dharmakaya's intent through *inspiration* and through *resplendence*.[107]

The first of these refers to how the essential identity of dharmakaya is awakened and remains as a wisdom body. This identity—a self-knowing that transcends dualistic intellect—knows itself to be threefold: empty in essence, cognizant by nature and unconfined in its capacity. This identity intends and transmits from within the natural state since all that arises from it also dissolves back into it, beyond the limitations of realizing and not realizing. *The Speech Tantra* describes this:

> Even speech is spoken through samadhi.
> Even hearing is heard through samadhi.

Next I will explain how intention and transmission through *resplendence* takes place. Since the *inspiration*—the wisdoms—is manifest within dharmakaya in a way that is spontaneously present, the natural radiance of these wisdoms therefore appears as colored lights:

Dharmadhatu wisdom, which is the empty essence of dharmata, appears as blue light. When acknowledged as the self-display of insight transcending the intellect, it matures to fruition in the form of Vairochana, and confers the empowerment of mind, the empty essence of which is dharmakaya.

Furthermore, from the essence—which is unconfined cognizance, mirror-like wisdom—appears its natural radiance as white-colored light. When acknowledged as the self-display of insight transcending the intellect, it matures to fruition in the form of Vajrasattva, and confers the empowerment of the mirror-like brightness of dharmakaya.

Again, from undivided aware emptiness, which is equality, appears its natural radiance as yellow light. When acknowledged as the self-display of insight transcending the intellect, it matures to fruition in the form of Ratnasambhava, and confers the empowerment of the undivided aware emptiness of dharmata.

From discriminating wisdom appears its natural radiance as red light, since intelligent wakefulness is unconfined within dharmakaya's emptiness. When acknowledged as the self-display of insight transcending the intellect, it matures to fruition in the form of Amitabha, and confers the empowerment of discerning wisdom.

From all-accomplishing wisdom which is unobstructed knowledge, appears its natural radiance as green light. When acknowledged as the self-display of insight transcending the intellect, it matures to fruition in the form of Amoghasiddhi, and confers the empowerment of the unobstructed knowledge of dharmakaya.

The *Tantra of the Storehouse of Magical Jewels* describes this:

> This is the origin of dharmakaya's teaching:
> Wisdom came from maturing into forms.
> Through the thought-free venue of enlightened mind
> They were taught by an inspired resplendence.

This was how the intention and transmission of the conquerors through the two aspects of inspiration and resplendence took place.[108]

Buddha Akshobhya

SECOND, HOW SAMBHOGAKAYA TEACHES OR INTENDS THROUGH ITS OWN IDENTITY:

As the radiance of the above-mentioned wisdoms matures into the bodies of fruition, they appear in the perceptions of the disciples who belong to their corresponding families.

Vairochana appears to the identity of the four families. Likewise, Akshobhya appears to the vajra family, Ratnasambhava to the ratna family, Amitabha to the lotus family and Amoghasiddhi to the karma family.

Moreover, these buddhas, the teachers of the five families, reside in a place with perfect attributes, the realm of Vajradhara. Their time is when awareness appears as objects. Their retinue is the male and female bodhisattvas of their family, as well as the bodhisattvas of luminous causation. To them they teach not through words and letters, but through the features of their bodily forms.

Here is how they teach through the *identity* of their respective thrones:

Gazing upon Vairochana seated upon a lion throne the retinue understands the fact of being indivisible from the three kayas.

Akshobhya seated upon a throne of elephants the retinue understands as the sign of unchanging dharmata.

Ratnasambhava seated upon the throne of eminent stallions the retinue understands as the sign of his capacity's unconfined strength.

Amitabha seated upon a throne of peacocks the retinue understands as the sign of involvement in the disciple's individual inclinations.

Amoghasiddhi seated upon a throne of *shang-shang* birds the retinue understands as the sign of unobstructed knowledge.

Furthermore, that these conquerors sit on sun and moon seats their retinues see and understand to be dharmakaya and the view, sambhogakaya and knowledge, nirmanakaya and capacity, means and knowledge, experience and emptiness, and so forth.

Their sitting on a lotus seat the retinue understands as the sign that dharmakaya while manifesting as the two types of rupakaya, is untainted by attributes, and that even though the rupakayas appear in disciples' perception, they are still untainted by the defilement of habitual tendencies.

Here is how the buddhas teach through the *identity* of the respective colors of their bodily forms:

Vairochana is shown as blue as the sign of unchanging dharmata;

Ratnasambhava is shown as yellow as the sign of developed qualities;

Amitabha is shown as red as the sign of guiding disciples through compassion;

Akshobhya is shown as white as the sign of being immaculate in essence;

Amoghasiddhi is shown as green as the sign of benefiting beings through the four activities.

This is also how their respective retinues realize and understand.

Here is how they teach by means of the *identity* of their hand-attributes:

Vairochana holds a wheel because dharmakaya is devoid of partiality, sambhogakaya is endowed with the major and minor marks, and nirmanakaya possesses discriminating knowledge, through which his retinue realizes and understands accordingly.

Akshobhya holds a vajra to signify that the five kayas and five wisdoms are not separate but unchanging as a single sphere, and through this his retinue realizes and understands accordingly.

Ratnasambhava holds a blazing jewel to signify that the fourfold modes of manifestation are unobstructed from within the precious sphere, through which his retinue realizes and understands accordingly.

Amitabha holds a lotus to signify that the dharmakaya is untainted by marks of concreteness and that the rupakayas are untainted by karma and habitual tendencies, through which his retinue realizes and understands accordingly.

Amoghasiddhi holds a vajra-cross to signify that the four activities accomplish the welfare of beings even though he in fact possesses no conceptual effort, through which his retinue realizes and understands accordingly.

Here is how they teach through the *identity* of their seated posture:

Since the reality of the basic state is without family, body color or hand-attribute, and does not change throughout the three times, they are all seated with legs in the vajra position, and the retinues realize and understand accordingly.

The *(Tantra of the) Storehouse of Magical (Jewels)* describes this:

Sambhogakaya's own approach of teaching
Is to teach through the particular identity.

THIRD, HOW NIRMANAKAYA TEACHES THROUGH COMPOSITION:

This will be explained under nine points: the nirmanakaya's cause and circumstance, manner of birth, virtues, disciples, attire, substance of teaching, superior qualities, extent of deeds, and passing beyond the world's sorrows.

FIRST, from the threefold state of essence, nature and capacity, Buddha Sky Essence and his consort Radiant Light's wisdom sphere, in fruition, is the co-emergent identity that remains as the very heart of self-existing awareness, and so forms the cause for manifestation.

SECOND, THE CIRCUMSTANCE was miraculous birth from an udumvara lotus flower.

THIRD, THE MANNER OF BIRTH. The teacher Vajrasattva appeared as an eight-year-old child.

FOURTH, THE VIRTUES. It is the expression of dharmakaya—virtues that lie beyond constructs—which manifests in the form of sambhogakaya, and it is sambhogakaya which then manifests as a self-existing nirmanakaya. Thus on the outer level Vajrasattva saw the displays of the six classes of beings as a magical illusion while, on the inner level, he saw the displays of spontaneous presence as sambhogakaya.

With six syllables in the six places of his bodily form, his spontaneous voice resounded instantaneously as he addressed sambhogakaya:

Royal sameness, Dharma lord of every family,
From the mandala of vajra space in Akanishtha,
Show this unexcelled and wondrous, supreme awakened state,
So that Vajrasattva may understand his mind.

Show the basic truth of buddha seen within oneself,
The self-existing mandala of space, also seen within,

Which once arisen never sets again.
Reveal it to all beings in the world.

Thus he requested, but sambhogakaya made no utterance whatsoever. And yet, the reality of no utterance itself communicated profoundly and extensively to Vajrasattva. Thus he realized dharmakaya to be an ineffable essence, the original wakefulness of basic space; he realized sambhogakaya to be the nature of total perfection; and he realized that he was the nirmanakaya that is the natural expression of unconfined capacity.

Glorious Vajrasattva then miraculously manifested six self-appearing forms of compassion, the extraordinary retinue as the seventh, the three bodhisattvas abiding on the levels, making ten, and the Lord of Secrets as the eleventh, all of whom accomplished the welfare of beings.

Shakra miraculously appeared from the crown of Vajrasattva's head, Splendid Robe from his nape, Shakyamuni from his heart center, Yamantaka from his aorta, Flaming Mouth from his navel, and Ox-Head from his mouth. Having appeared, they accomplished the welfare of the six classes of beings.[109]

Dharmevajra was emanated from Vajrasattva's nose out of five-colored light and established as the one to make the requests. Manjushri was emanated from his right ear, Avalokiteshvara from his left ear, and Prahevajra from between his brows; they established him to be holder of the buddha family.

Five self-existing goddesses appeared from the five pure essences of the elements: Alokema, Nordenma, Logpar Desöl, Shugdro Nampar Jema, and Yila Jugpey Tobdenma. These five resided in the wisdom lamps of Vajrasattva's eyes.

From within the expanse of natural space a stupa made of precious crystal with five ledges spontaneously appeared. On the first level appeared Amoghasiddhi, on the second Amitabha, on the third Ratnasambhava, on the fourth Akshobhya, and on the fifth appeared Vairochana; hence five self-appeared emanations. Above them, the five female buddhas spontaneously appeared, present as the nature of five-colored lights; and above them, the dome of nondwelling wakefulness.

These self-appeared buddhas, with the nature of light, appeared as the *Sources* of the precious doctrine, and descended onto Vajrasattva's left hand.

It was at the time of natural luminosity that all teachings that lie beyond concreteness manifested as suchness.

Similarly five mudras arose spontaneously, and from them appeared the *Body Tantra Swirling Lotus,* the *Speech Tantra Vajra Pinnacle,* the *Mind Tantra Jewel Heap,* the *Qualities Tantra Loving Mound,* and the *Activities Tantra Circle of the Sun,* all of which descended into his heart center.

At this time glorious Vajrasattva perfectly contained four rivers of empowerment, which were no different from him—the self-existing river of compassion, the five-grain river of bravery, the empowerment river of five wisdoms and the four great pronouncements as above. All flowed forth spontaneously and appeared naturally in his mind, so that he bestowed the empowerment of omniscient knowledge and wisdom.

Fifth, the disciples. He bestowed these rivers upon the requesting retinue such as Dharmevajra and others, upon the attendants such as the six Munis, upon the listening retinue such as the bodhisattvas on the ten levels, and upon the compiling retinue such as Prahevajra.

Sixth, the attire is that of Vajrasattva, Krodha the Powerful and so forth, to guide whoever is in need in whichever way is necessary.

Seventh, the teachings given. Vajrasattva, also known as Vajradhara the Sixth, appeared on the heavenly plateau of the Thirty-Three Gods, in the palace of complete victory, after magically assuming the form of Youth of Inconceivable Sublime Light. At this time the patrons were [Shakra, the king of the gods, and his four consorts[110]], the attendant was Excellent Starlight, and the retinue were seven in number—the six Munis and Prahevajra. Dharmevajra functioned as the compiler. They honored him with the three medicinal grains, syrup, molasses, honey and divine ambrosia, and with the sounds of musical instruments.

The teachings he taught were: externally, the six paramitas; internally, the six million four hundred thousand tantras of the Great Perfection; the three principles of ground, path and fruition; and the testaments of the buddhas.

Next, in the intermediate heavenly realm, the summit of Blazing Fire Mountain, Vajrasattva appeared in the garb of Krodha the Powerful. The rishi Garuda-Clawed Moonlight was the patron and the dakinis Conch of Brahma's Voice and Serene Purna were the female patrons and the Lord of Secrets was the attendant. In addition, there was a retinue of seven: the bodhisattvas Vigorous Cloud, Powerful Elephant, Delightful Youth, Eminent Samadhi, Jewel-Bearer, Vajra Cutter and Sun Circle.[111] With food that grants immortal life, and with offerings like those of the dakinis—flesh, blood, and bones, *bhandhas* and skull-drums, flutes and horns made of thighbones—they honored and praised him boundlessly.

Since dakinis cannot be influenced by teachings on karmic causation, as the essence of the teachings Vajrasattva exclusively gave the pointing-out instruction that shows how appearances are empty, and conferred the empowerment of awareness-display. Moreover he taught the *Bringing Face-to-Face,* the *Knowing One that Liberates All,* the *Equalizing Secret Tantra,* the *Tantra of the Blazing Crest,* as well as the *Eighteen Tantras of Mahayoga.*[112]

The teacher Vajrasattva then went to the last heavenly realm, Vulture Peak Mountain, where he magically appeared in the form of Buddha Kashyapa. The brahmin named Excellent Marks was the patron and the nun Lotus-Eyes the female patron. The bodhisattva Flawless Sandalwood was his attendant and seven virtuous lay-people presented the questions: the virtuous Eminent Youth, Moon Crest, Flawless Jewel, Brimming Vase, Immaculate Nectar, Noble Ornament and Boundless Jewel-Eyes.[113]

The teachings he gave included the *Cutting Insight Essence Tantra* along with the three aspects of the philosophical vehicle and the six paramitas.[114] He also taught the *Tantra of Secret Wonderment* as five root tantras, four instruction tantras and four child tantras—thirteen in all.

SEVENTH, THE QUALITIES are boundless, but they can be included under five types: those of body, speech, mind, qualities and activities.

For the first, the qualities of body, being born from a lotus flower Vajrasattva appears while remaining untainted by a womb and has therefore no concrete body of flesh and blood. He is endowed with the general thirty-two major and eighty minor marks of excellence. As for the extraordinary marks, Vairochana is seated at the crown of Vajrasattva's head with the mudra of composed mind illustrating that he is empowered with omniscient wisdom. Upon his tongue is Amitabha seated in equanimity and encircled by the four goddesses of speech, illustrating that he teaches the Dharma to beings while retaining the state of purity. In his heart center is Akshobhya with the mudra of the tathagatas, illustrating that he understands all phenomena within a single state of realization.

For the second, the qualities of speech, since the reach of Vajrasattva's tantras and statements is beyond thought and inexhaustible, they are understood in one's own language, show ripening and liberation, and are not of a concealed intention but stated definitively.

For the third, the qualities of Vajrasattva's mind which is endowed with five wisdoms. Having the identity of the wisdom of emptiness, its changelessness is dharmadhatu. Being unobscured and utterly pure, it is like a mirror. Since everything is by nature total purity, it is equality. All phenomena are clearly distinguished, just like the planets and stars reflected in water. The all-accomplishing quality is that without effort everything is spontaneously present and perfected. In short, within the precious, secret sphere, Vajrasattva is present as the wisdom beyond body, the intelligence beyond dualistic mind, the buddha beyond teachings, the natural radiance beyond elements, and as the self-display beyond words. In reality, he resides as the never-ending adornment wheel of omniscience in regards to all phenomena.

For the fourth, the unfolding of his qualities transcends dimension and description, in general, and, being part of his jewel-like mind, they are manifest as a fourfold display. Since they all naturally appear as spontaneous presence beyond struggle, naturally dissolve without effort, and are naturally present in his own state, the kayas and realms are therefore a spontaneous and pure unfolding.

For the fifth, since the activities arise from the compassion of all buddhas, they have an altruistic resolve, are uninvolved in the hardship of purification and journey, and appear naturally and spontaneously for the benefit of others.

THE EIGHTH, THE DEEDS accomplish the welfare of sentient beings by means of the four activities.[115] To benefit beings in the world he remained as Kashyapa the Elder for eight hundred thousand years.

THE NINTH, THE MANNER OF PASSING. Even though a buddha is not subject to aging and death, in order to rouse lazy people to the Dharma and to disillusion those who expect permanence, he dissolved all of appearance and existence into the expanse of dharmata, let the four major wisdom elements roar, and within a mass of light rays vanished into the open sky. Everything shifted, in the center and the four directions, so that one place seemed higher and another lower, and the entire world shook as the teacher left the wretched world in a mass of light, leaving no trace behind. At this, the master Prahevajra[116] cried out in despair:

Alas, alas! This world is bare and empty!
Bereaved, all beings, without parent or protector,
They have neither savior nor defender!
How can you turn away your caring eyes?

And for three days, he remained in a faint. When he had regained his senses, the words SARVA SIDDHIKA resounded from the sky.

[In Prahevajra's narrative:]

I, Prahevajra, looked up. My experience had changed without the scene changing—my awareness naturally arose as the awakened state and I was brought face-to-face with the great emptiness of the ground-display. Here, within the dharmata sky of personal experience, Vajrasattva appeared in a form of magical illusion and spoke from this expanse of light:

"Noble child, I have passed beyond sorrow and awakened to true and complete enlightenment. Having passed beyond beings needing guidance, all constructs have completely subsided. As my mind has passed beyond sorrow, thoughts have dissolved into basic space.

"Noble child, even though I have passed beyond sorrow, as the representation of body I have left behind a crystal stupa with five tiers.

"Even though my voice has passed beyond sorrow, I have left behind the tantras of *Refined Nectar*.

"Even though my mind has passed beyond sorrow, I have left behind a self-appeared symbol of wisdom, the lamp of awakened mind. Understand their significance and work for the benefit of beings."

Here Prahevajra understood that while Vajrasattva had left the wretched world, these representations resembled the teacher in person.

At that very moment the teacher extended the fingers of his right hand from within the sphere of light and a silver casket, one inch in size, descended upon the crown of Prahevajra's head. Then a gold casket, also one inch in size, landed in his right hand and into his left hand fell a turquoise casket, one inch is size as well. From the tip of his nose fell a statue of Vajrasattva, four finger widths tall.

When Prahevajra opened these and looked, from within the silver casket appeared the *Tantra of Self-Existing Awareness*. From within the gold casket appeared the *Tantra of Knowing One that Liberates All*. From within the turquoise casket appeared the *Tantra of the King of Knowing Awareness in Actuality*. When looking into the crystal image that came from the tip of Vajrasattva's nose, he beheld the countenance of the five families of conquerors.[117]

As Prahevajra swallowed the first of these caskets, all teachings became spontaneously known within his mind. By looking at the tantra in the second casket and scrutinizing its meaning, he knew all teachings as being one and became liberated in all. By reading the tantra in the third casket, he established the ninefold key points of natural awareness. By beholding the countenance of the five families, all mistaken perception manifested as pure experience, and all unwholesome concepts dissolved into dharmadhatu.

Up to this point was the way of transmitting the intent of the conquerors.

Thus, as the *Speech Tantra* declares,

In the first aeon the original dharmakaya buddha Changeless Light taught while in the manner of a seed. In the middle aeon Vajrasattva taught while in the manner of a seedling. In the last aeon the buddha Kashyapa the Elder taught while in the manner of a fully matured fruit.

The *Tantra of Arrayed Knowing* mentions,

The time for dharmakaya to teach through *inspired resplendence* is when the vajra of realization self-manifests. The time for sambhogakaya to teach through *identity* is when the sublime bodily form manifests. The time for nirmanakaya to teach through excellent verbal *composition* is when manifesting in accordance with the individual sentient beings to be inspired.

Moreover, transmitting through realization means samadhi, as the *Speech Tantra* says,

> The teaching too is done within samadhi.
> The hearing too is done within samadhi.

The way the vidyadharas transmit through symbols

The *Speech Tantra* says,

> One way to understand the word vidyadhara is *kula-dhara* (family-holder). Because of first originating from the *kula* (family), next carrying out its work, and finally not forsaking it, *kula-dhara* is therefore so described.

When, for instance, a prince is born to a *chakravartin* ruler, he grows up to uphold the family of his father, carrying out the exact same duties as his father. Next he performs the same deeds in his father's tradition. Finally he upholds it by not forsaking it.

In the same way, Vajrasattva as the king of Dharma, had a heart son Prahevajra. Just as Vajrasattva carried out the task of teaching, Prahevajra having received the mandate to transmit the teachings, also took up the task of benefiting beings. Finally, he never forsook Vajrasattva's teachings.

Here is how the symbolic meaning was transmitted. Vajrasattva magically appeared amidst the pure sky in the form of a *kalapinga* bird, being a bird with a fine beak, and uttered the four sounds of *rigpa*. "TRA TAH MA ZHA, TRA TAH MA ZHA," it sang, forming the basic dimension of sound. "TRA TAH ZHA, TRA TAH ZHA," it sang with the selective factors of sound. "HITIRI HITIRI," it sang with the benefiting factors of sound. "PRATINAMA" it sang with the establishing factors for sounds. On hearing these sounds, the pure being Prahevajra clearly perceived and comprehended the general and specific attributes of all phenomena.

The knowledge-holder Prahevajra proceeded to Lotus Mound and remained composed in meditation inside a grove of bodhi trees in the southern jungle known as Blissful Mingled Minds. Using as example the king of trees—the divine bodhi tree—he composed the Outer Cycle as the established root, the Inner Cycle as the connecting trunk, the Secret Cycle as the outstretched branches, the Secret Unexcelled Cycle as the radiant flowers, and the Innermost Unexcelled Cycle of the Precious Fruition as the ripened fruits.[118] All these cycles remained within the self-existing pagoda in Magadha, present in the sky before him, inside a mansion composed of seven types of precious substances.

Here is how the knowledge-holder Prahevajra appeared in this human world during the teachings of Shakyamuni.

Three hundred and sixty years after Buddha Shakyamuni's passing, in the fragrant valleys in the country of Uddiyana, there was a city known for the auspicious Shankara Kuta temple. In the main palace lived King Uparaja and his Queen Radiant Light. Prahevajra was born to their daughter, Princess Graceful Light, and he not only converted non-Buddhist teachers but also crushed vicious attacks from heretical teachers and demonic forces. Thereupon he went northward to Mount Brilliant Sun, where he remained composed in samadhi for thirty-three years.

After another thirty-one years the master Prahevajra went to Mount Malaya, the peak of heaped jewels. There he and two dakinis of vajra space—Blissful Loka Taste and Yellow Bliss-Giver of Boundless Qualities—spent three years writing down all the precious *Collections* spoken by the former truly and completely awakened one, but especially the natural Great Perfection in six million four hundred thousand sections that were present in Prahevajra's mind. Meticulously and correctly, together with the nirmanakaya, the dakinis wrote down the letters of self-occurring naturalness. The wise dakinis then received permission to venerate the teachings and placed them within the Freedom Cave of Dakinis.

Now the master went to the great charnel ground Cool Grove which is situated five leagues northeast of the Vajra Throne, flying astride one of the daughters of Vishnu, who was naked, her hair hanging loose. There Prahevajra taught the Dharma in a gathering of countless dakinis.

Later on, while he resided under the Bodhi Tree at the Vajra Throne, to the west was a city known as Two Stages. There the brahmin Benevolent Teacher and his wife Effulgent Lamp had a son by the name of Manjushrimitra, who became learned in the five sciences.

One day their son received this prophecy from noble Manjushri: "Pay heed, son of a noble family. If you wish to attain enlightenment within a single lifetime, go to Cool Grove charnel ground!"[119]

Manjushrimitra went there and met Prahevajra.[120]

Meanwhile in the Chinese region known as Shacheling, the householder Virtuous One and his wife Wise Light had a son they named Shri Singha, a child who became most erudite in the qualities of learning.

When Shri Singha was fifteen he took ordination with the Chinese master Hastibhala and studied the five topics of knowledge to perfection.[121] Shri Singha then resolved to visit the city of Golden Sanctuary situated to the west. During the journey Avalokiteshvara appeared in the sky and smilingly gave this prophecy, "Listen, worthy one. If you wish to attain the definitive fruition, go to the Bodhi Tree in the land of India!"

Shri Singha thought, "This prediction is most excellent. But I am still young." So he went to the Five-Peaked Mountain that lies in the eastern part of China where for seven years under the master Bhelakirti he studied all the available tantras, statements and instructions of the outer and inner sections of Secret Mantra. Shri Singha then remained in naturalness until the age of seventy-seven, until one day, while he was bathing in a pool to the east of the Five-Peaked Mountain, in an instant he experienced a nonconceptual samadhi and again received Avalokiteshvara's prophecy.

"The journey to India is long and strenuous," Shri Singha thought to himself, "I must ensure I do not succumb to obstacles." He then practiced samadhi for three years and attained both the siddhi of swift walking and the vidyadhara level of longevity. Moving with the speed of the wind and not touching the ground, he arrived at the Bodhi Tree in just four days, or nine day-nights[122]—in the presence of both Prahevajra and Manjushrimitra.

At that time the great master Prahevajra liberated both Manjushrimitra and Shri Singha by means of the *Five Symbols of the Practice Lineage,* the

Five Symbols of the Manifest and the *Five Symbols of the Deeds.*

To indicate these symbols succinctly Prahevajra showed a pure crystal, so that they understood the crystal to symbolize the primordially pure dharmakaya; they understood its five-colored light to be sambhogakaya, and the vivid presence of whichever object it displayed they understood to be nirmanakaya. Just as the crystal appears as any color or object, depending on how it is placed, and is seen to be transparent, with neither inside nor outside—while the crystal's identity remains unchanged—they understood all the phenomena of samsara and nirvana to be similar.

As Prahevajra pointed his finger at the sky they understood all the phenomena of nirvana to be empty and devoid of identity. Then he created boundless forms of beings belonging to the three realms and again dissolved them, and thus they understood that all conditioned phenomena are impermanent and painful.

When Prahevajra pointed his finger at his heart they understood that *jnana* resides as natural light within the *chitta*.[123] As his eyes looked heavenward, they understood that the eyes are the gates for *jnana* to manifest. When he looked into the ten directions they understood that the kayas and buddhafields will unfold.

Furthermore, placing a clay figurine inside an empty room with a flame and directing the five senses there, he showed the five senses to be lucid and nonconceptual, and he showed the figurine to be free of the concept of identity as well as clinging. While the basic identity is one, he showed that the venues of the five senses manifest in manifold ways but that the eyes are the primary ones. He showed that other than through the sense-doors the *jnana* is unable to manifest while bound by the body's seal. Crushing the figurine to let the flame shine through, he showed that *jnana*'s luminosity pervades the buddhafields when the body's seal is broken.

After showing many other similar kinds of symbolic indications, Prahevajra sang the words of this vajra song in a slow melody, in order to cut through extraneous concepts:

Kye ho.
If you should ask, "What is the view?"

The view is wakefulness, self-knowing.
Free of effort—how delightful!

And if you ask "What is the training?"
Training is the four times joined with sameness.
Transcending breaks and sessions both—how utterly delightful!

"What is the conduct?" you might ask.
Conduct is the great and natural freedom.
Neither keeping nor rejecting—how delightful!

"What is fruition?" you might ask.
Fruition is the triple kaya, spontaneously perfected.
No meeting and no parting—how delightful!

Upon hearing this song the two vidyadharas understood the meaning exactly.

The knowledge-holder Prahevajra then conferred upon them the stream of his empowerments, in the manner of one vase filling another to the brim, and explained in detail the meaning of the words. Thus he completely transmitted the Great Perfection's three cycles—the Outer, Inner and Secret Cycles—as well as the Secret Unexcelled Cycle of Fruition and the Innermost Unwritten Cycle and others, without a single exception.

For seventy-five years they remained together, serving the great nirmanakaya. It was at the source of the Dantig river that the nirmanakaya then entered the samadhi of great indivisibility and, after remaining in samadhi for three weeks, his physical body vanished into a rainbow-like mass of light.

On witnessing this, both Manjushrimitra and Shri Singha fell down in a faint, and exclaimed,

Alas, alas, the world is now empty!
When the doctrine's light has faded away,
Who will clear the world's darkness?

As they were crying out such words of sorrow, from the sky resounded "SATAKASHA," and when they looked up they saw Prahevajra appear within the *dharmata* sky of personal perception. He extended his right arm up to his elbow and, accompanied by a sound, a gold casket, one inch in size, landed in the hands of the two masters.

When they opened the casket and looked inside, they found that it contained Prahevajra's testament, written with self-engraved letters of the five precious substances on paper made of refined lapis. By simply beholding these letters the two masters were liberated into the naturally pure nature of all phenomena, so that they were then like vases that have been perfectly filled to the brim from another perfect vase. The time of Prahevajra reaching the exhaustion of phenomena coincided with the two masters' increase of experience.[124]

§

Eventually, while Guru Shri Singha remained in meditation in the Cool Grove charnel ground, I, Padma of Uddiyana was practicing the sadhana of Vishuddha Mind (Yangdag) in the great charnel ground Joyful Forest. It was then that I received this prediction from the Lord of Secrets:

> Pay heed, Dorje Tötreng Tsal,
> If you want the siddhi of Vishuddha,
> Go to meet the Lion Guru
> In the Cool Grove charnel ground,
> And request the teaching cycle on the *Unexcelled Fruition*.

The very moment Padmasambhava received this prediction, he went to meet Guru Shri Singha who bestowed upon him the Bindu Cycle of the Secret Edict together with its *Exposition Tantras, Mind Tantra,* the *Hearing Lineage,* and so forth, of which he understood all.[125]

After eight years had passed, he said to Guru Shri Singha, "Please hear me, great guru. I beseech you to give the extraordinary teaching, the Unwritten Cycle that brings enlightenment through being pointed-out the ultimate transmission."

Here is the Lion Guru's response,

> To point you out in just this way:
> Enclosed within four elements,

Within the trunk of a red bull,
A crystal shines with five-hued lights.
The bull's right eye your hand must cover.
Yank out the left and then return.

[In Padmasambhava's narrative:]

I, Padma, set out searching for the "bull." At a fork in the road, I met a maiden. "Lotus Master, where are you going?" she said, staring at me intently.

I repeated the above events whereupon the girl pointed a finger to her own heart, covered her right eye with her right thumb and then remained, with her left eye looking directly into midair. Understanding this to be the symbolic lineage of the ultimate transmission, I presented her with the buddhafields of the three kayas arranged as a mandala offering. When I asked her to explain the symbolism she introduced the hidden pathway and, when I had acknowledged this, she added, "This is indeed the way to awakening."

After returning I related it to the great guru. The Lion Master responded, "Son, within this state, look outward!" I looked and pure perception arose.

Then he said, "Look inward!" I looked and beheld the kayas and the wisdoms.

Looking in-between my experience arose as self-existing, empty cognizance, unimpeded wakefulness.

Thus I realized that self-existing wakefulness has no outside, inside nor an in-between.[126]

Let me explain the above symbols, unraveling the ultimate transmission:

The fork in the road symbolizes the girl, and the enclosure comprised of the four elements indicates this body made of the four elements. Right here, within this enclosure of means and knowledge, pointing her finger at her heart center meant that the self-existing five wisdoms dwell within the *chitta*. Nevertheless, the bull symbolizes a lack of knowing this.

Covering her right eye with her right hand symbolized first using a method and then forming the habit of clinging to the method. Letting her left eye look directly into midair symbolized that the eyes are the doorways for wisdom to manifest. In particular, this gesture pointed them out as a symbol for the unimpeded self-existing wakefulness having an unobstructed basis for arising.[127]

The fact that the girl was standing at a fork in the road indicated the following threefold essential pointing-out instruction, using the girl's own words:

> Whoever recognizes as their own experience
> This profound, symbolic meaning
> Of the undivided, unimpeded wakefulness,
> Attains complete awakening within a single instant.

And as she uttered this, I was liberated.

This was the Lions Master's lineage of insight through symbols that was transmitted into the heart of I, Uddiyana.

Three days later the Lion Master visited where I, Uddiyana, lived. While the world filled with sounds, lights and earthquakes, he awakened to true enlightenment without any remnants of the aggregates.[128]

At this time, as I, Uddiyana supplicated in request of a testament—just as the two masters mentioned above had beseeched Prahevajra—Guru Singha's light-body, visible yet insubstantial, appeared within a sphere of rainbow lights in the pure sky of personal experience. He placed his right hand upon the crown of my, Uddiyana's, head and spoke these words:

> Son of Amitabha's family,
> After having passed beyond the world of woe,
> These, the secret, self-existing tantras
> Will, through wearing, bring a definite result
> To sentient beings wandering in darkness.
> Uddiyana, keep them as your mind-support.

Having said this, the *Tantra Cycles on the Essence of Liberation Through Wearing* descended into my, Uddiyana's, three places.[129]

Up to this point I have explained how the vidyadhara's transmission of insight through symbolism occurred.

The explanation of how sublime individuals taught through oral transmission.

Last of the three general points is the oral transmission through sublime individuals.

The snow-filled kingdom of Tibet, a serene and lofty land, had become the sphere-of-influence of the glorious lords of the three families. And it was here that the great Dharma-king Trisong Deutsen—himself an incarnation of sublime Manjushri—had begun the construction of a temple to house the Buddha's teachings. But Tibet's malicious gods and demons prevented his noble wish from being fulfilled.

The abbot bodhisattva from Zahor offered this prediction, "In India lives the glorious master from Uddiyana known as Padma Tötreng Tsal, a great knowledge-holder of longevity, who has command over the phenomenal world and employs gods and demons as his own servants. If you invite this emanation of Buddha Amitabha, your wishes will be completed fulfilled."

So the king dispatched Dorje Dudjom of Nanam, Palgyi Senge of Shubu and Shakya Prabha of Chim, furnishing each with three *drey* of gold dust and three gold ingots as offerings for the invitation. The three Tibetans undertook a journey wrought with countless hazards, but with the blessings of I, Uddiyana, they arrived safely.

This was at a time when I, Uddiyana, was guru at the court of Surya Singha, the king at the Vajra Throne in India. The three lotsawas presented one *drey* of gold dust and one ingot to I, Uddiyana, and similarly one *drey* of gold dust and one ingot to the king. As well, they offered one *drey* of gold dust and one ingot to the five hundred panditas residing as the religious dignitaries at the court. When they then read aloud the Tibetan king's letter with his request, I, Uddiyana, knew that the time had come to accept these disciples. I accepted to go to Tibet and the Indian king and his court clerics gave their consent. Thus under the constellation of the Pleiades we set out on the journey to Tibet.

It then happened, on the eighth day of the second month of the year of the Male Tiger, under the constellation of Uttarasadha, that the foundation was laid in the Tamarisk Forest at Red Rock. Having performed the ceremony for taming the site the construction was begun. It seemed that the building grew taller at night with the help of gods and demons than the humans could build during the day. And before long, the great temple of Spontaneously Accomplished Wishes was completed.

On the fifteenth day of the second winter month in the year of the male Water Horse, under the Pushya constellation, I, Uddiyana, magically created myriad emanations and re-emanations who simultaneously performed consecration by means of one hundred and eight deities throughout the snowy ranges of Tibet.

Then, in order to ensure that the king's wishes were completely fulfilled and to ensure that the teachings would flourish, Vairotsana together with Ka and Chok began translating the *Collection of the Buddha's Words* in its entirety. Thereupon, I personally blessed the one hundred and eight major practice places of Tibet, headed by the Caverns of Chimpu, as well as the twelve hundred minor practice places, where I practiced and performed boundless deeds for the benefit of beings.

It was on such an occasion that I composed the innumerable instructions, which are the distillation of the heart essence, for the *Seventeen Tantras of Unexcelled Fruition of the Great Perfection,* the *Tantra of the Blazing Sun of the Brilliant Expanse,* the *Great Samayoga Tantra* and countless others. I concealed these instructions within treasure caches for the benefit of beings in future generations in all the cardinal and intermediate directions, since the time for their propagation had not yet come.

And now I shall explain about the *Heart Essence of the Brilliant Expanse,* a most unique terma treasure concealed within this land, the name of which is difficult to allow to pass one's lips.

Although there was the great King of Dharma and countless other disciples endowed with karmic fortune in Tibet, I have never spoken of this teaching, not even with one word. It was only to my heart son Namkhai Nyingpo and my qualified companion the Lady of Kharchen that I transmitted it in completeness among the rocky slates of the Chimpu charnel ground and at Kharchu in Lhodrak. Dividing it into three—the heart, the life-blood and the vital essence—they wrote the teachings down in detail on

Guhyachandra the Indian Siddha

the surface of the yellow parchment and finalized them within five chests of black rhinoceros hide. Three representations of enlightened body, together with the sadhana cycles that I composed, were consecrated within five red chests of black rhinoceros hide. And within the Splendid Long Cave that is the very center point of Kharchu in Lhodrak, on the tenth day of the Monkey month in the year of the male Earth Horse, I invoked all the knowledge-holders and celestial gurus, and, placing the caskets on the crown of the head of the translator Könchok Jungney of Langdro, I performed the complete entrustment ceremony for the teachings of the *Heart Essence.* Together with the aspiration and empowerment that he would meet with and utilize the teachings in the future, I performed the auspicious ritual, uttering verses of well-wishes such as those of the eight vidyadharas and the five consorts.[130]

Following that, on the tenth day of the Bird month, this teaching was concealed at Furrowed Red Rock[131] entrusting the Three Maroon Brothers with guarding the terma treasure. It was sealed together with this aspiration: "When fifty years marks the middle age of man, may this terma meet with the sublime heart son of I, Padma!

"And in future times, rife with the five degenerations, after having connected with this person possessing the karmic link, may I re-awaken the dormant hearing lineage and empowerment in either vision, actuality or dream.

"With my care several people with karmic destiny will spread the instructions in all directions so that the Buddhadharma will flourish everywhere. Thus this will benefit many beings in the future."

This described the oral transmission of sublime individuals as well as the entrustment and prediction of future disciples.

> Emaho
> Sublime quintessence, like the finest butter,
> Churned from the milky ocean of profound instructions
> Of Padma, I, the Lake-Born Vajra's heart.
> Like taking out a wishing-gem among the finest jewels,
> I hid an untold number of the deepest Dzogchen treasures.

Könchok Jungney of Langdro

But only this is ultimate—the quintessence of them all.
As this is Padma's purest life-blood,
I swear I have concealed it in no other terma more profound.

When fifty marks the middle age, may this unexcelled
    quintessence—
Through the strength of Padma's aspirations—
Meet my worthy heart son yet again!
Three Brother Guardians, I place this terma in your charge!

This completes *The Great History of Transmitting the Lineage of the Precious Teachings.*

SAMAYA. KHATHAM. SEAL, SEAL, SEAL.

ལས་རྣམ་རྩ་བཞིན་དུ་རྫི༔

In the year of the Hare, Ghuru Ratna Lingpa revealed this from within the rhinoceros chests at Sky Plain Cliff. I copied the yellow parchment, the length of one arrow and four fingers wide, at Dharma Fortress Hermitage, verifying it three times. May it be auspicious.

ௌ

Wellsprings is primarily a history book, but I felt it would be inappropriate not to include a couple of teachings as well. So here is an outstanding instruction that the great knowledge-holder Shri Singha gave to the Lotus-Born master. It forms the crown jewel among all the above-mentioned precious teachings from Ratna Lingpa's Brilliant Expanse (Longsal).

Shri Singha's
Heart Mirror

Homage to the vastness of primordial purity.

I, whose name is Lotus-Born,
Sought out the heart of conquerors in the three times.
And from the learned Splendid Lion
I was bestowed instructions on fruition in a single life.

With the intent to benefit the beings of the future,
This advice is kept concealed within three terma caskets.
I wrote it down in three distinctive versions,
But this especially is more profound so keep it in your heart.
May this meet with the person endowed with the right fortune!

⑤

The great master of Uddiyana addressed Shri Singha in these words, "Great guru, I beseech you to bestow upon me a perfect instruction with few words, deep meaning and which allows one to reach the awakened state."

Here are Shri Singha's words in reply:

As an incarnation of Amitabha and the Great Compassionate One in person, you have in reality transcended beyond all doubts. Nevertheless, it is excellent that you make this request for the benefit of beings. I shall give you a teaching, a jewel from my heart that is the quintessence extracted from all the tantras and Dharma teachings.

In general, all phenomena belonging to samsara and nirvana are, from the very beginning, spontaneously perfected as the essence of awakened mind. However, because of failing to realize and not knowing this to be just how it is, sentient beings circle among the three realms and continue to wander among the six abodes. In order to guide them, it is generally said that an inconceivable number of doorways to the Dharma belonging to the various vehicles have been taught, but these can all be contained within development, completion and the Great Perfection.

Moreover, there are the three sections of the philosophical vehicles belonging to nirmanakaya, the three sections of Kriya and Yoga belonging to sam-bhogakaya, and the three aspects of development, completion and the Great Perfection belonging to dharmakaya. Among these, I shall explain to you the Ati Yoga of Instructions, distilling its quintessence, which is the Innermost Vajra Essence of the Unexcelled Fruition. So listen, Padmasambhava.

This instruction on the awakened state as an intrinsic possession, a clear guidance instruction like pointing a finger at it, has these five aspects:

1. Resolving the essence by means of three summaries.

2. Eliminating the limits of permanence and nothingness by means of three seals.

3. Crossing the narrow gorge of pitfalls and obscurations by means of meditation practice.

4. Demonstrating the signs of progress in practice by means of three metaphors.

5. Stating the meaning of the title of this teaching.

1. Resolving the essence by means of three summaries.

For the first—the three summaries—resolve, absolutely, that all phenomena, the world and beings, included within samsara, nirvana and the path, are contained within the awakened mind of awareness; that all the eighty-four thousand types of negative emotions are included within the demonic belief in a self; and that all the eighty-four thousand entrance-doors to the Dharma are contained within the three pith instructions of one's guru.

That all phenomena are contained within mind is, for instance, like the analogy of all the things that you can dream of when asleep—horses, cattle, men and women, and sceneries of places to which you have not even gone—have no existence upon waking up, apart from having been the magical displays of one's own mind. Likewise decide that there are no phenomena besides the displays of blind habitual tendencies.

The way that negative emotions are included within the belief in a self is, for instance, like the analogy of the sprouts, stamen, leaves and kernels of a crop which may all appear to be separate while in fact they spring from the same root, which is the seed. Likewise, decide that it is due to the belief in the identity of a self that there is attachment, hate solidifying from aversion, the conceited indignation of thinking "I am" and the jealousy of clinging to the idea of "other." In short, no matter which negative emotion one personally feels, it is created from the cause, which is close-minded ignorance. And it is from these five negative emotions that many others proliferate, so that eighty-four thousand emotions stem from one and the same root.

Furthermore, the way that the eighty-four thousand Dharma-doors are contained within three pithy instructions of one's guru, is: the instruction in first cutting the all-ground (*alaya*) at its very root; the instruction in investigating the root of samsaric existence; and the instruction in naturally entering the state of original wakefulness.

First, to show that the natural state is contained within one's own mind, begin by scrutinizing the location from where this mind arrived, next how it dwells and finally where it departs to. Through this you will see that it does not arrive from anywhere at first, does not dwell anywhere in between, and at the end does not depart anywhere either. In this way mind is not found to possess an appearance of shape, form or color, but rather it is a lucid emptiness that defies every type of mental construct. And thus the very root of the all-ground has been cut through.

Investigating the root of samsaric existence means to look into where the insidious demon known as "I" or "me" is located—tracking it down as "there"—in the external environment, sensory data, cognitive acts, the world and beings, as well as your own body. Then looking to see if it is "here"—within the sphere defined as oneself. The very fact of being incapable of pinpointing its location and its identity means that the self cannot be proven to exist.

For the instruction in naturally entering the state of original wakefulness, relax your mind loosely in the very state of not finding—the state in which there is no ego. Free of using effort, train in being serene and calm, lucid and present, in a way that is naturally clarifying. In this way you will grow accustomed. Regard this as the key point of nirmanakaya.

2. Eliminating the limits of permanence and nothingness
by means of three seals.

Next, since this is for the purpose of enhancement, stamp the essence of the visible with the seal of being empty; stamp this empty nature with the seal of being visible; and stamp this nondual, visible emptiness with the seal of transcending limitations.

That is to say, when thoughts or other movements occur, they are bound by the principle of non-deviation: just like a fish never leaves the ocean's water no matter where it swims or like a bird never leaves the sky no matter where it flies. In the same way you should know that your mind never departs from its own nature no matter which thought may be stirred up.

SAMAYA. ፨ KHATHAM. ፨ SEAL, SEAL, SEAL. ፨

3. Crossing the narrow gorge of pitfalls and obscurations
by means of meditation training.

Next is to cut through pitfalls and obscurations by means of the three meditation trainings. Within the uncontrived natural state, first, when dull train in being wakeful; next, when scattered train in being collected; and when obscured train in disrupting.

For the first, train in being wakeful when you sink into sleepiness and the state of inert shamatha. For the second, train in being concentrated when you become dominated by events or sense objects. For the third, train in an invigorated and uplifted way when feeling deluded and stupid, or when one's mind is clouded.

4. Demonstrating the signs of progress in practice by means of three metaphors.

The next instruction also has three key points: To be like a lion is the sign of possessing confidence, to be like a crazy yogi is the sign of having a presence of mind that does not become overtaken by circumstances, and to be like a child is the sign of attachment having naturally fallen away.

The first metaphor is that of a lion who is fully confident, free of fear or timidity in front of any other animal. Similarly, the yogi—because of recognizing all appearances to be his own mind—is free of fear or timidity in the face of any adversity or difficulty.

Second, the yogi of medium abilities—just like a crazy person who is neither shy nor clings to concepts of clean and unclean—is someone for whom clinging naturally dissolves, having neither attachment to concepts of good and bad nor judgmental preferences.

Third—just like a child can remain unattached, without craving, and be very natural—it is taught that the yogi as well should be free of clinging and attachment.

These are true ways for a yogi to practice.

SAMAYA. ﮓ

5. Stating the meaning of the title of this teaching.

This practical instruction that places the very essence of the natural state right in one's hand is an advice that shows: how to identify the troublemaker and naturally dissolve concepts, how to cross the steep abyss of the six realms, how to extricate delusion, and how to seal samsaric existence. It is the instruction for transmuting thoughts into original wakefulness, like the key alchemical advice for transforming base metal into gold. It is the skillful method that allows you to realize dharmakaya within a single lifetime and then to work for the benefit of beings through the two types of rupakaya. Incarnated being, keep this extraordinary instruction within your heart!

These were the words that Guru Shri Singha spoke to I, Uddiyana.

§

These nectar-like and sacred words, so hard to utter,
The deepest method for dissolving thoughts in dharmakaya,
Profound and eminent quintessence, heart-jewel, as precious as
my eyes,
Were received by Padma who obtained the empowerment of
rigpa's play.

This wish-fulfilling jewel is difficult to teach,
So I have sealed it for the benefit of future generations,
And placed it as the background teaching's lucid pointing-out
instruction,
In the Trekchö manual for *Heart Essence of the Brilliant Expanse*.

When more lengthy, the wordiness is like a river's stream;
While this is like a boat upon the ocean to realize the natural
state.
So for certain people this has all the necessities complete.
And therefore I conceal it as a precious terma treasure.

May it be a guide for beings at the end of the ages in the future!
At the final time, when a mid-length lifespan reaches fifty years,
And the Buddha's teachings are like thunderclaps of summer,
People spread the unripe and pursue distorted teachings;
Practitioners and centers, temples, kingdoms, all are scattered to
the wind.
At this time toward the Kali Yuga's end,

May the worthy one connect with this my deepest treasure!
SAMAYA. ⟨⟩ KHATHAM. ⟨⟩ SEAL, SEAL, SEAL. ⟨⟩
Seal of mantra. ⟨⟩ Seal of concealment. ⟨⟩ Seal of entrustment. ⟨⟩
MANTRA GUHYA. ⟨⟩ SEAL. ⟨⟩

གཏེར་རྒྱ་ཟབ་རྒྱ་དུ་རྒྱ༔ ཁ་ཐམ་རྒྱ་རྒྱ་རྒྱ༔ སྔགས་ཀྱི་རྒྱ་གཏེར་གབ་རྒྱ་གཏད་རྒྱ༔ སྔ་ཀ༔ གུ་བ་ཡ་རྒྱ༔ ༔ རྒྱའོ་ཨ་ཨ་བ་རྒྱ༔
ན་མ༔ སྔ་ཧ་རྒྱ་རྒྱ། ༆བཀྲ་ཤིས་ཤཱུ་བ་ཨ་འ་འ་དྷ་དུ༔ ཚེ༔ ཛཿཝ༔ ཁ་གྲུ་དམར་ཁུག་ཉུ་རྣམས༔

I, Ratna [Lingpa], revealed this reply to a question, like a jewel in one's heart, at Furrowed Red Rock. At the end of this age may it be a guide for ignoble beings.

ༀ

The following two excerpts are from The Heart Essence of Vajrasattva, a terma treasure revealed by Kunkyong Lingpa in the 15th century from Padmasambhava's cave in the Zabbu Valley of Tsang. It has a unique manner of transmission in that Padmasambhava received the tantra and all the instructions directly from the magical incarnation Prahevajra.

Later on, while the Lotus-Born master stayed in the upper cave on the Juniper Ridge of Crystal Pearls in southern Tibet, he bestowed the entire transmission upon the great lotsawa Vairotsana as a special mandate. It was Vairotsana's future incarnations, as Dorje Lingpa and his rebirth, Kunkyong Lingpa, who would reveal these teachings. Taksham Samten Lingpa, the reincarnation of Vairotsana's scribe and disciple, Labu Dönyö Dey, revealed a third, identical version. In the 17th century, Vairotsana's reincarnation Pema Dechen Lingpa gathered all three streams and fused their blessings into one. This lineage still continues thanks to Jamgön Kongtrül's including this important treasure in the Rinchen Terdzö, the Treasury of Precious Termas in sixty-three volumes.

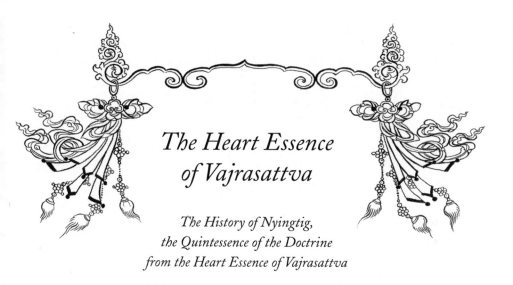

The Heart Essence
of Vajrasattva

The History of Nyingtig,
the Quintessence of the Doctrine
from the Heart Essence of Vajrasattva

ཉེ་ ༔ ༔ན་ཏ་ཀོ་ལ་ཧྲུག་རྩ་ཚང་༔ ཐ་ རཱུ༔ ༔ཐ་རག་ཚིག་ཀ་བ་ལ་ཏ་ས་ཧྲ་ཏ་ཧྲ་ས་ས་༔ ༔ན་ས༔ ཅོ་ཚ་ཀ༔ ཀྱི་ས༔

Homage to The exalted Vajrasattva. Homage to samsara and nirvana's vast
expanse, transcending all confines.

> For the precious human forms, comprised of fourfold elements,
> This exalted essence, Vajrasattva's heart,
> Which from Jambudvipa until now has remained unknown,
> Vividly reveals its face: intrinsic are the triple kayas—
> The quintessence of all yanas has arisen
> To illuminate the three times with unobstructed wisdom.

ᦋ

First the explanation of the way in which the insight of the conquerors has
been transmitted.

It was within the dharmadhatu's ineffable and vast expanse, that the timelessly awakened one—spontaneously perfected in his nature—arose as the identity of the conqueror, the glorious Samantabhadra. From his natural capacity,
the basic space beyond all constructs, rose the one whose name is Vajrasattva.

His form was adorned with flowers of the major marks and with the fruits
of minor marks of excellence. He was endowed with strength, the fourfold

fearlessness, as well as all the rest of the enlightened virtues. And crowned was he, upon his head, by buddhas of the fivefold families. He wore an upper garment of the whitest silk, a *pati* skirt of many colors, bedecked with a variety of precious jewelry. His form was bright and radiant, crystal-like in hue.

A jewel platform formed his throne and upon it was a seat of a lotus and a sun. It was supported by eight elephants—eight mahabodhisattvas who had magically appeared through the force of their noble aspirations. And there he sat, his legs in *sattva* posture, a vajra held before his heart, a bell supported on his thigh.

His form was such that one's gaze would never tire—extremely dazzling and resplendent, lucid in its serenity, so calm its brilliance—like a rainbow in the sky or like reflections in a mirror, not formed of earthly substance.

Amidst the blissful, pure expanse of basic space, he manifested as the never-ending wheel of ornaments—the body, speech, mind, as well as all the qualities and the activities of each and every tathagata. Within the realm of Akanishtha, the dharmadhatu sky, the vast expanse of basic space, this mansion beyond measure, timeless wakefulness was not subject to any obscuration.

The retinue that manifested from him consisted of the dharmakaya, which was his nature; the sambhogakayas, also his nature; and the nirmanakayas, his natural expressions; as well as earth and water, fire, wind and space, and the Kama Loka, Rupa Loka and the formless realms, and all the buddhas and the bodhisattvas of the past, the present and the future, and the mundane, supramundane, extremists and *sattvas*, and Vajrapani and, especially, the magical creation Prahevajra. Everyone resided in the great expanse, the single sphere.

That was the time he spoke this very tantra about the greatness that is present in oneself—OM VAJRA SATVA HUNG. And, in particular, and simply through his will, the magical creation Prahevajra was blessed spontaneously with all instructions, both the verbal and the ultimate, and having given these, he, Vajrasattva, then dissolved into his own expanse—in essence empty and in nature brilliant, and in capacity quite able to be seen in everyone, just like a rainbow in the sky or reflections in a mirror.

🌀

The Quintessence
of All Vehicles

The Ultimate Root Tantra
from the Heart Essence of Vajrasattva

§ད་ང་རྒྱུད་ཐུག་གི་ཐིག་ལེ་ཐེགཪ

In the Indian language: VAJRA SATVA CITTA TILAKA YANA SARVA
HRIDAYA TANTRA NAMA.

In the language of Tibet: *rdo rje sems dpa'i snying gi thig le theg pa
kun gyi yang bcud ces bya ba. rdo rje sems dpa'i snying thig las*§
rtsa ba'i don rgyud ces bya ba bzhugs so§

In the English language: *The Tantra of the Heart Essence of
Vajrasattva, the Quintessence of All Vehicles.*

Homage to the primordially awakened state, exactly as it is.

Here are the words that once upon a time, I then expounded.

It was within the all-pervasive realm of greatest bliss, in the vastness of
this basic space, the great immensity that is the unconditioned nature, that,
present by its own accord, the primordially awakened state was the Blessed
One, the Glorious Samantabhadra.

And from his power of expression appeared the teacher Vajrasattva, the
spontaneously perfected triple kaya. A throne of elephants, completely
stable, was his seat, and in his right hand he held a golden vajra level with
his heart, while in his left a silver bell was placed upon his thigh. Above his

head were seated all the buddhas of the fivefold families. His body, fully graced with every ornament, was white and brilliant, crystalline in hue. Adorned with countless of the major and the minor marks, his countenance was captivating, shining and resplendent. He had appeared spontaneously from within the source of dharmadhatu's empty vastness, in a form possessing face and arms.

Now it was that from the expressive strength of his capacity, a retinue no different from himself appeared: Ratnasattva, Padmasattva, Karmasattva, Dharmasattva and also female bodhisattvas, as well as Vajrapani and Prahevajra. As they were all his emanations, they remained together—within the basic space of wakeful vastness, the single nature of all things.

And then the teacher spoke and he proclaimed this tantra of intrinsic greatness that is the essence of all tantras, the root of all the statements, the quintessence of all instructions, the extract of all teachings, the mirror that shows the three kayas, the refinement of the three levels—the outer, inner and the innermost—the secrecy even greater than secrets, the unmistaken realization of Vajrasattva, the introduction to overturn samsara from its depths, and the way to awaken without cultivation.

OM VAJRA SATTVA HUNG

By simply proclaiming these words, the entire retinue was inspired by the unconditioned nature, and, with a single voice, they exclaimed:

Emaho, o marvel, Blessed Vajrasattva,
The sound of emptiness proclaimed,
This Secret Mantra of the greatest wonder
Has never reached my ears until this time,
So now I beg you, please explain its meaning.

As they beseeched using those words,
From within the vast, ineffable expanse
The teacher raised his voice and spoke:

Emaho, now listen, emanated retinue,
As I shall now explain the most sublime quintessence,

The true embodiment of every yana.
Retain it, with devout and unmistaken frame of mind.

Within the nature of this mind, pure from the beginning,
The unconfined expressions can be manifest as path,
So fruition of the great and primal liberation is achieved.
This quintessence of all vehicles
Is present in yourself—how wonderful!

These were the words he spoke.

And from the *Heart Essence, the Quintessence of All Vehicles*, this
was the first chapter, on the setting.

৯

Jamgön Kongtrül here describes Vimalamitra:

Attainer of the indestructible form of the rainbow body and crown ornament of five hundred panditas and siddhas—the master Vimalamitra arrived in Tibet where he bestowed the teachings of the Mahasandhi's Instruction Section upon Tingdzin Zangpo, the mendicant of Nyang, who had attained manifest clairvoyance and later also departed in a body of light. With Yudra Nyingpo as translator, Vimalamitra had the Thirteen Later Translations *of the Mind Section rendered into Tibetan. Tingdzin Zangpo received the oral lineage while the scriptures were concealed as a terma treasure, later to be revealed by Dangma Lhungyal who passed them on to Chetsün Senge Wangchuk in the eleventh century. As they gradually reached other masters, these teachings became known as* Vima Nyingtig, *the* Heart Essence of Vimalamitra.[132]

The first segment of this story, covering Uddiyana and India, can be found in Quintessential Dzogchen (Rangjung Yeshe 2006).

The Written
Narration: In Tibet

The Secret Heart Essence of the
Great Perfection, the Most Profound Quintessence.

Now follows the story of how the teachings were transmitted orally through sublime individuals to the Snowy Land of Tibet.

At this time and on this occasion, here in this central land of Tibet, the great Dharma-king Trisong Deutsen had built Glorious Samye. He had invited Padma, Bodhisattva and other masters from India. He had the lotsawas translate the sacred Dharma, and then promoted the Buddha's teachings to spread and flourish.

At this time, he thought, "I must make the Buddhadharma shine like the sun rising in the sky." So he sent the Indian king Singhabhadra[133] three *drey* of gold dust and [twenty-]five ingots of solid gold. He then dispatched Kawa Paltsek, Rinchen Chok of Ma and Chokro Lui Gyaltsen with this message:

> Singhabhadra, Dharma-king, pay heed!
> I offer you this gift of gold dust and ingots.
> In return, please send me a learned pandita
> With broad knowledge of the Sutra and Mantra teachings.
> In particular, I ask you to kindly consider Tibet,
> And send someone learned in the Secret Mantra.

These three envoys went to India and, upon reaching their destination, they presented the king with the written communication, the gold dust and the ingots. The king then went to the panditas gathered for a Dharma teaching to announce how the Tibetan king's messengers had arrived and what presents they had offered him.

Among the five hundred panditas, Jemalamudra[134] rose and said, "GUNA ATISHA ANG," which the envoys understood in three different ways. Kawa Paltsek understood it thus:

> When the boatman sitting in his boat
> Dares to take up oars and row,
> The boat will cross the waters.

According to the understanding of Chokro Lui Gyaltsen it meant:

> When the archer dares to let his arrow fly,
> Which his fingers' muscles have held back upon his bow,
> The arrow can then find its target.

Rinchen Chok of Ma understood it to mean:

> If you, the king, will dare to send
> Someone with the proper qualities,
> He will reach Tibet and bring great benefit.

Thus Jemalamudra consented to go. Then, to indicate his samaya, he brought a *kapali* four finger widths in size and also took along the mendicant Earth Essence as his attendant.

As the three Tibetan envoys escorted Jemalamudra, the Indian diviners of dreams all saw inauspicious signs. They dreamt that three Tibetan envoys carried off the sun and took it to Tibet. Some people adept in the art of swift feet were dispatched to spread the slander that the three Tibetan envoys who went to invite a pandita had brought back an adept of evil mantras to wreak disaster upon Tibet.

The three lotsawas then asked permission to invite the great pandita to Samye and meet with the Dharma-king, but the king said, "Tonight let him stay in the Golden Orphan Temple. I shall see him tomorrow."

It was then that the slander spread by the Indians was heard. The ministers said, "This man the three envoys have brought back is not a pandita but an *atasara* sorcerer. Please send him back to India."

The next morning the three lotsawas again asked permission to bring the pandita to see the ruler. The king said, "This pandita the three of you have brought back does not appear to be genuine. He must be examined."

The three lotsawas were downcast and depressed so that the luster on their faces faded. They then went to the Golden Orphan Temple and requested the pandita to pay his respect to the shrine objects. The pandita replied, "I do not pay homage to clay." The lotsawas thought to themselves, "I wonder, if someone does not pay homage to the shrine objects couldn't they be a *tramen* sorcerer?" The pandita perceived this and said:

> To Vairochana's form, a fabricated deity,
> I, Jemala, a deity of wisdom most sublime,
> Pays homage to the deity of fabrication.

Then by simply raising his right hand in the gesture of homage, all the statues of the deities turned to dust. The three lotsawas were amazed and conveyed this to the ruler but the Dharma-king responded, "So it is true: he is a tramen sorcerer. I didn't invite him here to destroy my statues."

The three lotsawas were now even sadder than before. The pandita perceived this and said:

> On the form body of Vairochana, the fabricated deity,
> Jemala, the supreme wisdom deity,
> Confers consecration and empowerment.

Placing his right hand where the head of the deity images had been, they reappeared even more splendid and blessed than before. The three lotsawas then related this story to the Dharma-king and upon hearing it he, his ministers and subjects were all overjoyed. So they made a welcome delegation, paid their respects and requested Vimalamitra to sit upon a three-tiered jeweled throne.

After presenting a mandala offering of gold and a lavish banquet, the king requested Vimalamitra to teach the Dharma. Consequently he [helped to] translate numerous teachings of the outer vehicle of philosophy and tantras, and scriptures of the inner Mantra. At night he taught all the tantras, statements and instructions of the Innermost Unexcelled Great Perfection to the great Dharma-king Trisong Deutsen and his sons, as well as to Tingdzin Zangpo the mendicant of Nyang, Kawa Paltsek and Chokro Lui Gyaltsen.

Henceforth, in the upper retreat place of the Stupa of Khardo, the great pandita Jemalamudra unfolded the mandala that subsumes the profound meaning of the *Secret Heart Essence of the Great Perfection* for the Dharma-king Trisong Deutsen, Prince Murub Tseypo, Tingdzin Zangpo of Nyang, Kawa Paltsek, Chokro Lui Gyaltsen, Drimey Dashar and other members of the court. Using numerous symbolic means he gave the pointing-out instructions. After having given the instructions on the development and completion of the *Secret Heart Essence* that subsumes the profound meaning, the *Essential Guidance* and the *Heart Essence*—the quintessence of his mind—that points out mind essence as being the guru and deity, he exhorted that these teachings be meticulously followed.

The four volumes of the profound *Secret Heart Essence* that contains the key points of instruction he concealed as a terma treasure at the Caverns of Chimpu; and after having given his final words known as *Three Statements of Pithy Advice* he departed for the Five-Peaked Mountain, Wu Tai Shan in China, without leaving a physical body behind. Thus, for as long as the teachings of the one thousand buddhas last, he will remain in the body of the great transformation for the benefit of beings. Every one hundred years he will miraculously appear once in the temples of Lhasa, Samye and other places where the people of pure karma can meet him in actuality and receive his instructions.

Following this, I, the mendicant of Nyang, made a volume of instructions that combine the four most profound scriptures of the *Secret Heart Essence*, and kept them in my custody.

᭝

Then follows the story of how Tingdzin Zangpo built the temple known as Uru Zhai Lhakhang, where he concealed the teachings of the Secret Heart Essence as a terma treasure and predicted that they would be revealed by a tertön named Ösel Gyuma Terzhey Tsal, a reincarnation of Prince Murub Tseypo, the son of King Trisong Deutsen, to appear in the sixteenth century.

Prahevajra's Three Words Striking the Vital Point is one of the famous "Testaments of the Vidyadharas." It has been translated into English innumerable times, pioneered by Tulku Thondup Rinpoche. Many readers may be familiar with Paltrul Rinpoche's wonderful poetic rephrasing of the Three Words and his auto-commentary. The account of how Manjushrimitra received this testament is found in several places in Wellsprings.

The following chapter presents the original scripture.

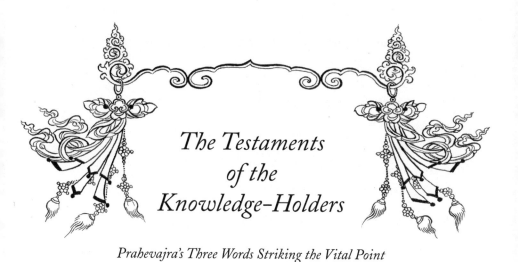

The Testaments
of the
Knowledge-Holders

Prahevajra's Three Words Striking the Vital Point

NAMO SHRI GURUYE
Homage to the confidence of realizing natural knowing.

> Since this awareness has no real existence
> Its natural radiance is totally unconfined,
> All that appears and exists manifests as the dharmakaya realm,
> And this manifestation is liberated in itself.

> This meaning that subsumes the insight of all sugatas,
> Three words of key advice, meant to revive your faint,[135]
> Resolves both samsara and nirvana,
> So bury these final words deep in your heart.
> A ITHI

Here is the instruction that utterly reveals awareness:
Recognizing your own nature,
Deciding on one point, and
Gaining confidence in liberation.

"Your own nature" being what is and "other" being what appears, you recognize their mingling. ITHI

Since all that appears is you and you are sovereign, you recognize your-self.

Recognize the mother as the mother.
Recognize the child as the child.
Recognize one within one.

Link yourself to this one knowing.
Link yourself to this one nature.
Link yourself to this one liberation.

Decide diversity within your nature.
Decide your displays within oneness.
Decide doubts within liberation. ITHI

To be certain of yourself is the confidence that is like a treasury.

To be certain of "other" is the confidence that is like a universal mon-arch.

To be certain of the state of liberation is the confidence that is like the sky dissolving into the sky. ITHI:

Free yourself within yourself.
Free one within one.
Unite mother and child. ITHI:

The "Seven Spikes of Shri Singha" is another of the famous testaments of the vidyadharas. The colophon mentions it was given at Auspicious Ten Thousand Gates in China.

How Jnanasutra received this testament from Shri Singha is told in source texts with similar wording:

"On the morning of the eighth day after his departure, a loud sound was heard. When Jnanasutra looked and saw the sublime master seated amidst a mass of light in the sky, he fell to the ground in a faint. After Jnanasutra had regained his senses, he saw that the heavens were illuminated amidst a mass of light and that all of the sky resounded with endless harmonies in the most melodious ways. The whole earth was quaking, trembling and shaking, and was covered with boundless heaps of flowers of gold, silver and other types. When he had uttered words of grief, Shri Singha's testament, the Seven Spikes, fell into the palm of Jnanasutra's hand."

The Seven Spikes
of Shri Singha

Shri Singha's testament to Jnanasutra

SARVA SANTIKA

Homage to lucid emptiness, the perfect insight.

All-pervasive, it appears in countless ways—
Wakeful knowing, boundless, undirected.
So I planted heavy spikes into the changeless ground,
Driving seven spikes between samsara and nirvana,
Changeless, greatest bliss arose within my mind.

Like a ray of sunlight to revive you from your faint,
This instruction in the ultimate has the secret meaning.
Open wide the treasure-door to a lucid insight
And, like a wish-fulfilling jewel, realize this meaning:

Drive the spike of unimpeded, lucid wakefulness between
    samsara and nirvana.
Drive the spike of the lamp of self-display between object and
    the knower.
Drive the spike of self-pure essence between mind and matter.

Drive the spike of unbound view between permanence and
nothingness.

Drive the spike of dharma-less knowing between dharmas and
dharmata.

Drive the spike of five wide-open doors between dullness and
agitation.

Drive the spike of primordially perfected dharmakaya between
appearance and emptiness.

ITHI: 𑁍

Your natural face unveiled by cognizance, to let self-freed insight be in
the face of "other" is like grass meeting fire.

Seeing appearances to be directly freed, to have gained mastery over
thought movement is like a dark room meeting light.

To truly see the fourfold meaning of the primordially pure knowing is
like an amorous man and woman meeting.

To transcend concerns, since your natural boundless wakefulness dawns
as your own state, is like a face meeting [itself in] a mirror.

Since the myriad thoughts, beyond view and meditation, dawn as a display, they are like frost being touched by the sun.

To see the equality of objects and their conditions, having primordially
sealed appearance and existence with the original state, is like meeting your
only child.

Since dharmakaya free from effort and striving has never been separable
from you, to let the world and beings dissolve in their natural state is like a
pauper finding a treasure.

ITHI: 𑁍

When Shri Singha was about to enter the state beyond the world's sorrow,
he ascended into midair engulfed within a mass of lights. Jnanasutra fell to
the ground crying out, "Alas, alas!"

Right then, he heard a voice from the sky. As he regained his senses he
looked up and from amidst the lights Shri Singha's right arm appeared and
to wake him from the faint a one-inch casket of precious gemstone landed

in the palm of his hand. The moment it touched his hand, he attained the confidence of realization.

This completes *The Seven Spikes*, which resemble leading a blind man, the testament of Shri Singha that was given at Auspicious Ten Thousand Gates.

ॐ

Nagarjuna

Some of the early Mind Section sources mention a few additional details of the lineage masters. Here are a few more:

Manjushrimitra was the son of Shri Kumara, the king of Singala. By practicing the Secret Manjushri Tantra he attained a vision of Yamantaka and received the yidam deity's prophecy. He gained certainty through the specific tradition of the Great Perfection, unmixed with other vehicles, fulfilled his guru's wishes and, to ensure that the teachings would endure for a long time, composed texts covering the seven qualities and twelve topics of training in the unconditioned awakened mind of the Great Perfection. In India's sandalwood forests he taught Dhanadala, a king from the east.

Bodhi the Yakshini, the daughter of Angiraja the king of the yakshas, was a disciple of Vajrapani. He took command over all the yakshas, and attained perfect realization of the Secret Mantra of the Mahayana in both view and conduct. She in turn taught Sarati the Courtesan.

Sarati the Courtesan was always engaged in the ten spiritual activities; she had a vision of the female deity Buddhalochana and composed the text on the Great Perfection known as Wheel of Life-Force. *She became the teacher of Brilliance in Kashmir's turquoise forest.*

Brilliance, the son of Eminent Moon, the king of Kashmir, was a master learned in the fields of knowledge. He attained a vision of the female deity Chunda and composed the scripture on the Great Perfection known as Sublime King Scripture of Awakened

Mind. *The Kashmiri master Brilliance became the teacher of the virtuous courtesan Arali in the Drumabriksha forest.*

Arali the Courtesan attained a vision of the heruka mandala through the practice of Buddha Samayoga and became capable of reducing the "cities of heretics" to dust. She composed the scripture on the Great Perfection known as Luminosity of Awakened Mind. *Arali became the teacher of Nagarjuna Garbha. This is the view of her realization:*

> *As I am Arali the Courtesan,*
> *I take my mind to be the king of all instructions.*
> *For whom that sees the nature of this mind*
> *That is itself the king of views.*

Nagarjuna Garbha, the son of a brahmin householder, was foretold in numerous sutras and tantras. He accomplished the Great Peacock dharani mantra and the alchemy of transforming base metal into gold through which he was able to benefit others. This bodhisattva who had attained the seventh level also composed the scripture on the Great Perfection known as Compendium of Awakened Mind. *He in turn taught Samanta.*

Samanta, the daughter of the courtesan Sucharya, a woman tireless in helping beings by means of the ten spiritual activities and the virtuous actions. She attained a vision of the goddess Tara and became the teacher of Kukkuraja, the second Dog King, at the ocean in the northwestern part of Uddiyana.

The following songs from the twenty-one learned ones of the Mind Section were revealed by the knowledge-holder Longsal Nyingpo (1625-1692) of the Katok tradition through the blessing he received from Vimalamitra. Longsal Nyingpo was one of the great tertöns responsible for the revival of Katok Monastery.

Before the actual songs, the Rangjung Nyagchik gives these details of the lineage through the twenty-one Indian panditas of the effortless vehicle. It is included since several of these teachers have varying names:

Samantabhadra; Vajrasattva; Prahevajra; Manjushrimitra; from him to (Dhahena Talo); Rajadheva the senior prince; from him to Princess Paramita; from her to Takshaka the naga king; from him to Bodhi the Yakshini; from her to Sarati the Courtesan (Parani); she taught Brilliance the Kashmiri scholar; he taught Maharaja the scholar of Uddiyana; he taught Princess Gomadevi; she taught Aloke the Atsantra; he taught Kukkuraja the Dog King; he taught Paramita the Rishi; he taught Purasati the Courtesan; she taught Nagarjuna; he taught Dog King the Younger (Kukkuraja Dhahuna); he taught Manjushri[mitra] the Younger; he taught Bhararaja Muletsün (Devaraja); he taught Buddhagupta;[136] he taught Shri Singha; he taught Kungamo the virtuous;[137] and she taught Vimalamitra.

Twenty-One Songs of Self-Existing Oneness

From the Self-Existing Oneness
of the Effortless Great Perfection: The Heart Essence of the
Realization of the Twenty-One Indian Panditas
of the Effortless Vehicle

Prahevajra sang to Manjushrimitra:

> I, Delightful Vajra,
> With the play of mind resolved,
> Realized this play to be dharmadhatu's light
> Thus the yidam Unity and I are two no more.

Manjushrimitra sang to Dhahena Talo:

> I, the kinsman of Manjushri,
> Resolved the play of rigpa and all wisdom displays
> To be naught but dharmadhatu's play—
> Now everything arises as adornment.

King Dhahena Talo sang to Rajadeva, the senior prince:[138]

> I am Dhahena Talo, who fathers
> All of dharmadhatu's plays.
> Phenomena are fully liberated
> By simply realizing this, the single door, the source of all.

Rajahasti sang to Princess Paramita:

> I am Rajahasti.
> When all arisings, means in its display,
> And the emptiness of insight have a single taste
> Everything is freed within this equal state.

Paramita sang to Takshaka, the naga king:

> I am Paramita
> Who sees the play of dharmadhatu.
> This multitude of thoughts are one in Mother's basic space;
> Not seen as two, they all dissolve in sameness.

Takshaka, the naga king, sang to Bodhi the Yakshini:

> I am Takshaka, the naga king.
> Self-dissolved, the poisons turned to nectar.
> Having seen my nature, like ambrosia,
> Everything is now dharmakaya's play.

Bodhi the Yakshini sang to the courtesan Sarati:

> I am Bodhi the Yakshini,
> Not two are mind and its own effulgence—
> Dharmas now subside into the vastness of their basic space;
> Freed as dharmakaya, they adorn my realization.

Sarati the Courtesan sang to Brilliance, the Kashmiri scholar:

> I am Sarati the Courtesan.
> I saw the fact that mind is neither male nor female;
> And seeing nonduality my duality dissolved.
> Behold the wakeful vastness of the total freedom!

Gomadevi the Princess

The Kashmiri scholar sang to Maharaja, the scholar of Uddiyana:

I, the scholar Brilliance,
Recognize that knowledge in its countless forms
Is the play of single wakefulness;
Now every aspect rises as adornment.

The scholar Maharaja sang to Princess Gomadevi:

I am Maharaja.
Accompanied by his retinue of unconfined display,
The sovereign of wisdom-play
Is the very essence of the kingdom of all-knowing.

Gomadevi sang to Aloke the Atsantra:

I am Gomadevi
For whom the play of wisdom, the expression of awareness,
And the wakeful vastness are no longer two—
An adornment that unfolds the twofold purpose.

Aloke the Atsantra sang to Kukkuraja the Dog King:

I am Aloke, the scholar.

Kukkuraja the Younger

As everything has but a single essence
Beyond both one and many,
Remain within this single vastness beyond all limitations.

Kukkuraja sang to the rishi Parati:

I am Kukkuraja.
The single taste of good and evil concepts
Is dharmakaya's ornament within the basic space,
The state of sameness that is not duality.

Parati the Rishi sang to the courtesan Putamati:

I am the rishi Parati.
Having gained a perfect insight into mind
All things are known by wakefulness—
Behold the inner confidence you too will find.

Putamati the Courtesan sang to Nagarjuna:

I am Putamati the Courtesan.
This wakefulness, pure from the beginning,
Enfolds within its space all thoughts and all emotions
And purifies desire into discriminating wisdom.

Nagarjuna sang to Kukkuraja the Younger:[139]

> I am Nagarjuna
> Whose passions have dissolved within the space of insight.
> With timeless freedom that transcends attachment,
> On dharmakaya's basic purity they are a splendid ornament.

Dhahuna the Dog King sang to Manjushrimitra the Younger:

> I am Kukku Dhahuna.
> The hordes of thoughts and of emotions I devoured
> To spread the glow of all five wisdoms,
> And now the perfect wisdom of the fourfold joys has manifest.

Manjushrimitra the Younger sang to Devaraja Muley Tsen:

> I, Manjushri the Younger,
> Have unlocked the secret of the wakeful mind,
> Fathomed the very depths of insight's wakefulness,
> And totally perfected them into splendid wisdom.

Devaraja sang to Buddhagupta:

> I am Devaraja.
> By the splendor of dharmata all dharmas are adorned.
> This very nature is itself adorned by total freedom,
> A state of total freedom that is one of greatest bliss.

Buddhagupta sang to Shri Singha:

> I am Buddhagupta;
> Clinging's tether has been cut with a capacity,
> The nonduality of essence and its nature,
> Freed into the cut without cutting.

Shri Singha sang to Kungamo the Virtuous:

> I am Shri Singha
> Who blossomed in the space of wakeful knowing
> And through the equal vastness of this vast and open space
> This wakeful essence is the perfect liberation.

Kungamo the Virtuous sang to Vimalamitra:

I am Kungamo the Virtuous.
In Prajnaparamita's vast, the basic space of things,
Great mother of all conquerors,
Your insight yields a true perfection.

ᛋ

Padmasambhava's more lengthy account of the twelve buddhas of the Great Perfection is presented here. It was revealed by Taksham Nüden Dorje (Samten Lingpa) in the 17th century. Another version with different details can be found within the Lama Gongdü *termas of Sangye Lingpa (1340-1396). There are also the pithy and profound* Testaments—*one for each of the twelve buddhas*—*revealed by Dorje Lingpa (1346-1405) within his amazing terma cycle the* Father Tantra View of Vastness. *Vimalamitra's and Padmasambhava's original narrations have been copied by historians innumerable times over the centuries.*

Besides the Vima Nyingtig, *this account is one of the longest versions I could find and deserved inclusion even though it seems to have only eleven Dzogchen teachers. Repeatedly copied by hand over the centuries, perhaps Youth Playful Grace and Gentle Splendor Protector Against Fear became counted as one where in other sources they are two.*

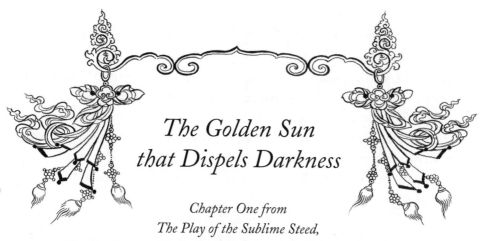

The Golden Sun
that Dispels Darkness

Chapter One from
The Play of the Sublime Steed,
The Confluence of Insight of All Yidams: the history that narrates
the sequence of transmission of the three yogas and the precious masters.

ग्रᨿᨩ᩠ᨶᨻᨯᨶ᩠ᨳᨦᩬ

Homage to the secret yidam deity.

From *The Play of the Sublime Steed, The Confluence of Insight of All Yidams,* here I shall explain the history that narrates the sequence of transmission.

To quote *The Self-Liberation of Samsara and Nirvana Root Tantra, the Instruction Tantra of the Play of the Sublime Steed*:

> Three teachers and their threefold places,
> Triple sphere of influence with a triad retinue,
> Times of teaching and so forth—fifteen are taught.

To explain this there are four chapters: how the mind lineage was transmitted, how the symbolic lineage was transmitted in the noble land, how the hearing lineage was transmitted to Tibet and how the blessings were transmitted to Tsogyal.

The Mind Lineage

Within the vastness of the basic space—which by nature is a total purity, the dharmadhatu palace of Akanishtha, unformed and from the very first spontaneously perfected, appearance and emptiness undivided, the union of means and knowledge—samsara and nirvana remained as natural liberation. This was the transcendent conqueror, the glorious Samantabhadra in union with his consort.

Let me explain. This dharmakaya immaculate, which in essence is comprised of nothing whatsoever, appeared in compassionate form with face and arms and adorned with all the major and the minor marks of excellence to the eyes of those to be inspired. And yet within the state that lies beyond every type of fabricated concepts, the place which is the Akanishtha palace, swirling in the fivefold hues of wisdom lights, he entrusted in completeness his insight to the great Vajradhara, the sixth conqueror, and anointed him to be his regent most sublime.

Having conferred this blessing, when the compassion spontaneously welled forth for all the beings to be guided, he showed himself within the spheres of their perception in countless forms possessing all the major and the minor marks. And so this conqueror, the great Vajradhara, many eons prior to the first kalpa in the realm Complete Array, presented the buddha Exquisite Flower with a golden vajra and formed the resolve [to attain supreme enlightenment]. Two lives later, in Swaying Array to the north, he was born as Jewel Garland. His father's name was Noble Giving and his mother was Sublime Giving. At the age of twenty-five he listened to the Dharma from the buddha Eminent Destroyer of Samsara.

Following that he took birth as Generous Hand, in the city of Sky-Holder on the continent Euphoria, to Lightning Flash and his wife Ravishing Beauty. He heard the Dharma from the buddha Virtuous Wisdom and for seven years remained in samadhi. At the age of seventy-five, on the peak of Mount Array of Precious Gems he awakened to true enlightenment. And then, in but a single instant, from within the vast expanse beyond mental constructs, his mind of the immense self-existing wakefulness was moved to manifest as the sambhogakaya and thus he remained as the teacher of the three kayas, accompanied by countless sugatas of the five families, who are the inexhaustible adornment wheels of body, speech and mind.

In the time of dharmakaya, within the domain of dharmadhatu, he perfected the deeds as the nature of the teacher Samantabhadra while surrounded by countless buddhas, a retinue magically emanated from his own wakeful knowing. The teaching was known as the natural vajra of dharmata not formed by anyone whatsoever. The time was that of purity, of seeing dharmata. At this time he displayed each of the twelve deeds of body, speech and mind; and he perfected the attributes of perfect enjoyment.

Following this he manifested in the form of sambhogakaya, in the place, the realm of Densely Arrayed, as the teacher Vairochana Immense Ocean. In his hands, in equanimity, there were twenty-one buddha fields tiered one above the other and beautifying each other like a dome of brocade. In each of these there were teachers and so forth, retinues and beings to be guided in fivefold aspects. Below his waist were sixteen realms shaped like a canopy, like evenly distributed heaps of grain. His retinues were boundless buddhas of the fivefold families. The teaching was the wisdom of speech, unformed by anyone, the unexcelled Secret Mantra. The time was that of dharmata unchanging. The deeds that he displayed were twelve in each of his activities of body, speech and mind.[140]

Nirmanakayas unfolded from sambhogakaya. As the discerning faculty of self-existing wakefulness faced outward, this sovereign of all the doctrines of awakened ones taught in actuality and as reflections. This time has no discernible origination since there was not an actual body of a buddha.

Furthermore, each of the triple kayas has a basic intent for the context of the wisdom body, speech and mind: the wisdoms of the dharmakaya's body, speech and mind, the wisdoms of the sambhogakaya's body, speech and mind, and the wisdoms of the nirmanakaya's body, speech and mind. And thus, wherever teachings were successively transmitted, from Samantabhadra onwards, the blessings were endowed with countless miracles.

The deeds of the nirmanakayas appear in manifold ways to cause beings to become expert in words. Due to understanding the nature beyond conceptual focus of the variegated sambhogakaya, beings become skilled in the Buddha's teachings. Due to understanding the dharmakaya insight in completeness beyond rejection, they become skilled in the transmission of the pith instructions of the masters. Even during the time of following generations, unless there is the mind transmission of the buddha's form, the ordinary body will not be liberated from samsara. Without the insight transmission of speech, the voice cannot be liberated. Without the insight transmission of mind, the mind will not be liberated from samsara.

To whom were these transmissions of body, speech and mind conferred? Dharmakaya transmitted to sambhogakaya, and sambhogakaya appeared as nirmanakaya and is thus known as nirmanakaya Vajradhara.

The first beings to be guided by this nirmanakaya—during the time when a lifespan could last an incalculable number of years, in the place known as the realm Abundant Delight—were the beings who were born with bodies of light, the subtle essences of the elements, and all took birth instantaneously. In order to guide them, Vajradhara appeared in the form of omniscient enlightenment upon a golden lotus with a thousand petals, to benefit beings and became renowned as Vajrasattva. At this time upon each lotus petal his body, speech and mind appeared with their own respective retinues. This occurrence of one thousand and two teachers was an auspicious sign that one thousand and two buddhas would appear in this Good Eon. This was when the deva children Brilliant Sun and Flawless Moon took miraculous birth. All the senses emerged; six million four hundred thousand radiant stars appeared in the sky; the cows of bounty, the horses of wisdom, the food of joy, pools of light and, together with the light of the sun and moon shining from oneself, a life could last an incalculable number of years.[141]

Every thousand years the lifespan diminished and emotions slightly increased so that merit waned until there gradually came a time when a lifespan would last ten million years. At that time the teacher Vajradhara took birth in the beautiful five-colored egg composed of the essences of the elements and appeared under the name Immutable Light.[142] The teacher's form and all other beings were born from eggs, so that their forms and countenance were extremely youthful, their senses natural and their radiant limbs all fully

Youth of Immutable Light

formed. All of them had the youthful forms and clear faculties of a sixteen-year-old. Each body was adorned with light extending one bow's length, and miraculously, like the flames of butter lamps, everyone appeared transparent. The teachings were the mother tantras, the Dharma of discriminating knowledge; the retinue was an assembly of two hundred thousand dakinis, who received this sublime teaching by means of which they, in their female forms, attained accomplishment. And there were auspicious signs that these two hundred thousand dakinis would awaken to buddhahood.

Eventually, in the Saha world-system, humans descending from devas in the realm the Four Great Kings indulged in desirous yearning, one of the four emotions. The four sections of tantras appeared among the Dharma of skillful means. The three poisonous emotions forced the three lower realms to be formed out of the negative actions of body, speech and mind, perpetuating karmic causes and effects.

At this time it was once more in the place of Tushita in the grand mansion that the teacher took birth from a womb and appeared in the form of a ten-year-old child. The name under which he became renowned was Youth Playful Grace (also known as Gentle Splendor Protector Against Fear).

In this manner, Shakra, the king of the gods, in his exquisite palace of total victory in the kingdom of the thirty-three devas arose to rule over all of the desire realms. In the exquisite site known as Healing Garden to the south of this palace, the teacher transformed himself into the body of a bodhisattva and, considering the six classes of beings outwardly, magically conjured forth the six Munis; and thus taught the Dharma of the six paramitas, to the retinue of seven successive buddhas. The compiler was the deva son Club Wielder, and the benefactor was Shakra himself.[143]

As sustenance he lived on herbal oils and to the retinue of seven successive buddhas, when the lifespan was seventy thousand years, he gave the teachings on the Great Perfection, the tantras beyond effort and remained doing so for seventy-five years. When the first light of dawn appeared he passed completely beyond sorrow and a testament fell into the hand of his attendant Manibhadra. Following that he remained for seven thousand years in the lion mountain samadhi.

Then again compassion moved the teacher's heart to consider sentient beings. In a barbarous, forbidden location on the northeastern side of Mount Sumeru was the mansion where the wrathful vajra bearers cavort known as Yaksha Palace. And it was there that he enacted the drama of entering the womb of Kameshvari, an abrasive and violent dakini who was the consort of a beastly yaksha by the name Lion Face the Raksha. The moment the teacher emerged from the womb, twelve moons rose simultaneously and the earth trembled seven times. Loud sounds of musical instruments were heard from all directions. This teacher named Powerful Warrior Youth had appeared in the terrifying form of a midget with three heads and six arms.

In this place lived countless dakinis and his retinue of seven, which included the bodhisattva Vigorous Cloud, were the above-mentioned six Munis and Manibhadra in the form of the yaksha Noble Conduct. Seated amidst masses of clouds, emerging from their waist up, they listened to the teachings with joined palms. The compiler was Vajrapani who emerged from the breath of his nostrils. The benefactors were the dakinis Serene Purna, Conch of Brahma's Voice, Lion Face, Peacock Neck, Mirror Face, as well as the rishi Moonlight and others.

Gentle Splendor Protector Against Fear

For the teachings he considered Maitreya and gave the outer father tantras, considering Vajrapani he gave the inner mother tantras, considering Amrita Kundali he gave the secret *Self-Arising Awareness* and considering all of them he taught the unexcelled *Self-Liberation of Samsara and Nirvana.* There he remained for one thousand years teaching the Dharma to the dakinis, and then, at the break of day, the teacher passed beyond sorrow. His testament was given to the yaksha son Noble Conduct.[144]

The merit of beings continued to decrease; it waned further and further every thousand years, so that the lifespan of people now could only stretch sixty thousand years. The teacher remained in the samadhi known as the majestically poised lion for a hundred thousand years. The one known as Noble Conduct was later to be born as Prahevajra.

Thereupon, when a lifespan could last ten thousand years, the teacher arose from his samadhi and, on an ocean isle in the western part of the Jambu continent, in the exquisite palace, a sanctuary known as Rakshapurna, in a domain where countless bodhisattvas lived—including Avalokiteshvara, Taradevi, Vajrapani, Manjushri and others—he was miraculously conceived as the son of the *raksha* Lion Face and his consort the *rakshini* Shamsham. When emerging from the womb, male and female devas honored him with clouds of offerings, and he was named Wrathful Sage King.

Encircled by a retinue of ten million rakshas the benefactors were assemblies of yakshas, rakshas and nagas. The teachings he gave were the Hayagriva tantras: *Horse Head Saccha* as the body tantra, *Supreme Steed Display* as the speech tantra, *Lotus Net* as the mind tantra, *Blooming Lotus* as the tantra of qualities and *Heruka Display* as the tantra of activities.

Moreover, he taught the *Kilaya of Peak Array,* the *Tantra of Kilaya Perfection,* the *Eighty Deeds of Yamantaka, the Magical Wheel of the Sun and Moon, Yamantaka's Cutting the Stream of Karma,* the *Ever-Excellent Salasakra of the Mothers,* the *Raksha Wish of the Black Mother's Secret Heart, Shri Ekajati Wrathful Mother,* the *Tantra of the Female Raksha Slayer.* Having considered their undisciplined demeanor he taught these and other such tantras to tame rough-minded beings. The compiler was the Ten-Headed Ravana of Lanka, and for two thousand years the teacher worked for their benefit. Finally he passed beyond this world's sorrow on the mountain where tigers and lions frolic to the northeast, without bestowing a testament, and then remained for five thousand years in the samadhi known as the sporting lion.

Thereupon, when a lifespan could last five thousand years, on the ornament of the Jambu continent known as Vulture Peak Mountain, in King Jawari's capital Rajgir, at the place replete with natural virtues, situated to the north of the source of shravakas, pratyekabuddhas and buddhas,[145] and which housed exceptional shrines including a *sharira*-filled stupa, the teacher entered the womb of Radiant, the magnificent wife of Excellent Lion. Upon his birth, dakinis, devas, nagas, yakshas, garudas and many other beings gathered in the skies like cloud banks, each carrying their own types of delightful offerings, and the teacher was named Sublime Golden Light. Fully grown by the age of three he became adept at sports and arts.

When the teacher reached twenty-five he went before the sharira-filled stupa, shaved his own hair and became a renunciate. His retinue was the eight noble shravakas endowed with miraculous powers and many others. The benefactors were King Jawari and the brahmin maiden Subahu. The teachings he taught were, among others, the Vinaya, the *Mother in Five Hundred Segments* and the *Seven Hundred Thousand.* The compiler was the noble Ananda and for seven years he fulfilled their wishes. It was in the time when a lifespan could last five thousand years.

When the lifespan of people could last one thousand years, in the center of the northern land of Turquoise-Browed Sogpos was the self-appeared stupa Shankara Kuta known as Enchanting Mound. At this site grew a bodhi tree and there, the teacher appeared in the form known as Lovingly Playful Wisdom.

His retinue was the eighth level bodhisattva Matibhadra and countless other bodhisattvas. The benefactor was Lion-Face of Turquoise-Browed Sogpos and the goddess Effulgence. The teachings he taught were the *Kulayaraja,* the *All-Creating King, Play of the Cuckoo Bird,* the *Great Prophecy of Awakened Mind,* the *Intrinsic Greatness of Samantabhadra,* the *Great Space,* the *Masterful Display,* the *Sublime Wisdom,* the *Slivering Wheel,* the *Essence Studded Tantra,* the *Great Blaze,* the *Studded Jewels,* the *Black Naga Tamer*

Truly Perfected King

Subsequent Tantra, the *Dark Red Jackal Tantra of the Mother Deities* and all the activity tantras. The compiler was the bodhisattva Akashagarbha and the teacher remained there for one hundred and twenty years.

When a lifespan could last five hundred years, it was in the southern Blissful Grove on the Vulture Peak from the plateau of the Thirty-Three Gods that the teacher considered sentient beings' suffering of old age and magically appeared in the form of Kashyapa the Elder.

His retinue was six arhats, emanations of the six Munis, and the rishi youth Guarded Mind. All seven of them magically assumed the forms of arhats and listened to the Dharma. The benefactors were the brahmin Good Sign and Virtuous Eyes. The teachings he taught were sutras, the *Array of Ati* and many others. Shariputra Noble Starlight compiled the teachings. Having resided there for seventy-five years Kashyapa the Elder proceeded to the bank of Narajara where he remained in austerity, not moving from the vajra-posture for a full seven years.

To the northeast of Vulture Peak he then took seat at the Vajra Throne with his back against the bodhi tree. At dusk he defeated the maras by remaining composed in the samadhi of courageous movement. At midnight he attained true enlightenment by remaining composed in the vajra-like samadhi. At the first break of dawn, he manifested the samadhi of magical illusion. As the day broke he departed in a mass of light together with the vanishing of his physical remains.

The testament bestowed upon the rishi youth Guarded Mind was *Single Child Seed Tantra* and the *Final Testament*.[146]

Thereupon, when a lifespan could last three hundred years, in the center of the Jambu continent, at the Vajra Throne, the source of every learned and virtuous master, the teacher magically emanated himself to be born as the son of Virtuous Goodness, a brahmin adept in the Vedas, and his wife, the dakini Splendid Giving. The teacher was given the name Truly Perfected King.

His retinue was comprised of the lords of the three families and others; the benefactor was Manibhadra, a prosperous trader's son. The Dharma he taught was exclusively the teachings on the definitive meaning, the *Final Subsequent Tantra Devourer of a Billion Worlds,* the *Lotus Segment* and others. The compiler was Subahu the Divine Giver. Having remained there for twenty-five years, he passed beyond the world of sorrow for the benefit of his last disciples, demonstrating the process of birth, old age, sickness and death.

When a lifespan could last one hundred years, to the east of Kapilavastu in India, the teacher then took birth in Anathapindada's pleasure grove and with the words "I am Shakya sage, exalted chief of teachers," he took seven steps in each of the four directions. A lotus sprung forth in each place he touched and he was named Shakyamuni.

Encircled by his retinue of five eminent ones, he taught the teachings of the four truths as the Dharma-wheel, turning it twelve times. He performed the play of twelve deeds and then, as his bodily form had vanished from the perception of disciples, the teaching through his physical form was completed.

ᠺ

Padmasambhava also explains that: "The remains of Buddha Shakyamuni filled eight drey measures. Seven were kept and honored by seven various kings while one drey was taken by the nagas. One of his four incisors was taken to the plateau of the Thirty-Three Gods, one remained in the town Graceful, one was kept as an object of veneration by the king of Kalingka, and the fourth by the naga king in the city Utrayana. His shroud, ashes, pyre, sarcophagus and the like were all carried off by various individuals to be placed as shrine objects in their respective homelands. His mind—within the continuity of unconditioned suchness—manifested in the form of the sixth great Vajradhara and appeared in Akanishtha."

The chapter concludes with Padmasambhava's explanation of the outer, inner and innermost aspects of the twelve deeds in regards to body, speech and mind, followed by the various terma lineages.

Moreover, Padmasambhava continues in the next chapter to mention that Prahevajra arrived three hundred and sixty years after Buddha Shakyamuni. Manjushrimitra appeared five hundred and forty-four years after Buddha Shakyamuni and passed away three hundred and twenty-five years after that. Shri Singha arrived eight hundred and thirty years after the Buddha, after having received the instructions from Manjushrimitra. Shri Singha passed the Heart Essence on to three: Padmasambhava, Jnanasutra and Vimalamitra with a seal of secrecy. At that time nine hundred and ninety-four years had passed since the Buddha's nirvana.

PART V
Chokgyur Lingpa's Revelations

This, the ultimate of all vehicles,
Was perfectly compiled by Vajrasattva,
Who, appearing as lords of the three families,
Spread it throughout the three realms,
Liberating countless beings into the body of light.
The master, Prahevajra,
Received it from Vajrasattva in person,
Then transmitted it to Manjushrimitra,
From whom Shri Singha received it;
This gracious master
Bestowed it upon me, Padmasambhava.
I now teach it to the king, subject and companion.
Conceal it as a treasure for the sake of the future.
SAMAYA. ༔

> —*From the Heart Essence of Samantabhadra,*
> *a terma treasure revealed by Chokgyur Lingpa.*

Sangye Lingpa the Treasure Revealer

About the Three Sections of the Great Perfection Jamgön Kongtrül wrote:

"Mind Section: the Outer Cycle, like the body, is the intent stated in such tantras and scriptures as Kulayaraja, the All-Creating King, the Eighteen Marvels of Mind and others.

"Space Section: the Inner Cycle, like the heart, is the meaning stated in such tantras and scriptures as Samantabhadra's Royal Tantra of All-Inclusive Vastness and others.

"Instruction Section: Similar to moxabustion applied directly to the vital point, this extraordinary Secret Cycle is like the heart-blood or the pure essence of the life-force, the intent stated in the Seventeen Tantras and other such scriptures—the Bindu Section of the Innermost Cycle that elucidates the key points of oral instruction."

In his empowerment manual for the Three Sections of the Great Perfection, *the* Dzogchen Desum, *Dudjom Rinpoche, an exceptional master of recent times, described this terma treasure in these words: "Among the innumerable teaching lineages for the unexcelled Ati Yoga, these are Shri Singha's instructions which contain the ultimate realization that he imparted to the lord of conquerors Padmasambhava and to the great translator Vairotsana. It is the refined essence of their personal practice—the sacred Dharma of the Great Perfection."*

In his memoir Blazing Splendor *Tulku Urgyen Rinpoche describes his great grandfather thus, "Chokgyur Lingpa was an authentic tertön. He was the reincarnation of Prince Murub, the second son of the great king Trisong Deutsen, who established Buddhism in Tibet. Another of his former lives was Sangye Lingpa.[147] Chokgyur Lingpa was the 'owner' of seven distinct transmissions and is often counted as the last of one hundred tertöns of major importance. He is regarded as the 'universal monarch of all tertöns,' in part because no other tertön has revealed a teaching that includes the Space Section of Dzogchen. There are several Mind Section revelations, and all major tertöns reveal the Instruction Section. But only Chokgyur Lingpa transmitted the Space Section. This is why his Three Sections of the Great Perfection is considered the most extraordinary terma he ever revealed."*

Jamyang Khyentse Wangpo taught that generally in the Dzogchen teachings, the outer Mind Section (semde) *mainly describes the luminosity, the inner Space Section* (longde) *mainly describes the emptiness, and the innermost Instruction Section* (men-ngagde) *describes luminosity and emptiness as a unity.*

The sections are actually quite similar, but those showing mind as mainly cognizant are called mind section, those showing it mainly to be empty are the space section, and those teachings that mainly teach it as the unity of being cognizant and empty, belong to the Instruction Section.

—*Tulku Urgyen Rinpoche, unpublished teaching, 1982*

Vimalakirti

Tulku Urgyen Rinpoche once asked Dzongsar Khyentse Rinpoche about the Three Sections of the Great Perfection:

He replied, "It is the combined heart essence of Padmasambhava, Vairotsana, and Vimalamitra that they received from their guru Shri Singha, their primary guru for the teachings of the Great Perfection.[148] So far it hasn't been widely propagated and practiced in Tibet; it's a concealed teaching, meant to be practiced in hidden places. I believe the time is yet to come when it will benefit a great many beings. I wouldn't suppose those three masters combined their efforts for no purpose—enlightened beings who can see the future wouldn't do something pointless, would they?" That's all he would say.

—*Tulku Urgyen Rinpoche,* Blazing Splendor

It is therefore an auspicious way to conclude this book by offering a selection of songs from the masters of these three sections.

King Jah the Worthy One

Vajra Songs from the Masters of the Outer Cycle

ཨོཾ་ སྭཱ་སྟི་སིདྡྷཾ༔

Here are the vajra songs from masters of the Outer Cycle.

These were the words Vimalakirti from the clan of the Licchavis
Sang in Jeweled Mansion at the early break of dawn:

A HO༔
For I, Vimalakirti, sky-yogi of the Secret Mantra,
Perceptions of sense objects are the basic space itself—
Naught but a freely resting knowing, left alone.
The inside and the outside, wide open and nondual, are a single
    lucid wakeful state.

These were the words the king of devas sang in the Victorious Mansion
At a time of greatest bliss transcending time:

As Shakra, king of gods, the lord of greatest bliss in natural
    clarity,
Clings not to blissful objects, realizing that displays are all
    illusion,
Self-liberated and beyond a focus, all appearances ineffable,

Meteor Face the Yaksha

In dharmata's vastness, self-arising self-dissolving has now
    reached completeness.

These were the words the yaksha Meteor Face sang below the Jeweled
Tree when mingling *sem* and *rigpa,* child and mother:

Dharmadhatu's natural clarity, contained by mind completely,
A vastness of the view, which even Ever-Excellent does not
    behold.
But not disproved as nothing, this essence of a lucid
    wakefulness;
As illusion's body breaks its seal, it mingles with the clear and
    perfect king of space.

Skillful Wisdom the Raksha sang these words on Blazing Fire Mountain's summit at the second part of dawn:

As I, the Skillful Wisdom, for whom arising and dissolving are
    concurrent,
Remain within the timeless state of undirected space,
The sun of pure and lucid wakefulness has risen in my mind;
And now this unity of empty knowing is like the sky suffused
    with brightest sunlight.

Bodhisattva, King of Nagas, sang these words in Jewel Mansion at the
time of discerning the nonduality of sem and rigpa:

Ignorance, this bond so tightly tied,
Loosed by no one else has come undone all by itself.
Seeing rigpa—timeless, self-existing—I am uncontrived, for
    nothing need be done.
In complete nondwelling, I am free from concepts of a
    meditation.

King Jah, the Worthy One, sang these words in the Grand Feast Hall of
Dakinis as the sun rose on the sky:

As I, King Jah, the Worthy One,
Made bliss illusory my path,

Skillful Wisdom the Raksha

By training in the Great Perfection
All sense perceptions of the sixfold types,
Now free from judgments of accepting and rejecting,
Are self-arising, self-dissolving blissful states.
I have realized the vast nonaction beyond concepts.

Prahevajra, the knowledge-holder, sang these words from the basic space of phenomena at the time when luminous mind-essence shone within Vajrasattva's vastness:

For I, the human knowledge-holder Prahevajra,
Since the perceiver has dissolved into itself, mind is no thing to
    view.
Free of concepts of a meditation, it transcends both clarity and
    vagueness.
And with no conduct to be carried out, I am free from making
    judgments.
Fruition is the natural freedom in the lucid essence's vastness.

Manjushrimitra, the acharya, leaned his back against the stupa in the charnel ground of Expanding Delight while practicing at dusk and sang this song of self-existing realization:

For I, Manjushrimitra, Prahevajra's heart-like son,
In all-pervasive wakefulness, there is no meditator on
    instructions;
No focus to behold, no iota of a reference point.
Timeless purity is emptiness, and yet the kayas and the wisdoms
    are a vivid presence.

As the incarnated great tertön, Chokgyur Dechen Lingpa decoded this from the yellow parchment revealed in the Cave of Lotus Crystal, this was written down by Khyentse Wangpo, a joyful servant of the Lotus-Born.

ॐ

The following songs express the profound insights of Samantabhadra, Vajrasattva, Prahevajra, Manjushrimitra, Shri Singha, Jnanasutra, Vimalamitra and Padmasambhava. They are from The Treasury of Nyingma Songs—a collection of realization poetry compiled by Kyungtrul Kargyam of Heru Gompa in Nangchen, one of Tulku Urgyen Rinpoche teachers.[149] These songs were also taken from Chokgyur Lingpa's revelation the Three Sections of the Great Perfection.

Songs from the Innermost Essence

Emaho, here is the vajra song of Samantabhadra's realization:

HUNG

Since primordial awareness, untouched by good or evil,
Knows the all-ground and the ground of both confusion and of
    freedom.
From its state transcending hope and fear,
This timeless liberation—free of effort, confident—sent forth
An emanation, at the eon's first beginning, to Tushita's deva
    realm.
Here Vajrasattva taught the buddhas by the thousands
To keep an undistracted knowing in a state that's uncontrived,
So ground-displays can now achieve their greatest strength.[150]

Here follows Vajrasattva's realization:

The king of views, I see, is free from limits and extremes.
The king of training, now I see, is spacious emptiness.
The king of conduct, I have fully seen: no deed is to be done.
Fruition's king, I realize, is the triple kaya's natural presence.

Prahevajra expressed his view in song:.

HOH

For I, by name Delightful Vajra,
Knowing in itself is emptiness,

Knowing's form is cognizance,
And knowing's strength is unconfined.
Know this to be just what it is.

Here follows the extent of Prahevajra's realization:

Basic purity, I see, transcends conceptual views.
Empty cognizance, I see, transcends the training's striving.
Self-freedom effortless, I see, transcends conduct's eight
    concerns.
The fruit intrinsic, now I see, transcends both hope and gain.

Manjushrimitra sang this song of realization:

HOH
For I, known as the Kinsman of Manjushri,
The minds of buddhas in the threefold time
And the thoughts of beings in the triple realms
Differ not in quality or number,
So realize that this transcends all words.

Here follows the extent of Manjushrimitra's realization:

The view, I see, is free from the confines of judgments.
The training, now I realize, is free from clinging thoughts.
The conduct, I have seen, is free from deeds and effort.
The fruit, I see, is inherent from the first.

Shri Singha sang this song:

HOH
For I, by name Resplendent Lion,
By cutting through the ego-view, the cutter has dissolved.
By looking into my own mind, the looker's substance lost.
By using remedies while practicing, the remedy dispersed.
Beyond thought, word and image, intermingled day and night,
My guru's word fulfilled, I toil for others' sake.

Here is the extent of Shri Singha's realization:

The view, I see, is free from words and bias.

The training, now I see, is natural presence undistracted.
The conduct, I have seen, is freedom from attachment.
The fruit, I realize is this: the highest vehicle of changelessness.

Jnanasutra sang this song of realization:

HOH

For I, by name Confluence of Wisdom,
Have nailed the fourfold lamp to basic space,
And thus have torn confusion from its root.
By reaching the four visions' end
All words and limits naturally are cut.
Crossing through the fourfold bardo state,
Samsara's seeds are now in flames consumed.
There is no teaching beyond this, I swear.

Vimalamitra sang this song of realization:

HOH

For I, by name Flawless Kinsman,
The words of learning are but empty sounds,
While all reflection intensifies delusion evermore,
And any effort to meditate lures one from the goal.
With relaxed body, silent voice and undistracted mind,
Train in freshness—undisturbed, natural clarity;
Thus even Dharma words disperse of their own accord.

Padmakara sang this vajra song:

HOH

For I, known as the Lotus-Born,
With the four empowerments matured, the fourfold kaya I have
    gained.
Taking an authentic consort, I am the knowledge-holder of
    longevity.
Mastering the channel-winds of mahasukha, insight blossomed
    in my mind.
Rousing Trekchö, Tögal both, I gained the great transference.

Compassionate emptiness fully trained, helping others is
    effortless.
Now like a brim-filled vase about to fill another,
May all of this pour into Vairotsana's learned heart.

Padmasambhava sang this song of realization:

The view, I see, is changeless, empty cognizance.[151]
The conduct, now I see, is nondoing without bias.
The fruit, I realize, is purity primordial, devoid of yearning.

Tsogyal, if this realization is how you wish to see,
Let your view be wordless, lucid in your natural state.
Let your meditation be unmodified, thoughtfree in pristine
    clarity.
Let your conduct be spontaneous within a state of effortless
    nonaction.
Let your fruition be free of hope or gain, as self-arising, natural
    liberation.

For samaya beyond parting, let be within the state of
    nonobserving, nonrejection.
Let scriptural and oral learning settle in the vast untaught.
Let your knowledge settle in the state devoid of knower and a
    known.
Let samadhi be, unfixated in natural clarity.
Let your aspirations rest, transcending hope and thought.

Thus he sang.

ⓢ

Rombuguhya the Indian Siddha

These songs—also from Chokgyur Lingpa's revelation the Three Sections of the Great Perfection—express the realizations of King Indrabhuti, Vimalamitra, Padmasambhava, Jnanasutra, Hungkara, Kala Heruka, Nagarjuna, Prabhahasti, Danasanskrit, Karmeshvari, Rombuguhya, and Shantimgarbha.

Vajra Songs from the Masters of the Innermost Cycle

ཨོཾ༔ ཙཽཪྞ༔

Here are the vajra songs from the masters of the Innermost Cycle.

NAMO GURU
From songs of masters of the Cycle Innermost,
This is king Indrabhuti's vajra song.
Inside the gandhola of the dakini palace,
Within the greatest bliss, the self-existing, purity of basic space,
King Indrabhuti realized the meaning unexcelled:

A HO
In this awakened state of basic space, spontaneously arising, self-
dissolving,
The view is natural clarity, untainted by the four extremes.
The training beyond conceptual mind is lucid wakefulness.
The conduct is to freely settle in the state devoid of action.
The fruition is the wonderment discovered in oneself.

The vajra song of master Flawless Kinsman,
Was sung while the dakini Dhatvishvari
Served her guru in the palace of Great Bliss,
Within the purity of wisdom's basic space.

A HO

Filling the sky, the greatest bliss is purified in space,
And melts into a wakeful vastness, rises and dissolves within
  itself.
Awareness and this space, not two, the unity resolved,
Samsara and nirvana both pervaded by this glorious heruka.

Immortal Lotus-Born expressed this vajra song
To show that dharmata arises and is freed in naturalness;
While he, Padmakara, was engaged in yogic conduct
Within the jungle of the Self-Formed Bamro Mounds.

A HO

In this aware immediacy, its arising and its freeing simultaneous,
I proceed in fearlessness, free of care, nongrasping.
And all the magical displays, appearing from the basic space,
Unfold within samsara and nirvana's equal state.

The master Jnanasutra's vajra song
On the timeless wakefulness of great bliss, most sublime,
Was sung for the dakinis while he spun the wheel of feast
At Jnanasutra's hermitage Red Cliff.

A HO

Dissolving blissfulness within a vast expanse,
A sky-like empty bliss spreads far and wide.
Within this wheel of bliss, transcending all attachment,
Your body, speech and mind arise as greatest bliss.

Here is Hungkara the master's vajra song
On rigpa's thunderbolt that burns delusion's jungle.
While in Cool Grove, composed in meditation
Hungchen was honored by a group of brahmin maidens.

A HO

Self-arising self-existence, the great and splendid heruka
Gulping down samsara's life-blood, joined with empty space,
Depth of brilliant awareness, in dharmata's open vast,
All appearance, every type, like clouds into this sky disperse.

Kala Heruka the Indian Siddha

Here is the vajra song of Kala Heruka
About the natural mind's perfection in the pristine state,
While partaking in the *bamchen* wheel of feast
In awesome Rugged Grove, where magic play runs rampant.

> A HO
>
> By severing the thoughts of ego-clinging at their roots,
> I spin in space a thousand life-wheels of awareness,
> To slay a million thoughts and poisonous emotions
> So now they dawn as wisdom's great adornment.

Here is the master Nagarjuna's vajra song
On realizing self-awareness, like magical conjuring.
Amidst five hundred panditas, upon the mountain Glorious,
Nagarjuna proclaimed this song on nonarising.

> A HO
>
> This luminous awakened mind is all-pervasive,
> While rigpa's natural strength commands appearance and
> existence,
> All that appears and that exists is mind present in this sphere.
> Behold the nonarising magic of every possible appearance.

Here is the master Prabhahasti's vajra song
About the vajra vastness that obliterates fixation.
On Lotus Mound, having attained great bliss,
This vajra song was sung by Prabhahasti.

> A HO
>
> Within awareness, undisturbed by circumstance,
> Bound by endless clinging, mind will taint.
> But in the self-arising vastness, lucid, unimpeded, free of
> clinging,
> This mind is truly clarified and lets awareness dawn.

Here is the master Dhanasanskrit's vajra song
On finding wakefulness beyond description.
Within the great *vihara* at the Vajra Throne,
The sovereign of all the lords of siddhas,

Prabhahasti the Indian Siddha

The fearless Dhanasanskrit sang this song.

A HO

Awareness need not gaze into the mind ineffable,
Since truly pure awareness is perfected by itself.
Awareness, unsullied and crystal clear,
Is now no different from channel-wind and the awakened mind.

Here is dakini Karmeshvari's vajra song
On the all-pervasive purity of basic space.
Great Karmeshvari, in the Palace of the Sun and Moon,
Sang this to a gathering of wisdom dakinis beyond number.

A HO

Dharmadhatu that cannot be apprehended,
Present everywhere, without delineation,
Single sphere, ineffable, this mahasukha state—
The unexcelled abode of all the buddhas.

Here is master Rombuguhya's vajra song
On arisings from the vastness freed again within this space.
In front of the great stupa of Nyagrodha,
During a break in Vairotsana's practice,
Rombuguhya spoke these vajra words.

A HO

Free of focus and transcending the confines of nihilism,
Everything arises and transcends the domain of permanence.
The unity of lucid emptiness, nondual space and rigpa,
Where everything can manifest—this is the natural state.

Here is the vajra song of master Shantimgarbha
On liberating thoughts within dharmata's space.
When at the stupa Brilliant Resplendence
He slayed a thousand haughty gods and demons,
Shantimgarbha sang this song of HUNG.

A HO

Within the state of nonarising, every thought I stamp with
HUNG.

Dhanasanskrit the Indian Siddha

Whatever rises, unconfined, I join with rigpa's HUNG.
The self-existing rigpa's HUNG destroys all ignorance
And HUNG's loud roar defeats all ego-based beliefs.
HUNG HUNG HUNG

These were the authentic vajra songs from the knowledge-holders of the Innermost Cycle.

SAMAYA. ⸖ SEAL, SEAL. ⸖

Shantimgarbha the Indian Siddha

The incarnated great treasure revealer Chokgyur Lingpa recovered a yellow parchment from the Lotus Crystal Cave, and as he gradually decoded it, (Jamyang) Khyentse Wangpo, a joyful servant of the Lotus-Born, wrote this down. May it be virtuous!

༄

The Song of Manjushrimitra[152]

I am the kinsman of Manjushri, Prahevajra's heart disciple.
No seeker can I find, a lucid wakefulness suffuses all.
That as well unfindable, even an atom is not found.
This basic purity is emptiness, the kayas and the wisdoms
    manifest.

༄

This song by Vima Mudra, one of the names of Vimalamitra, is a part of his vajra song entitled Flawless Ambrosia. *Here he plays on the word ambrosia—related to the Sanskrit amrita, the nectar of immortality—which in Tibetan is dütsi, "demon-crusher," overcoming the Mara of death. While the nineteenth century treasure revealer Chokgyur Lingpa "opened up" to the world for the first time Mount Wangzhu in Kham, a sacred place for both Vimalamitra and Padmasambhava, he had a vision of the great pandita within Vimalamitra's cave and received many teachings and blessings. One of Vimalamitra's specialties was alchemy, as he was the main lineage holder of the Amrita Heruka mandate, so it is apt that the portion of his beautiful and profound song presented here covers the view of transforming the five poisons, using the alchemy of self-existing awareness.*

Vimalamitra's Song of Flawless Ambrosia

This natural song, the view of the Flawless Ambrosia,
Was sung by Vima Mudra, a yogi of the sky.

The attitude of clinging to desire is a demon;
Let's crush it with the strength of rigpa undetached.
When naturally dissolved within a flawless, empty ease,
Discriminating wisdom is revealed.

The attitude of blatant hatred is a demon;
Let's crush it with awareness holding no duality.
As it naturally dissolves in flawless magic, empty presence,
The wisdom like a mirror is revealed.

The attitude of slothful dullness is a demon;
Let's crush it with awareness, lucid yet thought-free.
As it naturally dissolves in flawless, basic, empty cognizance,
The dharmadhatu wisdom is revealed.

The attitude of conceited pride is a demon;
Let's crush it with awareness, self-existing, ego-free.
As it naturally dissolves into the sphere of flawless, empty rigpa,
The wisdom of equality is revealed.

The attitude of painful envy is a demon;
Let's crush it with awareness beyond ceasing and arising.
As it naturally dissolves into the space of flawless feeling,
     insubstantial,
The wisdom all-accomplishing is revealed.

Primeval and self-existing purity of everything,
Root of knowing and its fivefold wisdoms,
From here spread the branches of every type of insight;
This I call the amrita of attributes.

Tasting this ambrosia, Mara's emotions of delusion
Are crushed by rigpa's undeluded wakefulness.
Like iron touching the philosopher's stone,
No division—kayas, wisdoms self-perfected.

༄

PART VI
Aspiration

On the swift and single path of all the conquerors,
In the Great Perfection's vehicle sublime, extolled by every conqueror,
May the old translation school of mighty Lotus Conqueror
Spread far and wide the teachings of the conquerors.

§

The Heart Essence of the Vast Expanse, Longchen Nyingtik is a Terma cycle revealed by the master Jigmey Lingpa. Since its inception in the late 18th century, it has become one of the most widespread sets of teachings in the Nyingma tradition. It is particularly known and loved for its extensive commentarial literature, which includes practice manuals such as the famed Yeshe Lama.

These teachings were originally transmitted by the master Padmasambhava to King Trisong Deutsen, the dakini Yeshe Tsogyal and the Lotsawa Vairotsana at Samye Monastery in central Tibet. As the time for these teachings to spread was not yet right, they were then written in symbolic script by Yeshe Tsogyal, entrusted to the dakinis, and hidden to be revealed at a later time. The king later reincarnated as the treasure revealer Jigmey Lingpa, who recalled the teachings he had received and, recognizing the time was ripe for them to be practiced, put them down in writing and began to teach.

Jigmey Lingpa, the tertön who revealed this cycle of teachings, was a reincarnation of two important masters, Vimalamitra and King Trisong Deutsen. As the embodiment of these two figures, Tibet's two primary Dzogchen lineages were combined in Jigmey Lingpa—the Vima Nyingtik and Khandro Nyingtik—both of which are contained in the Nyingtik Yabzhi. Hence, the Longchen Nyingtik terma cycle is considered a condensation of these profound teachings.

The texts that were revealed by Jigmey Lingpa, in their present-day form, comprise three volumes, known as the Nyingtik Tsapö. The numerous treatises, sadhanas and prayers it contains deal primarily with tantric practice, in particular the stages of development, completion and Dzogchen.[153]

An Aspiration for the Ground, Path and Fruition

Homage to Glorious Samantabhadra.

The natural state, primordial, its nature unconstructed,
Is not a thing that does exist, and which the conquerors can see,
Nor is it nothingness, this basis of samsara and nirvana,
    everything.
While not a contradiction, it defies the reach of spoken words.
May we realize the natural state, the ground of Great Perfection.

Empty in its essence, the limit of a permanence is freed.
Cognizant by nature, it defies as well the limit of a naught.
Unconfined in its capacity, the base for myriad emanations.
Though seen as three, in fact, there is no separation.
May we realize the natural state, the ground of Great Perfection.

Well beyond the reach of thought, free of every fancy concept,
Beliefs in biased "is" and "isn't" fully crumble
And even Buddha's tongue falls short if this fact must be
    spoken:
A wakeful depth of open space beyond beginning, end or
    middle.
May we realize the natural state, the ground of Great Perfection.

Jigmey Lingpa

And while the natural state is perfect, nonarising and pristinely
  pure,
Its unformed radiance shines forth, which is spontaneous
  presence.
These two are not apart, the greatest unity, a knowing that is
  empty,
Which, when it's realized, fulfills the basic state.
May we transcend both fault and error in the key points of the
  path.

The purity primordial removes the names for something viewed.
The knowing of the natural face unpacks the peels of
  meditation.
The absence of a reference point undoes the conduct's chains,
Converging in the natural matrix's unconstructed, naked state.
May we transcend both fault and error in the key points of the
  path.

Unhampered by the prejudice of good and evil thoughts,
And not suspended in indifference, in an absent-minded state,
This spontaneous expanse where rising and dissolving are
  unjudged and unrestrained,
Is a state of natural, total knowing, basic voidance of selective
  bias.
May we transcend both fault and error in the key points of the
  path.

Within the pristine, space-like state of universal ground
The ground-displays of rigpa have dispersed like cloudbanks in
  the sky,
As outward wakefulness reverses back within,
Into the Youthful Vase Body, the sphere endowed with six
  distinctions.
May we seize command over the royal stronghold of fruition.

Within Samantabhadra, the pristine and natural knowing,

All ambition for achievements vanish into basic space.
Concepts of effort all transcended, Great Perfection's natural
state,
The spacious sphere of Kuntu Zangmo which is rigpa's
openness.
May we seize command over the royal stronghold of fruition.

The nature of the Middle Way is a complete nondwelling,
While Mahamudra's state is open vastness, all-pervasive,
And spaciousness beyond confines, the key point of the Great
Perfection;
The sphere where path and levels' virtues are completely present,
naturally, within the ground.
May we seize command over the royal stronghold of fruition.

—Revealed by Rigdzin Jigmey Lingpa

ऊँ

Endnotes

1   Tulku Urgyen Rinpoche, *Vajra Speech*.

2   The word *buddha* was translated into Tibetan as *sangye* which means purified and perfected.

3   Traditionally, these three principles would be the first three of the "six special qualities" of Samantabhadra: he ascended from the ground, saw the displays to be his own nature and thus made the distinction.

4   Tulku Urgyen Rinpoche, *As It Is*, Vol. 1, p. 107

5   Read more details in *The Flower Ornament Scripture (Avatamsaka Sutra)* and *Myriad Worlds*.

6   Tulku Urgyen Rinpoche told me many stories about one of his teachers, whom he always referred to as Bomta Khenpo. In *A Marvelous Garland of Rare Gems*, excellently translated by Richard Barron, this same teacher is called Polu Khenpo Dorje. The pages xxv–xxvi and 530–2 include a profound story of mind transmission and his biography.

7   Saha can also mean 'undivided' because the karmas and kleshas, causes and effects, are not separately divided or differentiated.

8   Jamgön Kongtrül describes in more detail this perspective: *Myriad World*, pages 95–105.

9   Tsele Natsok Rangdröl continues to give examples of the scriptures that describe Vajradhara's journey to enlightenment. Next he gives an explanation of Vajradhara's attributes, etc. Forgive me for not including them here in the Dzogchen context. These details can be found in the part of his *Collected Works* reproduced from the Tsibri woodblocks, [tbrc pdf file 1289, pages 462–468].

10 This quote explains the literal meaning of Vajradhara, vajra-holder or vajra-bearer.

11 The ancient *yojana* unit of distance which according to Abhidharma equals approximately four thousand fathoms (eight km) but in Kalachakra is defined as two thousand fathoms (four km).

12 These quotes are from the *Hevajra* and the *Kulayaraja* tantras, respectively.

13 Flawless Light Ray is Drimey Özer alias Longchen Rabjam.

14 The *Tantra of the All-Creating King*, in Sanskrit *Sarva Dharma Mahasanti Bodhichitta Kulayaraja (chos thams cad rdzogs pa chen po byang chub kyi sems kun byed rgyal po)* is contained in both the various editions of the *Hundred Thousand Nyingma Tantras* and in the Derge edition of the *Kangyur*, Vol. 97. The famous tantra in 84 chapters was, as the colophon narrates, "translated and edited and thereby established by the Indian pandita Shri Singha Natha and the monk Vairotsana." *See Supreme Source.*

15 Dilgo Khyentse Rinpoche's describes the meaning of Mahasandhi as "great state of perfect mental stability" (*yang dag pa'i bsam gtan chen po*).

16 The three sections successively transcend the limit of discards, the limit of their remedies and both of them altogether.

17 An alternate source reads: Unchanged the basic space of this yogi's mind remains.

18 The text inserts the note that Khangbu is also spelled Khambu.

19 Prahevajra is here referred to as the "re-emanation" since the earlier Prahevajra lived on Mount Sumeru.

20 An "incalculable eon" is measured by a number of years of ten followed by fifty-two zeros.

21 One of the versions add one sentence here which could mean: "Unless you have such a teaching, sooner or later will people not be confused about the way and not know how to get there?"

22 See Chapter 5 The History of the Effortless Ati Doctrine Flourishing in India pp.48–62 in *The Great Image*, translated by Ani Jinpa Palmo (Shambhala 2004).

23 The swastika is an ancient insignia of the changeless inherent nature.

24 Barani the Courtesan is also known as Sarati in other sources, not to be confused with the Parani who was Prahevajra's mother.

25 The state of fearless courage is here a synonym for awakened mind.

26 Ati, Chiti and Yangti are one of the way of subdividing the Instruction Section of Ati Yoga. Jamgön Kongtrül defines Chiti as teaching the profound tantric meanings of the general key points in the Instruction Section (*man ngag sde'i rgyud don zab mo spyi'i gnad ston pa spyi ti yo gar grags pa*) and Yangti as teaching the innermost and extraordinary Hearing Lineage (*yang gsang thun mong ma yin pa'i snyan brgyud ston pas yang ti yo gar grags pa*).

27 The seven successive buddhas are Vipashyin, Shikhinra, Vishvabhukra, Krakuchanda, Kanakamuni, Kashyapa and Shakyamuni.

28 The seven bodhisattvas endowed with the strength of bodhichitta are: Vigorous Cloud, Powerful Elephant, Delightful Youth, Eminent Samadhi, Jewel-Bearer, Vajra Cutter, and Sun Circle. Ratna Lingpa's terma on the *Brilliant Expanse* indicate that these seven were emanations of the six Munis and Prahevajra.

29 The lords of the three families are Avalokiteshvara, Manjushri and Vajrapani.

30 The sixty aspects are the number arrived at by adding together each of the twelve buddha's five perfections: teacher, place, retinue, teaching and time.

31 The literal meaning of *mind transmission* (*dgongs pas brgyud pa*) here is *"to transmit through intent."*

32 The word *buddha* in Tibetan combines *cleared* (*sangs pa*) and *perfected* (*rgyas pa*).

33 The word *history* (*lo rgyus*) combines *years* (*lo*) and *account* (*rgyus*).

34 This story follows closely a version revealed by Sangye Lingpa in the *Lama Gongdü* cycle. Vol 1871, pages 251

35 Presumably the *Great Array of Ati*.

36 Usually *vidya* (rig pa) is translated as knowledge, but here the word is spelled *family* (rigs) which refers to Vajradhara being of the sixth family. So instead of the usual translation of knowledge-holder the sense here is rather 'upholder of the family line.'

37 *The Nyingma History* by Dudjom Rinpoche says: "six thousand and eight hundred small temples"

38 These are, respectively, the fourth and third of the four visions in Dzogchen.

39 The eight gauris, or keurimas in Tibetan—names after the first of the eight—are often called the eight mamos of the sacred places: Gauri, Cauri, Pramoha, Betali, Pukkasi, Ghasmari, Smashani and Candali.

40 The *Turquoise Scripture* in the *Vima Nyingtig* cycle mentions the birthplace as being Koshaling (ko sha'i gling) and that the Tibetan for Shri Singha is Palgyi Senge (dpal gyi seng ge). Soshaling should not be confused with the charnel ground Sosadvipa which lies in India.

41 Shri Singha concealed texts on astrological calculations with these titles: (*gto sbyor gnad kyi rgya chen po*), (*dngos po sgyur byed gto'i yi ge*), (*brtag pa dpyad kyi yi ge*), (*'phrog byed khram gyi yi ge*) and many others texts.

42 Guru Tashi's *Nyingma History* as well as Jigmey Lingpa identify him with Nagaraja Patri, a reincarnation of the naga king Nanda. Before meeting Shri Singha, he studied many teachings from the Mind Section with King Hasti (Rajahasti) and Princess Prarani.

43 Guru Tashi's version says: "Through the *master's* blessings he reached there, covering the distance in a single *day* which would otherwise take nine months."

44 These are the practices known as *rushen*, which may be likened to preliminary practices for the teachings of *Trekchö* and *Tögal*.

45 One reasonable estimate is that one *drey* equals approximately two pounds or one kilo. But since it is an ancient volume measure equivalent to about one liter or two pints, one *drey* of gold would then have to weigh about thirteen kilos.

46 Persevering action is one of the synonyms for all-accomplishing wisdom. Sometimes it also describes one of the five aspects of this wisdom.

47 It was here that he concealed the eighteen tantras and the instructions later revealed by Pema Lingpa.

48 These three guardians refer to Rahula, Ekajati and Vajra Sadhu.

49 In Padmasambhava's commentary *stong gsal ti la mtha' dbus bral* is part of the homage, not the title.

50 Padmasambhava's commentary has an alternative wording for this line: *brtags shing bcangs pas 'khor ba stongs*, which alters the meaning slightly to: "Voids samsara when it's worn and kept."

51 King Uparaja often means the king in charge of secular affairs.

52 In explaining the transmission through the intention of the conquerors Nyoshul Khen Rinpoche's *Lapis Garland* follows this text almost word for word.

53 The *Lapis Garland* says Densely Arrayed Realms of Total Purity

54 It is in the *Jewel Garland Records* that Longchenpa mentions that Sudharma in Tibetan is (*chos kyi sde*) and that Garab Dorje's name is Vajra Prahe.

55 From this point onwards the wording is almost of identical with what Vairotsana dictated to his disciples as recorded in the *Drabag Chenmo (The Great Image* pp. 35–47).

56 Rather than "teaching through his identity of natural luminosity" (*rang gsal ngo bos gsung*) the *Drabag Chenmo* says, "teaching through showing the natural luminosity" (*rang gsal ngo sprod kyis gsung*).

57 An expression of surprise and wonderment.

58 The *Ati Zabdön Nyingpo's* history slightly differs: "Being called upon with those words, Shri Vajrasattva emanated from his heart a wheel of self-radiating jewels, which he placed in the Vajra Being's hand, and spoke."

59 The Vajra Being here is Vajrapani.

60 *Bairo Gyübum*, Vol. KA, pages 177 onwards gives a similar story.

61 There are slight variations between Longchenpa's version and *Drabag Chenmo:* 'primordially complete' instead of 'complete within the ground', the nature of everything' instead of 'self-existing', and 'manifests' rather than 'endowed with'. I have combined the two versions.

62 Longchenpa's version has: 'Can never change into samsaric thought'.

63 The first line of the famous tantra of the same name.

64 The three with the name Putra, according to Shechen Gyaltsab's *Pool of White Lotus Flowers,* Uparaja's sons Shakputri, Nagaputri and Guhyaputri.

65 The "finality of time" is a concept often used in Abhidharma to describe the shortest time fraction.

66 The Ninefold Space refers to the principles of view, conduct, mandala, empowerment, samaya, wisdom, meditation state, path, and fruition.

67 The *Drabag Chenmo* says (*'o cag skyengs par gyur to zhes ngo nag por gyur*): "Some of the panditas showed disapproval and said, 'That would humiliate us.'

68 This is another name for Samvaragarbha before he receives the name Manjushrimitra.

69 For this line Terdak Lingpa's revelation *Ati Zabdön Nyingpo* reads, "While everything is natural knowing, nonarising, free from bounds" (*chos rnams rang rig skye med mtha' bral la*).

70 Instead of "they cling to basic space as having sides," the *Ati Zabdön Nyingpo* reads "they cling to forms of intellectual positions" (*grub mtha'i dbyibs la zhen*).

71 The *Ati Zabdön Nyingpo* version has two extra lines: "In true reality the knower and the object known, / are cleared when you apologize / within the effortless expanse of sameness."

72 The *Ati Zabdön Nyingpo* reads, "Once you realize that everything's true nature is equality" (*chos kun mnyam nyid yang dag don rtogs nas*).

73 In *Ati Zabdön Nyingpo* Princess Parani is called Radiant Flower.

74 More information on these lineages can be found in *Bairo Gyübum,* Vol. KA, pages 134-8.

75 The third level of the second dhyana abodes within the heavenly Form Realms.

76 To teach "through your identity" is in the style of the sambhogakaya buddha.

77 The three incarnated vidyadharas being Padmasambhava, Vimalamitra and Vairotsana.

78 To quote *The Lotus-Born* biography: "The top floor of the triple-styled central temple was built in the Indian style, as India was the source of the tradition of Dharma. The middle story was built in the Chinese style as China was the matriarch, and the lower story was built in the Tibetan style since Tibet was the patriarch."

79 A teaching that liberates upon encounter—through seeing, hearing or touching.

80 The princess is Lhacham Pema Sal, the daughter of King Trisong Deutsen, who later reincarnated as Longchenpa.

81 The reader can find the full details of the great Tibetan translator Vairotsana in his biography *The Great Image,* translated by Ani Jinpa Palmo. Shambhala Publications.

82 A barb at Tibetans based on the old legend of the Tibetan race originating from a monkey and a demoness.

83 This fits very well with the destruction of Buddhism in India some centuries later.

84 The *gongpo* demon personifies the insidious evil spirit of egotism and self-centered ambitions.

85 This is an attempted translation for *sa'i ngad pa 'gam du 'jug pa.*

86 We assume it is Padmasambhava who spoke to Yeshe Tsogyal.

87 In the pure aspect, these three are the wisdom wind, rigpa and dharmadhatu. In the impure, distorted form which leads to samsara, they are the wind of karma, *sem* and the all-ground.

88 This is quite a clear criticism of the incorrect state of shamatha, which fixates on thoughtfree stillness rather than simple nondistraction, and therefore hampers the unfolding of true vipashyana, the source of all enlightened qualities.

89 "The three sections of Kriya and Yoga" is a way of referring to the Three Outer Tantras—Kriya, Upa and Yoga. They are mentioned as two since Upa combines the conduct of Kriya Tantra with the view of Yoga Tantra.

90 The view of and subsequent training in distinguishing dualistic *consciousness* and nondual *wakefulness* (*sem* and *yeshe*) are the main principles in the practice of the Great Perfection.

91 Rigdzin Natsok Rangdröl (Adzom Drukpa) adds a note in his text: "This is because of not realizing self-existing luminosity exactly as it is."

92 Rigdzin Natsok Rangdröl: "This is due to being closer to realizing luminosity."

93 Rigdzin Natsok Rangdröl: "In the bardo, which corresponds to the Secret Cycle."

94 In the dharmakaya realm of the Luminous Vajra Essence, the realm of the great all-pervasive dharmadhatu, Padmasambhava is the original protector Changeless Light, the teacher of complete mastery in that realm. Changeless Light is another name for the dharmakaya buddha Samantabhadra.

95 About semi-manifest nirmanakaya: Due to the power of compassion, the expression of the inner wisdom manifests outwardly in the realms of those to be influenced. Thus, all of the outwardly visible and semi-manifest realms, teachers, retinues, etc. are the manifest aspect of both the buddhas and bodhisattvas. The realm of Great Purity refers to the first of the two types of nirmanakaya, the natural nirmanakayas and the nirmanakayas who guide beings. The realms of the five families of Great Purity are Sukhavati and so forth with the five teachers being the five buddha families of Amitabha, etc.

96 A "nirmanakaya who guides beings" appears in the six realms of samsara as opposed to an emanation in a "natural nirmanakaya realm" such as Buddha Amitabha's pure land Sukhavati.

97 Guru Nyima Özer is Padmasambhava, now known under his new name.

98 Instead of *Assemblage of Vidyadharas,* other sources list this scripture under the title *Assemblage of Precious Gemstones.*

99 Instead of *Awakened Mind,* other sources list this scripture under the title *Nonarising Natural Mind.*

100 In the fourteenth chapter of *The Lotus-Born,* the life-story of Padmasambhava, telling how Vairotsana of Pagor went to India in pursuit of the Dharma, we find a slightly different list of the *Eighteen Marvels of Mind* and the *Eighteen Major Scriptures* (*lung chen po bco brgyad*). They are located in Vol. KA of the *Nyingma Gyübum.*

101 Chiti Yoga is one of three subdivisions of Ati: Ati, Chiti and Yangti.

102 Please compare with the list of these eight in *The Lotus-Born,* Chapter 12.

103 The word *naljor* is Tibetan for *yoga,* which is Sanskrit. The meaning is "connecting with the real."

104 *The Great Perfection of the Black Quintessence* includes fifteen tantras: *yang ti nag po gser gyi 'byu gcig, 'jam dpal yang tig gi rgyud, lta ba zang thal chen po'i rgyud, dgongs pa srog gi spu gri'i rgyud, srog gi 'khor lo'i rgyud, snang byed pu tra'i rgyud, kun tu bzang po'i srog gi thig pa, 'bras bu ye grol chen po'i rgyud, srog gi mkhyen pa thugs kyi srog, rig pa srog gi 'khor lo'i rgyud, rig pa rang byung srog gi bdal ba srog gi mkhyen pa, kun tu bzang po'i srog lan, rdo rje sems dpa' srog gi yang snying, ye shes 'khor lo'i rgyud, thig le nyag gcig gi dgongs pa.* These are the modes of the Black Quintessence. The modes of the *Great Perfection of Chiti* are numerous, including *'jam dpal nam mkha' dang mnyam pa'i rgyud, nam mkha' chen po'i rgyud, spyi rgyud chen po,* and so forth.

105 Padmasambhava's *Innermost Essence* is concealed as a terma treasure for future generations while Vimalamitra's is passed on as both an oral and a terma lineage.

106 Another source text with almost identical words, not included in this book (*Great General Background for the History of the Authentic Lineage,* according to the *Direct Revelation of Samantabhadra's Mind*) mentions the conquerors mind transmission under three headings: "There are three aspects to how the mind transmission of these precious teachings was passed on: how the dharmakaya of the ground of awareness taught through blessings, how the sambhogakaya of the fruition taught through its own identity, and how the nirmanakaya of compassion taught through excellent composition."

107 Dharmakaya's twofold way of transmission—here translated as "intending through inspiration" (*byin gyis dgongs pa*) and "intending through resplendence" (*rlabs kyi dgongs pa*) uses the two parts of the word for *bestowing blessing* (*byin gyis rlabs pa*).

108 Please notice that the contraction of "inspiration and resplendence," *jinlab*, is usually translated as blessings. The conquerors' mind transmission is here phrased as (*dgongs shing rgyud pa*) "intended and transmitted."

109 These are also known as the six Munis, the buddhas who appear for beings in the six realms.

110 Using the *Great General Background for the History of the Authentic Lineage*, I filled in words that were missing in the original text.

111 Notes in the original text indicate who these seven were: the bodhisattvas Vigorous Cloud and the first six were emanations of the buddhas of the six realms, while Sun Circle was an emanation of Prahevajra.

112 The *Great General Background for the History of the Authentic Lineage* mentions that Vajrasattva taught the *Purity of the Five Poisons, Appearance and Existence as the Manifest Ground*, the *Tantra of the Great Equalizing of Buddhahood*, and only these teachings from the *Innermost Unexcelled Cycle*.

113 As above, these seven were emanations of the six Munis and Prahevajra.

114 The three aspects of the philosophical vehicle are Sutra, Vinaya and Abhidharma.

115 The four activities are pacifying, enriching, magnetizing and subjugating.

116 Prahevajra, here, is the past life of the human knowledge-holder Prahevajra.

117 The *Great General Background* describes this event, "When Prahevajra opened these and looked, from within the silver casket appeared the *Tantra of Self-Existing Awareness;* from within the gold casket appeared the *Tantra of the Single Child of the Buddhas*, the *Tantra of the Secret Seed of Conduct*, and the *Knowing One that Liberates All;* from within the turquoise casket appeared the *Tantra of the King of Awareness in Actuality;* and when looking into the crystal from the tip of Vajrasattva's nose, he beheld the countenance of the five families of conquerors."

118 The *Great General Background* describes the last as "and the *Innermost Unexcelled Cycle of the Precious Fruition* in the manner of the ripened fruits."

119 Manjushri Tikshna gave this prophecy in the great charnel ground Excellent Valley.

120 The *Great General Background* adds, "Prahevajra taught these cycles, entitled Renowned as the Great Perfection, to five hundred panditas headed by Manjushrimitra. Following that, the master taught the *Six Dharma Sections of the Great Perfection that Reveal Dharmata in Actuality*, which were hidden within the treasure mine of his mind, to his two destined disciples Manjushrimitra and Shri Singha."

121 China is the translation of the Tibetan name Gya Nagpo (*rgya nag po*), nowadays the common name for China.

122 Nine *day-nights* mean five nights and four days.

123 In other words that the original wisdom resides within the heart chakra of the vajra body.

124 The four stages in Dzogchen practice are also known as the four visions. These four stages are manifest dharmata, increased experience, awareness reaching fullness, and exhaustion of concepts and phenomena.

125 The *Great General Background* adds that the *Bindu Cycle of the Secret Edict* had one hundred thousand instructions.

126 In the *Great General Background*, Padmasambhava adds "The wondrous and marvelous Dharma that requires neither cultivation nor effort was transmitted to my, Uddiyana's, heart through the symbols that indicate insight."

127 The *Great General Background* adds, "That the cognizant yet thoughtfree, natural awareness is endowed with a natural expression of this awareness as five-colored light is, for instance, symbolized by a crystal."

128 Without leaving physical remains behind, i.e. Shri Singha departed in a rainbow body.

129 The *Great General Background* names these texts *Three Liberation Through Wearing Tantras*.

130 The eight vidyadharas are: Manjushrimitra, Nagarjuna, Hungkara, Vimalamitra, Prabhahasti, Dhana Sanskrita, Shintam Garbha and Guhyachandra.

131 The great treasure revealer Ratna Lingpa, the king of Dharma, recovered this terma at Furrowed Red Rock at Sky Plain Castle .

132 History of Vimalamitra's lineage of the *Secret Heart Essence;* from *Dzogchen Sangwa Nyingtig, Rinchen Terdzö*, Vol. LI, pages 16–26 Tibet.

133 A note within the original text says: Also known by the name Dharmapala.

134 The *Turquoise Scripture* in the *Vima Nyingtig* cycle mentions that Vimalamitra's other name was Jemalamudra, which, Longchenpa explains, in Tibetan is translated as Seal of Vastness.

135 The testament to Manjushrimitra was given after he had fallen unconscious from grief, seeing that his guru, Prahevajra, had passed away in a body of rainbow light.

136 We assume that Butakutam is a misspelling for Buddhaguhya. Elsewhere in other sources, he is also spelled Bhutakugta, Butakuta, and Buddhagupta.

137 The manuscript contains the notes of the names included here in round brackets. The last note, inserted at this spot says "This was on the outer leaf."

138 Rajadeva and Rajahasti are identical here.

139 Kukkuraja the Younger is also known as Dhahuna the Dog King.

140 The verb tense here is past but could just as well be present, since dharmakaya and sambhogakaya are unchanging in being unformed and perpetual in continuity.

141 The phrase "incalculable number of years" is sometimes counted as a fixed number defined as ten followed by 50 zeros. Padmasambhava mentions in the *Lama Gongdü* terma 6.4 million being the omen for the appearance of an equal number of *shlokas* of the Great Perfection, seventeen of them being especially bright as an omen for seventeen essential teachings that would embody them all.

142 The *Lama Gongdü* terma mentions his name as the teacher Endowed with Omniscient Wisdom (ston pa kun mkhyen ye shes dang ldan pa).

143 The *Lama Gongdü* terma interjects: "Since he considered the six classes of beings on the outer level, the six Munis on the inner and the six paramitas on the innermost, he became known as the Sixth Vajradhara. Moreover, this teacher Youth Playful Grace taught the following tantras on the effortless Dharma: the Vajrapani tantra *Flame Garland* (*phyag na rdo rje me lce 'phreng ba'i rgyud*) in nine chapters to Vajrapani, the Avalokiteshvara tantra *Lion's Roar* (*spyan ras gzigs seng ge sgra'i rgyud*) in thirteen chapters to Avalokiteshvara, and the Manjushri tantra *Wisdom Adornment* (*'jam dpal ye shes brgyan gyi rgyud*) in seven chapters to Manjushri. In particular, for the seven successive buddhas he taught (*yongs su bshad pa'i rgyud*) in fifty chapters and the (*thig le mchog gi rgyud ye shes kun tu gsal ba*) in seventy chapters. He taught these and others such tantras belonging to the effortless Great Perfection."

144 The testament of Powerful Warrior Youth is known as the *Second Testament* (*sangs rgyas kyi 'das rjes gnyis pa*).

145 The source being the Vajra Throne at Bodhgaya.

146 In the *Lama Gongdü* terma Padmasambhava adds: "This rishi youth Guarded Mind was also the one later known as Prahevajra, and he received the realization of all the teachings—like a perfect vase filled to the brim from another. He became fully perfected, in no way different from all the qualities of the teacher himself."

147 Sangye Lingpa was the great tertön who revealed the *Lama Gongdü* cycle of teachings.

148 Interestingly, these four masters were all from different countries: Padmasambhava from Uddiyana, Vairotsana from Tibet, and Vimalamitra from Kashmir, while their guru, Shri Singha, was born in China, probably in one of the Central Asian countries beyond the Pamir and Karakoram mountain ranges. They all met Shri Singha in Bodhgaya, though not at the same time.

149 For more on this great master see the chapter entitled Meetings with a Remarkable Teacher in *Blazing Splendor* (pages 247–259).

150 It seems three phonemes were doubled from the line above, and in want of a second copy, the verse was truncated here.

151 The verse-line about meditation might be missing in the original. If found, may it be inserted at a later time.

152 The original scripture has Manjushrimitra's song of realization on a separate page by itself at the end.

153 This introduction to the *Longchen Nyingtik,* authored by Cortland Dahl, is found on www. DHARMADICTIONARY.NET.

Index